THE CONSTITUTIONAL CASE FOR RELIGIOUS EXEMPTIONS FROM FEDERAL VACCINE MANDATES

THE CONSTITUTIONAL CASE FOR RELIGIOUS EXEMPTIONS FROM FEDERAL VACCINE MANDATES

Religion and Law Series, Volume Nine

George J. Gatgounis

WIPF & STOCK · Eugene, Oregon

THE CONSTITUTIONAL CASE FOR RELIGIOUS EXEMPTIONS
FROM FEDERAL VACCINE MANDATES

Religion and Law Series, Volume Nine

Copyright © 2022 George J. Gatgounis. All rights reserved. Except for brief quotations in critical publications or reviews, no part of this book may be reproduced in any manner without prior written permission from the publisher. Write: Permissions, Wipf and Stock Publishers, 199 W. 8th Ave., Suite 3, Eugene, OR 97401.

Wipf & Stock
An Imprint of Wipf and Stock Publishers
199 W. 8th Ave., Suite 3
Eugene, OR 97401

www.wipfandstock.com

PAPERBACK ISBN: 978-1-6667-5948-8
HARDCOVER ISBN: 978-1-6667-5949-5
EBOOK ISBN: 978-1-6667-5950-1

VERSION NUMBER 102622

To Professor Alan Dershowitz, Harvard Law School,
who kept me on the edge of my seat

CONTENTS

INTRODUCTION | ix

MEMORANDUM OF LAW *CONTRA* FEDERAL COVID VACCINE MANDATE(S) | 1

I. THE UNITED STATES CONSTITUTION AND FEDERAL LAW LIMIT THE FEDERAL GOVERNMENT'S POWER TO FORCE SPECIFIC INDIVIDUAL CITIZEN'S ACTIONS. | 1

II. THE FIRST AMENDMENT'S FREE EXERCISE CLAUSE STILL LIMITS FEDERAL POWER. | 9
   A. Federal employees are entitled to pursue religious discrimination exemptions from mandates and religious discrimination claims against their federal employer. | 9
      1. The Federal Employee Vaccine Mandate fails constitutional scrutiny | 11
      2. Even if the mandate would survive scrutiny, once an employee establishes his or her sincere religious belief, the government is constitutionally required to accommodate the religious belief unless the government can prove undue hardship if such an accommodation was granted. | 17
         i. Sincerity of religious belief is a credibility test, not a government assessment of a believer's strict adherence to doctrines of known religions. | 17

CONTENTS

      ii. Offering a reasonable accommodation is an affirmative duty to the particular employee absent undue hardship under that employee's job and circumstances. | 22
   B. Although different rules govern military personnel, religious exemptions still must be evaluated based on individual members' sincere beliefs and accommodations made based on job duties and undue hardship. | 27
   C. The Federal Government's Vaccine Mandate for Defense Contractors exceeds its power under the Constitution and Federal laws. | 33

DIGEST OF SOUTH CAROLINA LAW ON RELIGION-RELATED MATTERS | 40
   I. South Carolina Constitutional and Statutory Provisions | 40
   II. Religion-Related Torts | 43
   III. Splitting Denominations or Congregations | 47
   IV. Free Exercise | 57
   V. Establishment Clause and Separation of Church and State | 61

EVIDENCE ATTACHMENT A: CHURCH COMPLAINT | 67

EVIDENCE ATTACHMENT B:
RELIGIOUS REQUEST FORM | 137

EVIDENCE ATTACHMENT C: POPE LETTER | 140

EVIDENCE ATTACHMENT D:
CATHOLIC EXEMPTION TEMPLATE | 144

EVIDENCE ATTACHMENT E:
CONTRACTOR GUIDANCE | 148

EVIDENCE ATTACHMENT F: MISSOURI V. BIDEN | 166

EVIDENCE ATTACHMENT G: NAVY RULING | 203

INTRODUCTION

What are the legal rights of federal employees, contractors and military members opposing mandatory COVID-19 vaccination on religious grounds under the United States Constitution, Religious Freedom and Restoration Act ("RFRA"), 42 U.S.C. § 2000bb-1, Title VII Civil Rights Act of 1964 § 703, 42 U.S.C.A. § 2000e-2(a)(1) and other federal laws?

An uphill battle awaits potential plaintiffs due to the numerous federal cases supporting the government's authority to mandate vaccines for the public's health on a rational based standard.

Legal recourse for federal employees is especially problematic. Since the President has substantial power over his employees, federal employees must file for exemption, been denied, and exhausted administrative appeal process before seeking judicial review. See:

> "If plaintiff intends to allege a First Amendment violation, he must articulate what conduct establishes that violation and it must be separate from the conduct he alleges to establish a Title VII or ADEA violation." *Santiago v. DeJoy*, No. 20-CV-1571 YGR, 2020 WL 6118528, at *5 (N.D. Cal. Oct. 16, 2020). "A court may not entertain discrimination claims by a federal-employee plaintiff under Title VII unless the plaintiff alleges that he has first exhausted the administrative process as required by federal statute. *Brown v. General Serv. Admin.*, 425 U.S. 820, 832-33 (1976). Allegations of discrimination falling outside the scope of the administrative complaint must

INTRODUCTION

be dismissed. *Vasquez v. County of Los Angeles*, 349 F.3d 634, 644 (9th Cir. 2003)."

Santiago, 2020 WL 6118528, at *6; *see also Steven Church v. Biden*, "Church," 2021 WL 5179215, *10 (Dist. Ct. D.C., November 8, 2021) (Federal Employee religious discrimination claim against COVID-19 vaccine mandate dismissed for failure to exhaust administrative remedies); *Holly v. Jewell*, 196 F. Supp. 3d 1079, 1085 (N.D. Cal. 2016) (dismissing constitutional claim arising from alleged First Amendment religious discrimination, and claim under the Religious Freedom Restoration Act of 1993, as covered exclusively by Title VII for federal employees).

Military members' cases are even harder to pursue because the federal courts are especially reluctant to interfere in military officials' decisions and cannot adjudicate claims until military administrative proceedings have been exhausted as well. *Church*, 2021 WL 5179215, at *11.

On the other hand, federal contractors and subcontractors have a strong argument that the mandate is an illegal extension of the federal executive's power because it is not supported by the United States Constitution's commerce clause, nor any federal law enacted by Congress.

MEMORANDUM OF LAW
CONTRA FEDERAL COVID VACCINE MANDATE(S)

I. THE UNITED STATES CONSTITUTION AND FEDERAL LAW LIMIT THE FEDERAL GOVERNMENT'S POWER TO FORCE SPECIFIC INDIVIDUAL CITIZEN'S ACTIONS.

"Under guiding principles of federalism, our Constitution preserves the power of the States, within constitutional limits, to adopt laws to provide for public health and safety." *Klaassen v. Trustees of Indiana Univ.*, No. 1:21-CV-238 DRL, 2021 WL 3073926 (N.D. Ind. July 18, 2021).

Court challenges to the exercise of that power via vaccine mandates in the United States are not new. Since the early 20th century, those court challenges almost exclusively centered on *state or local* vaccine mandates. Accordingly, the courts ordinarily found that the mandates were a legitimate exercise of the *state's* police power, if rationally related to a health emergency. *Roman Cath. Diocese of Brooklyn v. Cuomo*, ___U.S. ___, 141 S. Ct. 63, 67, 208 L. Ed. 2d 206 (2020) (Gorsuch, J., concurring) (explaining that *Jacobson v. Massachusetts*, 197 U.S. 11, 25 S. Ct. 358, 49 L.Ed. 643 (1905) is "essentially . . . rational basis review"); *Harris v. Univ. of Mass.*, 2021 WL 3848012, at *6 (D. Mass. Aug. 27, 2021) *Prince v.*

RELIGIOUS EXEMPTIONS FROM FEDERAL VACCINE MANDATES

Massachusetts, 321 U.S. 158, 166-67, 64 S. Ct. 438, 88 L. Ed. 645 (1944); *Zucht v. King*, 260 U.S. 174, 175 (1922); *Jacobson*, 197 U.S. 11, 25 S. Ct. 358, (the state's compulsory small pox vaccination law upheld); *Compagnie Francaise De Navigation a Vapeur v. Bd. of Health of State of La.*, 186 U.S. 380, 22 S.Ct. 811, 46 L. Ed. 1209 (1902) (Louisiana law requiring involuntary quarantine during a yellow fever outbreak was a reasonable exercise of state police power); *See also Johnson v. Brown*, No. 3:21-CV-1494-SI, 2021 WL 4846060, at *13 (D. Or. Oct. 18, 2021); *Zulay Rodriguez-Velez, et. al. v. PedroR. Pierluisi-Urrutia.* (D.P.R. Nov. 1, 2021); *Travis Wise, et al., v. Governor Jay Inslee, et. al.*, No. 2:21-CV-0288-TOR, 2021 WL 4951571, at *2-4 (E.D. Wash. Oct. 25, 2021); *Norris v. Stanley*, No. 1:21-CV-756, 2021 WL 3891615, at *1 (W.D. Mich. Aug. 31, 2021); *Harris v. Univ. of Mass.*, 2021 WL 3848012, at *6 (D. Mass. Aug. 27, 2021); *Bridges v. Houston Methodist Hosp.*, No. CV H-21-1774, 2021 WL 2399994, at *1 (S.D. Tex. June 12, 2021); *Klaassen v. Trs. of Ind. Univ.* ("Klaassen II"), 7 F.4th 592 (7th Cir. 2021); *Dixon v. De Blasio*, ___ F.Supp.3d ___, ___, 2021 WL 4750187, at *8 (E.D.N.Y. Oct. 12, 2021); *Middleton v. Pan*, No. CV 16-5224-SVW (AGR), 2016 WL 11518596, at *6 (C.D. Cal. Dec. 15, 2016), report and recommendation adopted, No. CV 16-5224-SVW (AGR), 2017 WL 10543984 (C.D. Cal. July 13, 2017); *Workman v. Mingo Cnty. Bd. of Ed.*, 419 Fed. Appx. 348, 356 (4th Cir. 2011). "The 'police power' is the general power of governing possessed by the States. *Nat'l Fed'n of Indep. Bus. v. Sebelius*, 567 U.S. 519, 132 S. Ct. 2566, 183 L. Ed. 2d 450 (2012) (emphasis added).

The 1905 *Jacobson* case is repeatedly asserted as the primary authority behind a state's right to mandate vaccinations to protect the health of the state's citizens. In *Jacobson*, the Massachusetts legislature enacted a statute which allowed a local Board of Health to mandate vaccination of individuals 21 years or older in their town or city. 197 U.S. 11, 25 S. Ct. 358. The Court upheld the law as a valid exercise of the state's police power. *Id.* However, the United States Supreme Court cautioned against an overextension of its ruling in the future beyond reason and authority. *Id.* Notably, the Court recognized that a state may exercise its power in such circumstances by regulations so arbitrary and oppressive that the courts must interfere to prevent wrong and oppression. *Id.* at 38.

The Supreme Court further elaborated, "We are not inclined to hold that the statute establishes the absolute rule that an adult must be vaccinated if it be apparent or can be shown with reasonable certainty that he is not at the time a fit subject of vaccination or that vaccination, by reason of his then condition, would seriously impair his health or probably cause his death .... '[a]ll laws,' this court has said, 'should receive a sensible construction. General terms should be so limited in their application as not to lead to injustice, oppression, or an absurd consequence. It will always, therefore, be presumed that the legislature intended exceptions to its language which would avoid results of this character. The reason of the law in such cases should prevail over its letter.'" *Id.* at 39. (Internal citations omitted).

Conversely, the *Federal* Government only possesses enumerated powers. In other words, the United States government can exercise only the powers granted to it by the United States Constitution. U.S. Const., Amdt. 10; *Nat'l Fed'n of Indep. Bus. v. Sebelius*, 567 U.S. 519, 534–35, 132 S. Ct. 2566, 2577 (2012) (Citing *McCulloch v. Maryland*, 4 Wheat. 316, 405, 4 L. Ed. 579 (1819)). "If no enumerated power authorizes Congress to pass a certain law, that law may not be enacted, even if it would not violate any of the express prohibitions in the Bill of Rights or elsewhere in the Constitution." *Nat'l Fed'n of Indep. Bus.*, 567 U.S. at 535, 132 S. Ct. at 2577.

In *Nat'l Fed'n of Indep. Bus.*, the Supreme Court determined that the Patient Protection and Affordable Care Act's (PPACA or ACA) health-insurance mandate was not a legitimate exercise of Congress' power to regulate interstate commerce under Art. I, § 8, cl. 3. 567 U.S. at 550, 132 S. Ct. at 2586. The Court opined that the Commerce Clause allows regulation of economic activity only:

> The individual mandate, however, does not regulate existing commercial activity. It instead compels individuals to *become* active in commerce by purchasing a product, on the ground that their failure to do so affects interstate

> commerce. Construing the Commerce Clause to permit Congress to regulate individuals precisely *because* they are doing nothing would open a new and potentially vast domain to congressional authority. Every day individuals do not do an infinite number of things. In some cases, they decide not to do something; in others they simply fail to do it. Allowing Congress to justify federal regulation by pointing to the effect of inaction on commerce would bring countless decisions an individual could *potentially* make within the scope of federal regulation, and—under the Government's theory—empower Congress to make those decisions for him.

Id. at 552, 132 S. Ct. at 2587.

The Court continued to express its concern over a potentially alarming expansion of federal government's power over individual choices if the Commerce Clause were construed to allow such power:

> Indeed, the Government's logic would justify a mandatory purchase to solve almost any problem. See *Seven-Sky v Holder*, 661 F.3d 1, at 14–15 (D.C. Cir. 2011) (noting the Government's inability to "identify any mandate to purchase a product or service in interstate commerce that would be unconstitutional" under its theory of the commerce power). To consider a different example in the health care market, many Americans do not eat a balanced diet. That group makes up a larger percentage of the total population than those without health insurance. See, e.g., Dept. of Agriculture and Dept. of Health and Human Services, Dietary Guidelines for Americans 1 (2010). The failure of that group to have a healthy diet increases health care costs, to a greater extent than the failure of the uninsured to purchase insurance. See, e.g., Finkelstein, Trogdon, Cohen, & Dietz, *Annual Medical Spending Attributable to Obesity: Payer-and Service-Specific Estimates*, 28 Health Affairs w822 (2009) (detailing the "undeniable link between rising rates of obesity and rising medical spending," and estimating that "the annual medical burden of obesity has risen to almost 10 percent of all medical spending and could amount to

$147 billion per year in 2008"). Those increased costs are borne in part by other Americans who must pay more, just as the uninsured shift costs to the insured. See Center for Applied Ethics, Voluntary Health Risks: Who Should Pay? 6 Issues in Ethics 6 (1993) (noting "overwhelming evidence that individuals with unhealthy habits pay only a fraction of the costs associated with their behaviors; most of the expense is borne by the rest of society in the form of higher insurance premiums, government expenditures for health care, and disability benefits"). Congress addressed the insurance problem by ordering everyone to buy insurance. Under the Government's theory, Congress could address the diet problem by ordering everyone to buy vegetables. See Dietary Guidelines, supra, at 19 ("Improved nutrition, appropriate eating behaviors, and increased physical activity have tremendous potential to ... reduce health care costs").

People, for reasons of their own, often fail to do things that would be good for them or good for society. Those failures—joined with the similar failures of others—can readily have a substantial effect on interstate commerce. Under the Government's logic, that authorizes Congress to use its commerce power to compel citizens to act as the Government would have them act.

That is not the country the Framers of our Constitution envisioned. James Madison explained that the Commerce Clause was "an addition which few oppose and from which no apprehensions are entertained." The Federalist No. 45, at 293. While Congress' authority under the Commerce Clause has of course expanded with the growth of the national economy, our cases have "always recognized that the power to regulate commerce, though broad indeed, has limits." *Maryland v. Wirtz*, 392 U.S. 183, 196, 88 S.Ct. 2017, 20 L.Ed.2d 1020 (1968). The Government's theory would erode those limits, permitting Congress to reach beyond the natural extent of its authority, "everywhere extending the sphere of its activity and drawing all power into its impetuous vortex." The Federalist No. 48, at 309 (J. Madison). Congress already enjoys vast power to regulate much of what we do. Accepting the Government's theory would give Congress the same license to regulate what we do not do, fundamentally changing the relation between the citizen and the Federal Government. *Nat'l Fed'n of Indep. Bus.*, 567 U.S. at 553–55, 132 S. Ct. at 2588–89.

The individual mandate also could not be sustained under the Necessary and Proper clause of the United States Constitution as alleged by the government. *Id.* at 521, 132 S. Ct. at 2573. Instead, the Supreme Court surprisingly held that the individual mandate was a proper exercise of the federal government's power to "lay and collect Taxes." Art. I, § 8, cl. 1. *Id.* at 521, 132 S. Ct. at 2573.

In the above situations, the discussion centered on Congress' powers or delegation of such legislative powers.[1] More alarming is such concentrated powers assumed by unelected officials in the Executive branch, or even by one man, the President, by mandating individuals obtain a specific medical treatment, i.e., a vaccine, a mandate which is backed by the power of force of the federal government. Undoubtedly, this is not a country that the Framers of our Constitution envisioned.

In fact, the United States Supreme Court rang such alarm bells in a more recent case, *Alabama Ass'n of Realtors v. Dep't of Health & Hum. Servs.*, 141 S. Ct. 2485 (2021), concerning a nationally imposed eviction moratorium because of the pandemic. In July 2020, the Director of the Centers for Disease Control imposed this eviction moratorium after the Congressional moratorium had expired under the Coronavirus Aid, Relief, and Economic Security Act. Pub. L. 116–136, 134 Stat. 281. *Id.* The CDC's moratorium even expanded its mandate to cover all residential properties nationwide and imposed criminal penalties for violators. *Id.* The CDC based their authority for this mandate "in reliance on a decades-old statute that authorizes it to implement measures like fumigation and pest extermination." *Id.* at 2486. More specifically, the CDC relied on delegated powers from the Surgeon General

---

1. Congress may seek to impose a vaccine mandate through its enumerated Spending power in the constitution which allows it to tax and spend for the general welfare. The validity of this authority is debatable, and any law would need to meet certain conditions. *See South Dakota v. Dole*, 483 U.S. 203, 211-212 (1987).

under § 361(a) of the Public Health Service Act which essentially enable the agency, with the approval of the Secretary of Health and Human Services (HHS), to enforce regulations related to the prevention of the spread of communicable diseases from foreign countries by providing for "inspection, fumigation, disinfection, sanitation, pest extermination, destruction of animals or articles found to be so infected or contaminated as to be sources of dangerous infections to human beings." *Id.* at 2487. It is indisputable that there is a significant difference between agency action and an executive order, so one may try to distinguish its worth. However, the overarching principle remains.

Aghast at the CDC's bold usurpation of such excessive power, the Court quipped: "It strains credulity to believe that this statute grants the CDC the sweeping authority that it asserts." *Id.* "Originally passed in 1944, this provision has rarely been invoked—and never before to justify an eviction moratorium. Regulations under this authority have generally been limited to quarantining infected individuals and prohibiting the import or sale of animals known to transmit disease." *See, e.g.*, 40 Fed. Reg. 22543 (1975) (banning small turtles known to be carriers of salmonella). *Id.* at 2487. In short, "Agencies are not permitted to act unlawfully even in pursuit of desirable ends." *Id.*

Several courts have raised grave concerns about unlawful or unconstitutional vaccine mandates and have issued injunctions against them.

1. In the Western District of Louisiana, a court granted a temporary restraining order (TRO) against a medical school's vaccine mandate because it was not granting religious exemption requests when reasonable accommodations were possible, and the mandates were not the least restrictive means to protect the school's students. *Magliulo v. Edward Via Col. Of Osteo. Med.* No. 3:21-CV-2304, 2021 WL 36799227 (W.D. La. Aug. 17, 2021).

2. A court in the Western District of Michigan also granted a TRO against the university for similar reasons as in the

Louisiana case. *Dahl v. Bd of Trustees of W. Mich. Univ.* No. 1:21-CV-757, 2021 WL 3891620, *2 (W.D. Michigan. Aug. 31, 2021). The Sixth Circuit affirmed that ruling. *Dahl v. Bd. of Trustees of W. Mich. Univ.* No. 21-2945, 2021 WL 4618519 (6th Cir. Oct. 7, 2021)

3. The United States District Court for the Northern District of New York and the Second Circuit Court of Appeals granted injunctive relief against New York State's vaccine mandate on healthcare workers as it expressly excluded religious exemptions. See *Dr. A. v. Hochul,* No. 1:21-CV-1009, 2021 WL 4734404 (N.D.N.Y. Oct. 12, 2021); *We the Patriots, U.S.A. Inc. v. Hochul,* No. 21-2179, dkt, 65 (2d cir. Sept. 30, 2021)

4. In the Northern District Court of Texas, the court stayed United Airlines' vaccination mandate until final resolution could be determined in a hearing. The court raised grave concerns about the enormous impact on people's lives if the TRO was not granted: "If the parties' stipulation were to expire without temporary injunctive relief in place, nothing would prevent hundreds of workers from ostensibly either: (1) being compelled to take a vaccination in violation of their religious beliefs or medical restrictions, or (2) being placed on indefinite unpaid leave by United. To be sure, the Court is not currently ruling on the merits of the parties' arguments on these points. Rather, the Court seeks simply to avoid the risk of irreparable harm to the parties and to maintain the status quo while the Court holds an evidentiary hearing on the Motion for Preliminary Injunction and issues an Order on the same." *Sambrano v. United Airlines, Inc.,* No. 4:21-CV-1074-P, 2021 WL 4760645, at *1–2 (N.D. Tex. Oct. 12, 2021)

5. The Fifth Circuit issued a stay of enforcement of the Occupational Health and Safety Administration's Director's vaccine mandate, via an Emergency Temporary Standard, against all businesses in the United States with over 100 employees. *BST Holdings, et. al. v. OSHA,* No. 21-60845 (5th Cir. Nov. 5, 2021).

Despite such warnings against unbridled federal usurpation of power, the same administration unlawfully executed edicts, and likely will continue to do so, which will try to force everyone in the United States to get the COVID-19 vaccine. In effect, these edicts are "empowering" federal executive officials (not elected officials of Congress) to make individual health choices for Americans throughout the United States on a specious claim of power, in an alleged pursuit of some desirable end. Previously, there had been no federal law mandating vaccines, except in limited circumstances for immigrants or the military.[2] This memorandum focuses on the mandates against federal employees, federal contractors, and military members. Their situations are certainly a bellwether for things to come for many other individuals.

II. THE FIRST AMENDMENT'S FREE EXERCISE CLAUSE STILL LIMITS FEDERAL POWER.

A. Federal employees are entitled to pursue religious discrimination exemptions from mandates and religious discrimination claims against their federal employer.

On September 9, 2021, President Joseph Biden signed Executive Order (EO), 14043 (Federal Employee Vaccine Mandate), which required that all federal employees receive the COVID-19 vaccine, "with exceptions only as required by law." The Federal Employee Vaccine Mandate instructed each of the federal agencies to implement a vaccination program for employees. *Id.* Previously, EO 13991 established the President's Safer Federal Workforce Task Force,[3] ("Task Force"), to provide "ongoing guidance to heads of

---

2. Immigrants had to present documentation proving they had received certain vaccinations, under 8 U.S.C. §1182(a)(1)(A); military members were required to get the anthrax vaccine. *Doe v. Rumsfeld*, 297 F. Supp. 2d 200 (D.C. Dist. Ct., Jan. 7, 2004).

3. The Safer Federal Workforce Task Force is led by the White House COVID-19 Response Team, the General Services Administration (GSA), and the Office of Personnel Management (OPM). Task Force members include: the Centers for Disease Control and Prevention (CDC), the Department of Veterans

agencies on the operation of the Federal Government, the safety of its employees, and the continuity of Government functions during the COVID-19 pandemic." 86 Fed. Reg. 7045-7046. The Federal Employee Vaccine Mandate required the Task Force to issue further guidance on the mandate within seven days of the EO.

Critically, the Federal Employee Vaccine Mandate primarily rests its authority to issue a federal vaccine mandate on § 7301 of Title 5, United States Code: "The President may prescribe regulations for the conduct of employees in the executive branch." The President's authority under § 7301 is not absolute. The Federal Employee Vaccine Mandate, and the subsequent guidance from the Task Force, recognized that the vaccine mandate must be constrained by a religious exemption, and medical exception, as allowed by law for all American citizens. *See* Safer Federal Workforce, Template for Request for Religious Exception to the COVID-19 Vaccination Requirement (Religious Exception template), https://perma.cc/6a6d-EPH9; *Steven Church v. Biden,* "Church," 2021 WL 5179215 (Dist. Ct. D.C., November 8, 2021) and for medical exemptions (Medical Exception template). https://www.saferfederalworkforce.gov/downloads/DISABILITY%20REQUEST%20FORM%20-%2020211004_510pm%20-%20MH508.pdf. However, the Task Force never published its guidance in the Federal Register for public comment before it became effective. (Exhibit A, Task's Force COVID-19 Workplace Safety: Guidance for Federal Employees).[4]

Religious discrimination by employers violates the Free Exercise clause of the First Amendment of the United States Constitution, and Title 7 of Civil Rights Act of 1964 § 703, 42 U.S.C.A. § 2000e-2(a); 42 U.S.C.A. § 2000e-2(j) ("Title VII"); *See Holly v. Jewell,* 196 F. Supp. 3d 1079, 1085 (N.D. Cal. 2016) (dismissing

---

Affairs (VA), the Federal Emergency Management Agency (FEMA), the Federal Protective Service (FPS), the Office of Management and Budget (OMB), and the United States Secret Service (USSS); See https://www.saferfederalworkforce.gov/.

4. Originally, Public employees whose religious beliefs prohibit them from vaccinating need not invoke the religious exception at all and can bypass the sworn declaration requirement by submitting a weekly negative COVID-19 test. A follow on EO removed weekly testing option.

constitutional claim arising from alleged First Amendment religious discrimination, and claim under the Religious Freedom Restoration Act of 1993, as covered exclusively by Title VII for federal employees).

To assert a claim for religious discrimination, federal employees need to file for an exemption with their employer-agency and proceed through administrative reviews of appeals of exemption denials before seeking judicial review. *See Church*, 2021 WL 5179215. Federal employees who are members of a union may also need to follow union grievance procedures depending on language in the union agreement. *See U.S. Equal Emp. Opportunity Comm'n v. Consol Energy, Inc.*, 860 F.3d 131 (4th Cir. 2017). The Federal Employee Vaccine Mandate states that employees who fail to comply with the vaccination deadline and "have neither received an exception nor have an exception request under consideration" are "subject to discipline, up to and including termination or removal." EO 14043. Any discipline or termination will be stayed pending completion of exemption review and appeals. Yet, the Task Force Vaccine Guidance further stated: "If an employee's request for a religious exception is denied, then the employee must receive their first (or, if a one-dose series, only), dose within two weeks of the final determination to deny the accommodation."

1. The Federal Employee Vaccine Mandate fails constitutional scrutiny

"Under the Free Exercise Clause, a law that burdens religious practice need not be justified by a compelling governmental interest if it is neutral and of general applicability." *Church of the Lukumi Babalu Aye, Inc. v. City of Hialeah*, 508 U.S. 520, 521, 113 S. Ct. 2217, 2220, 124 L. Ed. 2d 472 (1993) (Citing Employment Div., Dept. of Human Resources of Ore. v. Smith, 494 U.S. 872, 110 S. Ct. 1595, 108 L. Ed. 2d 876.) "However, where such a law is not neutral or not of general application, it must undergo the most rigorous of scrutiny: It must be justified by a compelling governmental interest and must be narrowly tailored to advance that interest. Neutrality and general applicability are interrelated, and failure to satisfy one requirement is a likely indication that the other has not been satisfied." *Id.* Such is the case here.

A law is not generally applicable where it has built-in exemptions which do not extend to accommodate religious exercise. *Legacy Church, Inc. v. Kunkel*, 472 F. Supp. 3d 926, 1016 (D.N.M. 2020), aff'd sub nom. *Legacy Church, Inc. v. Collins*, 853 F. App'x 316 (10th Cir. 2021). The federal government has issued a mandate which is not generally applicable since it exempts some federal employees. The Federal Employee Vaccine Mandate, E.O. 14043, only includes employees and agencies as defined by 5 U.S.C. 105. Thus, this vaccine requirement does not apply to several agencies, and their employees, such as the White House, CDC, National Institute of Health (NIH), and National Institute of Allergy and Infectious Diseases (NIAID).

A law may also evidence its lack of neutrality and religious animus in how it is applied in practice. *Masterpiece Cakeshop, Ltd. v. Colorado C.R. Comm'n*, 138 S. Ct. 1719, 201 L. Ed. 2d 35 (2018) ("The Free Exercise Clause bars even subtle departures from neutrality on matters of religion.") There are strong indications that the Federal government has been pressuring employees to submit religious exemption requests as quickly as possible so that they can evaluate the scope of federal employees seeking exemptions. (See Evidence Attachment A. Church Complaint.) Verified Complaint for Declaratory and Injunctive Relief, "Church Complaint," *Steven Church, et. al. v. President Biden, et. al.*, Civil Action No. 1:21-cv-xxxx, United States District Court for the District of Columbia, pp. 23-25).

On pages 23-24 of this Complaint, federal employees specifically allege a scheme by the Task Force to try to circumvent religious exemption laws. Besides direct allegations from the federal employees, the Complaint references notes made by Samuel Berger from a COVID-19 Guidance Zoom Meeting, SAFER FEDERAL WORKFORCE TASK FORCE, on October 8, 2021, on page 24, note 12 and attached as Exhibit 5 to the Complaint; *See also* https://www.facebook.com/fedfire1592/posts/438564490947629.

Apparently, during this recorded Zoom conference with over 400 federal personnel, the Task Force advised the attendees essentially to pretend to press deadlines so people would quickly submit their exemption forms. However, the federal officials were advised to pause decisions and evaluations until all are forms are in and they can assess the scope.

According to the plaintiffs, the video showed that the Task Force was requiring this because "once you grant exemption to an individual in a job category, it is very hard to say that you are not going to grant (an exemption) to a similarly situated person." (Evidence Attachment A, *Church* Complaint, p. 24, ¶55.) There is one template for religious exemption form with a few questions. (Evidence Attachment B, Religious Exemption Request Template.)

However, it appears that the Task Force stressed a much wider range of questions at the Zoom which the Task Force felt necessary to collect a lot of information about the federal employee. (Evidence Attachment A, *Church* Complaint, p. 25, ¶¶56-57.) The Task Force allegedly then told each agency that they can refuse accommodations "under whatever circumstances each agency so chooses." (Evidence Attachment A, *Church* Complaint, p. 25, ¶57.)

Obviously, decisions are being made prior to any evaluation as the Task Force "emphasized how important it is for the agencies to 'figure it out as quickly as possible ... because the agencies are not going to run an accommodation in those places—and that's totally fine.'" (Evidence Attachment A, Church Complaint, p. 25, ¶58.) There was very little guidance given at this meeting about how to evaluate the religious exemption requests.

In short, the government is trying to circumvent individual assessment of religious exemptions and undue harm on the government by collecting information so that it can essentially grant blanket denials due to the overall impact on the agencies. No doubt numerous federal officials are discussing retiring or resigning over the vaccine mandate. See https://www.govexec.com/workforce/2021/10/meet-federal-employees-who-will-refuse-covid-19-vaccine/186180. However, this fact only hurts the government's position that the mandate is rationally based. Loss of valuable federal personnel, including a doctor at the CDC, in a time of such crisis weighs public interest against this government mandate. *Id.* Even the EEOC warned against vaccination mandates! Regardless, the mandate does not justify government officials' planning of blanket or predetermined religious-exemption denials.

Based on the foregoing, the Federal Employee Mandate must be held to strict scrutiny standard. Strict scrutiny demands that the Government "demonstrate that the compelling interest test is satisfied through application of the challenged law 'to the person'—the particular claimant whose sincere exercise of religion is being burdened. This requires us to look beyond broadly formulated interests and to scrutinize the asserted harm of granting specific exemptions to particular religious claimants." *Burwell v. Hobby Lobby Stores, Inc.*, 573 U.S. 682, 727 (2014). Thus, "the government must show with 'particularity how [even] admittedly strong interest[s] . . . would be adversely affected by granting an exemption' to a particular claimant." *Hobby Lobby*, 573 U.S. at 728. The Federal Employee Mandate specifically states it is imposing this mandate to try to halt the spread of the COVID-19 virus, including the new Delta variant. Although there may be some public interest in encouraging vaccination, it is questionable if there is a compelling public interest to mandate vaccination for several reasons.

First, as stated previously, many federal employees may leave as a result, which will dramatically affect government operations. The problems are already evident in states with mandates as national guard members are called out to be bus drivers, replace healthcare workers, nursing home attendants, etc.[5] Who will replace the National Guard members deployed at their jobs?

---

5. See https://www.nytimes.com/2021/09/25/world/americas/health-workers-ny-vaccine.html; https://www.mcknights.com/news/unvaccinated-workers-at-nursing-homes-could-be-replaced-by-national-guard-official-says/; https://www.npr.org/2021/09/26/1040780961/new-york-health-care-worker-vaccine-mandate-staffing-shortages-national-guard; https://www.nydailynews.com/news/politics/new-york-elections-government/ny-covid-hochul-orders-national-guard-to-fill-hospital-shortages-20210927-eqm-7blbxxfd7fhcigsnd7f5rga-story.html; https://www.businessinsider.com/

Second, since many federal employees are not included in the mandate's definition, how much of an impact will there really be on the virus transmission?

Third, how compelling is the basis to justify a mandate when healthcare workers who were on the front lines throughout the epidemic crisis in 2020 question the vaccine's effectiveness?

Fourth, the government's push for a vaccine mandate continually ignored any evaluation of necessity of vaccination for those with natural immunity as part of the discussion. Two scientific studies counter vaccine necessity for those with natural immunity.[6] As noted in this Washington Post article,

> More than 15 studies have demonstrated the power of immunity acquired by previously having the virus. A 700,000-person study from Israel two weeks ago found that those who had experienced prior infections were 27 times less likely to get a second symptomatic covid infection than those who were vaccinated. This affirmed a June Cleveland Clinic study of health-care workers (who are often exposed to the virus), in which none who had previously tested positive for the coronavirus got reinfected. The study authors concluded that "individuals who have had SARS-CoV-2 infection are unlikely to benefit from covid-19 vaccination." And in May, a Washington University study found that even a mild covid infection resulted in long-lasting immunity. Marty Makary, *Natural immunity to covid is powerful. Policymakers seem afraid to say so*, Washington Post, September 15, 2021. https://www.washingtonpost.com/outlook/2021/09/15/natural-immunity-vaccine-mandate/[/EXT]

connecticut-vaccine-mandate-governor-lamont-replace-unvaccinated-staff-national-guard-2021-10;

6. One study from Israel: https://www.medrxiv.org/content/10.1101/2021.08.24.21262415v1; https://www.clarkcountytoday.com/news/israeli-study-shows-natural-immunity-delivers-13-times-more-protection-than-covid-vaccines/ ; Another natural immunity study from Cleveland: https://www.medrxiv.org/content/10.1101/2021.06.01.21258176v3; Marty Makary, *Natural immunity to covid is powerful. Policymakers seem afraid to say so,* Washington Post, September 15, 2021. https://www.washingtonpost.com/outlook/2021/09/15/natural-immunity-vaccine-mandate/

Lastly, the vaccine mandate decision did not seem even to consider vaccine injuries in the process. Jenna Greene, "COVID vaccine injury claims mount, but recourse is lacking for those harmed," Reuters, October 19, 2021. https://www.reuters.com/legal/government/covid-vaccine-injury-claims-mount-recourse-is-lacking-those-harmed-2021-10-19/.

Courts have upheld vaccine mandates which were narrowly tailored "in that it applies to specific sectors whose employees are essential to combatting COVID-19 and who come into regular contact with vulnerable segments of the public." *Travis Wise, et. al., v. Governor Jay Inslee. Et. al.*, No. 2:21-CV-0288-TOR, 2021 WL 4951571, at *2–4 (E.D. Wash. Oct. 25, 2021).

In contrast, the Federal Employee Vaccine Mandate is certainly not tailored to the least restrictive means. The mandate covers not only those at federal work facilities but those who are (and have been) working at home.

Arguably, reaching into the homes of federal employees far exceeds the power of the President. Since those workers at home are not potentially infecting those at the workplace, the mandate dramatically expands, instead of narrowly tailoring, its power in order to meet the federal government's interest.

In fact, "under the 'exceptionally demanding' least-restrictive-means test, 'if there are other, reasonable ways to achieve those [interests] with a lesser burden on . . . protected activity, [the government] may not choose the way of greater interference.'" *Dunn v. Blumstein*, 405 U.S. 330, 343 (1972). Eliminating the weekly testing as an accommodation exacerbates the problem with the Executive Order. As seen in recent actions by the federal government now to include all businesses with over 100 employees, the federal government chooses to expand, rather than to tailor to, what is necessary. Even if this mandate is only subject to the rational basis standard, the foregoing factors establish that the federal government's vaccine mandate was arbitrarily and capriciously made. In short, it was rash, not rational.[7]

---

7. Considering such lack of deliberations over material, scientific and practical concerns, any of the agency's mandates may conceivably violate the

2. Even if the mandate would survive scrutiny, once an employee establishes his or her sincere religious belief, the government is constitutionally required to accommodate the religious belief unless the government can prove undue hardship if such an accommodation was granted.

I. Sincerity of Religious Belief is a Credibility Test, Not a Government Assessment of a Believer's Strict Adherence to Doctrines of Known Religions.

Title VII prohibits an employer, inter alia, from discriminating against "any individual with respect to his compensation, terms, conditions, or privileges of employment, because of such individual's race, color, religion, sex, or national origin." 42 U.S.C. § 2000e-2(a)(1). *Brennan v. Deluxe Corp.*, 361 F. Supp. 3d 494, 504 (D. Md. 2019); *U.S. Equal Emp. Opportunity Comm'n v. Consol Energy, Inc.*, 860 F.3d 131, 141 (4th Cir. 2017). A federal employee can challenge religious discrimination by the employer by filing an administrative complaint alleging religious discrimination in violation of Title VII of the Civil Rights Act of 1964 § 703, 42 U.S.C.A. § 2000e-2(a); 42 U.S.C.A. § 2000e-2(j) (Title VII) with the Equal Employment Opportunity Commission (EEOC).

To establish a prima facie case of religious discrimination under Title VII, the employee must show that (1) she holds a sincere religious belief that conflicts with the employment requirement, (2) she has informed the employer about the conflicts, and (3) she was discharged or disciplined for failing to comply with the conflicting employment requirement. Civil Rights Act of 1964 § 703, 42 U.S.C.A. § 2000e-2(a); 42 U.S.C.A. § 2000e-2(j). *Beckerich*

Administrative Procedure Act: "An agency action usually is arbitrary or capricious under the Administrative Procedure Act (APA) if the agency has relied on factors which Congress has not intended it to consider, entirely failed to consider an important aspect of the problem, offered an explanation for its decision that runs counter to the evidence before the agency, or is so implausible that it could not be ascribed to a difference in view or the product of agency expertise. 5 U.S.C.A. § 706(2)(A)." *Rempfer v. Von Eschenbach*, 535 F. Supp. 2d 99 (D.D.C. 2008), aff'd sub nom. *Rempfer v. Sharfstein*, 583 F.3d 860 (D.C. Cir. 2009).

v. St. Elizabeth Med. Ctr., No. CIV 21-105-DLB-EBA, 2021 WL 4398027 (E.D. Ky. Sept. 24, 2021), reconsideration denied, No. CV 21-105-DLB-EBA, 2021 WL 4722915 (E.D. Ky. Sept. 30, 2021).

Courts have protected an individual's decision to refuse unwanted medication, especially when based on the person's sincere religious belief. *Cruzan v. Director, Mo. Dep't of Health*, 497 U.S. 261, 270, 278 (1990). "Religion" is defined to include "all aspects of religious observance and practice, as well as belief." *Brennan*, 361 F. Supp. 3d 494, 504–05 (D. Md. 2019). According to EEOC statutory language, "religious practices" include "moral or ethical beliefs as to what is right and wrong which are sincerely held with the strength of traditional religious views." 29 C.F.R. § 1605.1. *Westbrook v. N. Carolina A & T State Univ.*, No. 1:12CV540, 2013 WL 1668247, at *5 (M.D.N.C. Apr. 17, 2013), report and recommendation adopted in part, rejected in part, No. 1:12CV540, 2013 WL 3766083 (M.D.N.C. July 16, 2013).

A religious belief must satisfy two requirements. First, the belief must be "sincerely held." *Geerlings v. Tredyffrin/Easttown Sch. Dist.*, No. 21-CV-4024, 2021 WL 4399672, at *6 (E.D. Pa. Sept. 27, 2021) (Citing *Africa v. Pennsylvania*, 662 F.2d 1025, 1030 (3d Cir. 1981). This is a question of fact. *United States v. Seeger*, 380 U.S. 163, 185 (1965). Second, it must be "religious." *Id.* In other words, the claims must be rooted in religious belief. *Wisconsin v. Yoder*, 406 U.S. 205, 215 (1972). The sincerity inquiry questions "whether a given belief occupies in the life of its possessor a place parallel to that filled by the God of those admitted qualifying for the exemption." *Seeger*, 280 U.S. at 176. However, the EEOC and the court can only judge the sincerity of a plaintiff's religious belief, and not the validity or veracity of such belief. *Carter v. Centura Coll.*, No. CIV.A. 2:10-907-CWH, 2011 WL 7429447, at *4 (D.S.C. June 16, 2011), report and recommendation adopted in part, rejected in part, No. CIV.A. 2:10-00907, 2012 WL 638800 (D.S.C. Feb. 27, 2012); *See also E.E.O.C. v. Alliant Techsystems, Inc.*, No. CIV.A. 98-0084-R, 1998 WL 777015, at *5 (W.D. Va. Sept. 18, 1998) ("I think the defendants are hard-put to mount a challenge as to the sincerity of Mr. Jones' religious beliefs. Moreover, Jones' concern about the union's support of candidates who did not oppose abortion and homosexuality—which Gentry classified as political beliefs—are clearly mainline religious tenets.")

Simply stated, the Free Exercise Clause of the First Amendment demands that the federal government not assume the role of telling religious believers what is and is not important to their religion. *On Fire Christian Ctr., Inc. v. Fischer*, 453 F. Supp. 3d 901 (W.D. Ky. 2020); *See also Fallon v. Mercy Cath. Med. Ctr. of Se. Pennsylvania*, 877 F.3d 487, 490–91 (3d Cir. 2017) (no court should inquire into the validity or plausibility of the beliefs).

Absent religious animus, insincerity can be easily established. Examples of insincere religious belief are seen in the following cases: *United States v. Bauer*, 84 F.3d 1549, 1559 (9th Cir. 1996); *see also International Soc'y for Krishna Consciousness, Inc. v. Barber*, 650 F.2d 430, 441 (2d Cir. 1981) ("[A]n adherent's belief would not be 'sincere' if he acts in a manner inconsistent with that belief . . . or if there is evidence that the adherent materially gains by fraudulently hiding secular interests behind a veil of religious doctrine.") (internal citations omitted); *United States v. Messinger*, 413 F.2d 927, 928-30 (2d Cir. 1969) (referencing a Justice Department recommendation that a defendant-draftee's "long delay in asserting his conscientious objector claim" was evidence of religious insincerity where his claim came two years after his Selective Service registration).

However, sincerity must not be viewed with a narrow or biased focus. The covered religious belief embraces all religions and non-traditional religious beliefs, and only excludes political, sociological, or philosophical views. *Seeger*, 280 U.S. at 172-80. One such example of a non-religious view was found in *Friedman v. Southern California Permanente Medical Group*, where a medical group's temporary employee refused to be vaccinated with the mumps vaccine because he was a "strict vegan." 125 Cal. Rptr. 2d 663 (Cal. Ct. App. 2002).

However, to be sincere, the believer does not have to be a perfect adherent to the doctrines of a particular faith or even to his own standards. *Moussazadeh v. Texas Department of Criminal*

Justice, 703 F.3d 781 (5th Cir. 2012) (Jewish inmate who wanted kosher foods can still be found to be a sincere believer even though he does not always follow the tenants of orthodox Jewish religion or always eat kosher foods). In *Moussazadeh*, the Court noted the subtlety and sensitivity needed for this task: "[t]hough the sincerity inquiry is important, it must be handled with a light touch, or 'judicial shyness'. Courts must limit themselves to "almost exclusively a credibility assessment" when determining sincerity. "To examine religious convictions any more deeply would stray into the realm of religious inquiry, an area into which we are forbidden to tread." *Id.* at 792 (internal citations omitted). This inquiry and the government's duty mirror assessments of conscientious objector status at issue in *Seeger*, 380 U.S. 733.

Title VII applies a much broader definition of covered religious belief:

> In most cases whether or not a practice or belief is religious is not at issue. However, in those cases in which the issue does exist, the Commission will define religious practices to include moral or ethical beliefs as to what is right and wrong which are sincerely held with the strength of traditional religious views. This standard was developed in *United States v. Seeger*, 380 U.S. 163 (1965) and *Welsh v. United States*, 398 U.S. 333 (1970). The Commission has consistently applied this standard in its decisions. The fact that no religious group espouses such beliefs or the fact that the religious group to which the individual professes to belong may not accept such belief will not determine whether the belief is a religious belief of the employee or prospective employee. The phrase "religious practice" as used in these Guidelines includes both religious observances and practices, as stated in section 701(j), 42 U.S.C. 2000e(j).

29 C.F.R. § 1605.1. Accordingly, it is unlikely that the EEOC will scrutinize an applicant's belief even it is not tied to a specific tenant of a church's faith.

As specifically applied to the Federal Employee COVID-19 Vaccine Mandate, no doubt many people have various and very different religious views about the COVID-19 vaccines, even if believers are from the same religion. For example, many Christians, both Catholic and Protestant, are concerned about the vaccines because of its link, albeit possibly indirect, to aborted fetuses.[8] Pope Francis in the Roman Catholic Church has written a letter directly to Catholics concerning his views which supports getting the vaccine. (Evidence Attachment C, Pope Francis' letter.) However, it is a pastoral letter of persuasion, not doctrinal dogma of the church. The Pope even advises those who by their own personal religious belief think otherwise. Many Christians may assert that getting the vaccine may violate their biblically based belief that the body is the temple of the Holy Spirit. [9] (i.e.,: See Evidence Attachment D, Template for Catholic Religious Exemption from the National Catholic Bioethics Center.) Additionally, Muslims may object to the vaccine because they believe you should trust God to cure disease.[10] Other vaccines such as varicella, the vaccine for chicken pox, implicated problems for Muslims because they may contain hydrolyzed gelatin and fetal bovine serum, both of which are non-halal animal byproducts which would be injected or

---

8. Pontifical Academy for Life Statement, Moral Reflections on Vaccines Prepared from Cells Derived from Aborted Human Fetuses, http://www.immunize.org/talking-about-vaccines/vaticandocument.htm (last visited Dec. 20, 2020) (Medical Research Council 5 (MRC-5), which was developed with human lung fibroblasts from a 14-week male aborted fetus.).

9. *See, e.g.*, 1 Corinthians 6:19-20 (New International Version) ("Do you not know that your bodies are temples of the Holy Spirit, who is in you, whom you have received from God? You are not your own; you were bought at a price. Therefore, honor God with your bodies."); 1 Corinthians 6:16-17 (New International Version) ("Don't you know that you yourselves are God's temple and that God's Spirit dwells in your midst? If anyone destroys God's temple, God will destroy that person; for God's temple is sacred, and you together are that temple."); 1 Corinthians 10:31 (New International Version) ("So whether you eat or drink or whatever you do, do it all for the glory of God.").

10. Qur'an 6:17 (translation ed) ("And if Allah touches thee with affliction, none can remove it but He: if He touches thee with happiness, He has power over all things."); Qur'an 95:4 ("We have indeed created humankind in the best of molds."). For additional Biblical references linked to vaccines see *infra*.

ingested in violation of their faith.[11] Many people, many beliefs—the First Amendment protects them all.

II. Offering a Reasonable Accommodation is an Affirmative Duty to the Particular Employee Absent Undue Hardship Under That Employee's Job and Circumstances.

Under Title VII, it is "an unlawful employment practice for an employer . . . to discharge any individual . . . because of such individual's religion." 42 U.S.C. § 20003-2. This provision not only requires that an employer refrain from discriminating based on religion, but it also imposes an *affirmative duty* to reasonably accommodate an employee's religious beliefs and practices. *EEOC. v. Ilona of Hungary, Inc.*, 108 F.3d 1569, 1574 (7th Cir.1997); *Carter v. Centura Coll.*, No. CIV.A. 2:10-00907, 2012 WL 638800, at *10 (D.S.C. Feb. 27, 2012)

Once an employee notifies his or her employer about a sincere religious conflict with a job requirement, the employer must provide a reasonable accommodation for that religious belief, unless the accommodation would cause the employer undue hardship. *EEOC v. Firestone Fibers & Textiles Co.*, 515 F.3d 307, 312 (4th Cir. 2008) (internal quotation marks omitted); *U.S. Equal Emp. Opportunity Comm'n v. CONSOL Energy, Inc.*, No. 1:13CV215, 2016 WL 538478, at *2 (N.D.W. Va. Feb. 9, 2016), aff'd, 860 F.3d 131 (4th Cir. 2017). Reasonableness and undue hardship are separate but related inquiries:

> For instance, an accommodation that results in undue hardship almost certainly would not be viewed as one that would be reasonable. Likewise, the failure to consider alternative accommodations that pose no undue hardship may, generally speaking, influence the determination of

11. *See* CENTER FOR DISEASE CONTROL, EPIDEMIOLOGY AND PREVENTION OF VACCINE-PREVENTABLE DISEASESS, Appendix B-8 (Jennifer Hamborsky, et al. eds., 13th ed. 2015) (available at https://www.cdc.gov/vaccines/pubs/pinkbook/downloads/appendices/B/excipient-table-2.pdf).

whether an employer's offered accommodation was reasonable. *Cf. Ithaca*, 849 F.2d at 118 (finding the employer had violated Title VII given its "absolute lack of effort at accommodation"). Taken together, these standards ensure that while an employer must "actively attempt to accommodate an employee's religious expression or conduct," *Chalmers*, 101 F.3d at 1018, it is not required to do so "at all costs," *Philbrook*, 479 U.S. at 70, 107 S.Ct. 367.

Firestone Fibers & Textiles Co., 515 F.3d at 314–15.

"The EEOC has stated that employers may institute a mandatory COVID-19 vaccine requirement but noted that employers must provide a reasonable accommodation to employees requesting a religious exemption and can only lawfully exclude those employees if a reasonable accommodation is impossible." Mary-Lauren Miller, *Inoculating Title VII: The "Undue Hardship" Standard and Employer-Mandated Vaccination Policies*, 89 Fordham L. Rev. 2305, 2321 (2021). The EEOC also expressed previous preference for encouraging vaccination versus mandating it. *See Pandemic Preparedness in the Workplace and the Americans with Disabilities Act*, U.S. Equal Emp. Opportunity Comm'n (Mar. 21, 2020), https://www.eeoc.gov/laws/guidance/pandemic-preparedness-workplace-and-americans-disabilities-act [https://perma.cc/X7DD-QKP4]; *see also* Teri Dobbins Baxter, *Employer-Mandated Vaccination Policies: Different Employers, New Vaccines, and Hidden Risks*, 2017 UTAH L. REV. 885 n.8 at 920-21 (discussing the EEOC's position on mandatory vaccinations); Vimal Patel, *Employers Can Require Workers to Get Covid-19 Vaccine, U.S. Says*, New York Times (Dec. 18, 2020) https://www.nytimes.com/2020/12/18/us/eeoc-employers-coronavirus-mandate.html [https://perma.cc/YFE4-898M] (noting that public-health experts believe that employers may play a key role in vaccinating enough of the population to achieve herd immunity).

The EEOC has previously asserted religious discrimination claims against hospitals which failed to reasonably accommodate employees who had a religious objection to getting the flu vaccine. *See Mission Hospital Agrees To Pay $89,000 To Settle EEOC*

Religious Discrimination Lawsuit, EEOC News Release, 2018 WL 401505; Joint Motion for Entry of Consent Decree, *EEOC v. Saint Vincent Health Ctr.,* No. 1:16-cv-234 (Sept. 22, 2016); Press Release, EEOC, *Saint Vincent Health Center to Pay $300,000 to Settle EEOC Religious Accommodation Lawsuit* (Dec. 23, 2016), 2016 WL 7438696 (E.E.O.C.); https://www.eeoc.gov/eeoc/newsroom/release/12-23-16.cfm; Joint Motion for Entry of Consent Decree, *EEOC v. Mission Hosp., Inc.,* No. 1:16-CV-00118 (Jan. 12, 2018); Press Release, EEOC, *Mission Hospital Agrees to Pay $89,000 To Settle EEOC Religious Discrimination Lawsuit* (Jan. 12, 2018), https://www.eeoc.gov/eeoc/newsroom/release/1-12-18.cfm. "Title VII requires employers to make a real effort to provide reasonable religious accommodations to employees who notify the company that their sincerely held religious beliefs conflict with a company's employment policy," said Lynette A. Barnes, regional attorney for the EEOC's Charlotte District Office. "As a result of this lawsuit, Mission now has practices in place to better ensure that this happens." 2018 WL 401505.

Assuredly, consent decrees above appropriately included instructions to the employer on how to assess future religious belief exemption requests from vaccines or other work requirements: when considering requests for religious accommodation, the Health Center must adhere to the definition of "religion" established by Title VII and controlling federal court decisions, a definition that forbids employers from rejecting accommodation requests based on their disagreement with an employee's belief; their opinion that the belief is unfounded, illogical, or inconsistent in some way; or their conclusion that an employee's belief is not an official tenet or endorsed teaching of any particular religion or denomination. *Saint Vincent Health Center to Pay $300,000 to Settle EEOC Religious Accommodation Lawsuit,* 2016 WL 7438696.

As noted in Section IIA(1) above, there are serious concerns regarding the federal government's handling of religious-exemption accommodation. Assuredly, the federal employees in the *Church* Complaint are likely not alone in their experiences with their religious-exemption requests. Unfortunately, the D.C. Court dismissed their case because the plaintiffs' administrative remedies had not been exhausted, and in most of the cases, no decision has been made yet on their exemption request, so they lack standing. *Steven Church, et al. v. Joseph R. Biden, in his official capacity as President of the United States, et al*, No. CV 21-2815 (CKK), 2021 WL 5179215 (D.D.C. Nov. 8, 2021). Before the final decision, the court set forth the Task Force Vaccine Guidance effective October 29, 2021:

> The Task Force Vaccine Guidance recognizes that certain federal employees may be eligible for an exception to the vaccine requirement in "limited circumstances" in which "the law requires an exception":
>
> [A]n agency may be required to provide a reasonable accommodation to employees who communicate to the agency that they are not vaccinated against COVID-19 because of a disability or because of a sincerely held religious belief, practice, or observance. Determining whether an exception is legally required will include consideration of factors such as the basis for the claim; the nature of the employee's job responsibilities; and the reasonably foreseeable effects on the agency's operations, including protecting other agency employees and the public from COVID-19. Because such assessments will be fact- and context-dependent, agencies are encouraged to consult their offices of general counsel with questions related to assessing and implementing any such requested accommodations.

Church, 2021 WL 5179215, at *2–4

The D.C. Court also noted that it discussed with counsel about potential adverse actions against the plaintiffs before their exemptions were evaluated. *Id.* at *5-6. The government affirmed that no adverse action would be taken *while their religious exemption requests are pending,* "and will generally have two weeks from any final determination denying the request in which to begin the vaccination process." Notice ¶ 1, ECF No. 8. *Id.* at *6. Unfortunately, the Court left one question unresolved: What is considered "final determination denying the request"? In other words, will employees be forced to start the vaccination process while they exhaust administrative remedies? Certainly not a positive situation for those employees. Critically, religious-exempt employees must not be subject to more stringent job restrictions which impact their future status than medically excepted employees. *See Magliulo v. Edward Via Coll. of Osteopathic Med.*, No. 3:21-CV-2304, 2021 WL 3679227 (W.D. La. Aug. 17, 2021).

Notably, the Federal Employees Vaccine Mandate is distinguishable from other mandates in which some federal courts found support for constitutional violations or preliminary injunctive relief lacking. For example, in *John Does, 1-3, et. al v. Mills*, several unvaccinated Maine health care workers sued under Title VII to bar enforcement of Maine's vaccine mandate for healthcare workers which allowed medical exemptions but not religious exemptions. *Does 1-6 v. Mills*, 16 F.4th 20 (1st Cir. 2021). First, the Maine vaccine mandate applied to all healthcare workers, with only one exception for medically unadvisable. *Id.* The Federal Employee Vaccine Mandate only includes federal workers under title V of the United States Code. Additionally, the First Circuit opined that the Maine vaccine mandate did not "invite the government to consider particular reasons for a person's conduct by providing 'a mechanism for individualized exemptions.'" *Does 1-6 v. Mills*, No. 21A90 ,2021 WL 5027177, *2 (Mem) (U.S. Sup. Ct. Oct. 29, 2021); *See also Fulton v. Philadelphia*, 593 U.S. ___, ___ __ ___, 141 S. Ct. 1868, 1876-1877, 210 L. Ed. 2d 137 (2021) (quoting *Smith*, 494 U.S. at 884, 110 S. Ct. 1595) (alteration in original). In other words, Maine's emergency rule did not allow any government official discretion to consider the merits of an individual's request for an exemption. *Id.* Thus, heightened scrutiny was not required. Lastly, the Maine vaccine mandate was strictly tailored to healthcare workers who obviously cannot work from home and are in close contact with many vulnerable people.

None of these circumstances are present with the Federal Employee Vaccine Mandate. First, the Task Force's meeting with federal officials clearly indicated each agency had unfettered discretion in adjudicating religious exemptions. Additionally, not all federal workers who work onsite were included in the mandate, so it was not generally applicable. The government's mandate cannot meet strict scrutiny. Most importantly, the mandate was not narrowly tailored to the government's interest since working remotely or weekly testing was not an option. Based on the foregoing, the federal employees' case will support all steps needed for injunctive relief as enumerated in Section IIC below, after exhaustion of administrative remedies or at least some injury has occurred.

B. Although different rules govern military personnel, religious exemptions still must be evaluated based on individual members' sincere beliefs and accommodations made based on job duties and undue hardship.

The United States Supreme Court stated long ago that "the military is, by necessity, a specialized society." *Parker v. Levy*, 417 U.S. 733, 743, 94 S. Ct. 2547, 41 L. Ed. 2d 439 (1974). "Accordingly, the fundamental necessity for obedience, and the consequent necessity for imposition of discipline, may render permissible within the military that which would be constitutionally impermissible outside it." *Levy*, 417 U.S. at 758, 94 S. Ct. 2547. *United States v. Schwartz*, 61 M.J. 567, 569–71 (N-M. Ct. Crim. App. 2005), aff'd, (C.A.A.F. Sept. 28, 2006) (other internal citations omitted). Thus, military members must follow Department of Defense and individual service agency directives or regulations, in addition to other federal laws and the Uniform of Code of Military Justice. Undoubtedly, military members sacrifice some aspect of their constitutional rights upon entering the military due to the impact on military readiness, unit cohesion, and good order and discipline. Vaccine mandates are certainly nothing new for military members. *See Doe v. Rumsfeld*, 297 F. Supp. 2d 200 (D.C. Dist. Ct., Jan. 7, 2004) (Anthrax vaccine mandate upheld). Thus, over 40 years ago, the Defense Department was permitted to mandate vaccination for its members. *United States v. Chadwell*, 36 C.M.R. 741, 749–50, 1965 WL 4806 (N.B.R.1965).

Based on the foregoing, the military may be the most experienced in dealing with religious objections to service requirements since they have been dealing with conscientious objectors for a very long time. *See Seeger*, 85 S. Ct. 850; *Zulay Rodriguez-Velez, et. al. v. Pedro R. Pierluisi-Urrutia*. (D.P.R. Nov. 1, 2021); *See* Ben Adams and Cynthia Barmore, *Questioning Sincerity: The Role of the Courts after Hobby Lobby,*" 67 Stan. L. Rev. Online 59, 60 (2014). Although the court in *Seeger* determined conscientious objector status based on a federal statute, the court set the standard for determining religious belief under the Establishment Clause and RFRA: "*Seeger* illustrated that for a religiously based exemption statute to withstand constitutional scrutiny, the definition of religion must be sufficiently broad to include not only traditional theistic religious beliefs, but also nontheistic religions and moral and ethical beliefs held by individuals." *Travis Wise*, 2021 WL 4951571, at *3. Accordingly, the Department of Defense and individual services have established rules and regulations in place to handle religious exemptions and immunizations. The key, though, is that military leaders and personnel must be held accountable to follow them.[12]

Department of Defense Instruction (DoDI) 1300.17, Religious Liberty in the Military Services, specifically provides for accommodations for religious belief objections to requirements of service. U.S. DEP'T OF DEF., INSTR. 1300.17, RELIGIOUS LIBERTY IN THE MILITARY SERVICE, ¶ 1.2.b (Sept. 1, 2020) [hereinafter DoDI 1300.17]. DoDI 1300.17 states that the Services

---

12. "However, statutory provisions addressing conscientious objection provide a good framework for addressing this issue (religious objection to vaccination mandate). Conscientious objectors are those who, "by reason of religious training and belief, [are] conscientiously opposed to participation in war in any form."305 A conscientious objector may apply for noncombat service, and therefore continue to serve and support the mission.306 Congress should amend the statute addressing conscientious objection, Section 3806 of Title 50, to add a provision directing the Secretary of Defense to promulgate rules permitting involuntary separation of officers in this limited situation. Lieutenant Colonel Christopher J. Baker, *Over Your Dead Body: An Analysis on Requests for Religious Accommodations for Immunizations and Vaccinations in the United States Air Force*, 81 A.F. L. Rev. 1, 72 (2020).

will accommodate a member's sincerely held religious beliefs if the accommodation does not have an adverse impact on military readiness, unit cohesion, and good order and discipline.

DoDI 1300.17 does not specifically address immunization, but it does require that the Services consider religious beliefs as a factor for the waiver of required medical practices, and the request "must be consistent with mission accomplishment, including consideration of potential medical risks to other persons comprising the unit or organization." *Id.* at ¶ 3.3.c.

Military members will need to review their specific service regulations and directives to discern religious exemption and administrative appeal process. For example, "The Air Force Instruction for immunizations is a combined instruction: Army Regulation 40-562/BUMEDINST 6230.15B/AFI 48-110_IP/CG COMDINST M6230.4G, Immunizations and Chemoprophylaxis for the Prevention of Infection Diseases, 27 (hereinafter AFI 48-110_IP). The Instruction explains that the Air Force does not grant "permanent exemptions for religious reasons" and MAJCOM commanders are the approval authority for temporary (up to 365 days) exemptions. AFI 48-110_IP states that while medical exemptions may be temporary (up to 365 days) or permanent, it is currently Air Force policy not to grant permanent exemptions for religious reasons. Lieutenant Colonel Christopher J. Baker, *Over Your Dead Body: An Analysis on Requests for Religious Accommodations for Immunizations and Vaccinations in the United States Air Force*, 81 A.F. L. Rev. 1, 10 (2020).

The Marine Corps' policy guidance on religious exemption requests and accommodations is found in Marine Corps. Order (MCO), 1730.9. For more details on some Services policies, *see Church v. Biden*, 2021 WL 5179215, at *3-4.

Without a doubt, military cases facial judicial reticence to entertain suits "which ask the court to tamper with the established relationship between enlisted personnel and their superior officers." Id. at *5 (Citing *Bois v. Marsh*, 801 F.2d 462, 478 (D.C. Cir. 1986). Accordingly, courts will only reluctantly grant injunctive relief which interferes with a military service's corrective measures while the administrative process is still pending. *See Roe v. Department of Defense*, 947 F.3d 207, 2018 (4th Cir. 2020).

Since those original vaccination cases were issued, RFRA has been enacted by Congress. Unlike federal employees, military members' religious discrimination claims can be pursued under RFRA. This presents an opportunity for relief for military members if religious exemptions are denied and that denial is upheld through the administrative process.

Under RFRA "religious exercise" includes "any exercise of religion, whether or not compelled by, or central to, a system of religious belief." *Kaemmerling v. Lappin*, 553 F.3d 669, 678 (D.C.Cir. 2008) (citing 42 U.S.C. §§ 2000bb-2(4), 2000cc-5(7)). Additionally, "[a] religious exercise implicates 'not only belief and profession but the performance of (or abstention from) physical acts' that are 'engaged in for religious reasons.'" *Zulay Rodriguez-Velez*, (D.P.R. Nov. 1, 2021) (Citing *Burwell v. Hobby Lobby Stores, Inc.*, 573 U.S. 682, 710 (2014)).

Most importantly, RFRA applies strict scrutiny to laws which impact an individual's exercise of religious beliefs. *Id.* Thus, any pre-Smith court cases, or other applying strict scrutiny, are most applicable to review under RFRA. In *United States v. Meyers*, the 10th Circuit directly lays out the conditions for meeting the "religious exercise" component of RFRA. 95 F.3d 1475, 1482 (10th Cir. 1996).[13]

In sum, the government can only deny an RFRA accommodation if there are no less restrictive means to accomplish the compelling governmental interest. The government also bears the burden of showing that "application of the burden to the person . . . is the least restrictive means of furthering" its compelling interest. *Id.*

---

13. "In *Meyers*, the defendant, facing charges related to marijuana distribution, claimed he was the founder and Reverend of the Church of Marijuana, and it was his sincere belief that his religion commanded him to use, possess, grow, and distribute marijuana for the good of mankind and the planet earth." Lieutenant Colonel Christopher J. Baker, *Over Your Dead Body: An Analysis on Requests for Religious Accommodations for Immunizations and Vaccinations in the United States Air Force*, 81 A.F. L. Rev. 1, 14 (2020).

A military member may want to seek injunctive relief based on RFRA and violation of the member's First Amendment right to free exercise of religion especially if the member is court-martialed or disciplined for failure to follow a military order. "Unlike duress, conscientious objection is generally not a defense to the offenses of failure to obey lawful orders or missing movement. Our superior court many years ago reaffirmed that "conflict with religious scruples . . . [is] 'insufficient as a defense' to a charge of disobedience." *United States v. Webster*, 65 M.J. 936, 942 (A. Ct. Crim. App. 2008) (Citing *United States v. Wilson*, 19 U.S.C.M.A. 100, 101, 41 C.M.R. 100, 101, 1969 WL 6300 (C.M.A. 1969)).

The lawfulness of a military order is purely a legal question for the military judge to decide at trial. *United States v. Schwartz*, 61 M.J. 567 (N-M. Ct. Crim. App. 2005), aff'd, (C.A.A.F. Sept. 28, 2006). However, in *Schwartz*, the Military Court of Appeals found that the military order to receive anthrax vaccine was lawful because the order had a valid military purpose of retaining readiness capability in face of biological attack, and was clear, specific, and narrowly drawn. *Id.*

Defense Secretary mandated the COVID-19 vaccine for all military members regardless of the member's job duties or unit's mission. Mem. For Dep't of Def. employees (Aug. 9, 2021), https://perma.cc/H5G8-T62L. Remarkably, Secretary Austin only mandated use of vaccines which receive full licensure from the FDA. See DoD Instruction 6205.02, DoD Immunization Program,[14]

Presently, only one of the vaccines has received full approval: the Pfizer-BioNTech COVID-19 vaccine known as Comirnaty. This, of course, limits vaccines available for military personnel who are not already vaccinated.[15]

Regardless, DOD directives for the COVID-19 vaccine do not have the same connection to military duty as the anthrax

---

14. *See* Press Release, FDA, FDA Approves First COVID-19 Vaccine (Aug. 23, 2021); https://www.fda.gov/news-events/press-announcements/fda-approves-first-covid-19-vaccine.

15. The DOD directive considers members vaccinated with the other "emergency use only" vaccines as "fully vaccinated."

vaccine did, nor was it being imposed because it does. The DOD COVID-19 Directives and order can simply not satisfy strict scrutiny. There is only the general interest related to all Americans. The Defense orders and directives are not specifically targeted to military duties which subject vulnerable and unvaccinated individuals to unvaccinated military members which would establish a compelling interest to *mandate* vaccination. The DOD directive or orders are certainly not tailored to do so.

The D.C. District Court case *Singh v. McHugh* is most illustrative of when a court can intervene in military determinations of religious accommodation. 109 F. Supp. 3d 72 (D.C. Dist. Ct. 2015). Mr. Singh wanted to enlist in Hofstra University's Army ROTC program. Since he was a Sikh Muslim, he could not cut his hair or beard and had to wear a turban, according to his religious beliefs. *Id.* After reviewing its policies and norms, the Army asserted that it could not provide accommodation to Mr. Singh because it would be detrimental to unit cohesion and morale, and good order and discipline. *Id.* at 82-83. Although the Court acknowledged that ordinarily the Court grants great deference to the military on such matters, the Court stated that it needed to "determine whether defendants have proved that the decision to deny this plaintiff a religious accommodation that would enable him to enroll in ROTC actually furthers the compelling interests defendants have identified." *Id.* at 93-94. The Court determined the Army had not proven justification for denying accommodation to Mr. Singh. *Id.* The Army's argument was undermined by the fact that the Army routinely granted grooming and dress exceptions or accommodations. *Id.* at 95. In sum, Mr. Sing was entitled to a reasonable accommodation since the Army failed to show that it considered the least restrictive means to achieve its interest. *Id.* at 103.

Just as in the case of Mr. Singh, there are certainly many more accommodations which can be made and would be the least restrictive means and with a lesser burden on the protected activity. "RFRA . . . contemplates a 'more focused' inquiry: It requires the Government to demonstrate that the compelling interest test is satisfied through application of the challenged law 'to the person'—the particular claimant whose sincere exercise of religion is being burdened. This requires us to look beyond broadly formulated interests and to scrutinize the asserted harm of granting specific exemptions to particular religious claimants." *Burwell v. Hobby Lobby Stores, Inc.,* 573 U.S. 682, 727 (2014). The "least restrictive means" test requires that the government earnestly must evaluate reasonable and possible accommodations and choose the one least burdening on the members' rights, but still meet the government's interests. *Dunn v. Blumstein,* 405 U.S. 330, 343 (1972). The military services could temporarily grant accommodation or allowance to not be vaccinated until the member is ordered to deploy. This would be especially desirable if the member is due soon to reenlist, separate or retire. The military could also grant exceptions to those with natural immunity or who carry the antibodies.

It may also be possible for the military temporarily to reassign members to less vulnerable positions, or non-deployable positions, until herd immunity is reached, or the virus has been contained. Ultimately, these assessments are intensely fact-based and require determination. However, it is critical that military officials individually assess each religious exemption request to meet strict scrutiny.

C. The Federal Government's Vaccine Mandate for Defense Contractors exceeds its power under the Constitution and Federal laws.

None of the primary case authority previously cited herein involved mandates against defense contractors, as set forth in EO 14042. EO 14042, the "Federal Contractor Vaccine Mandate," was signed on September 9, 2021. This Federal Contractor Vaccine Mandate directed the executive departments and agencies, including independent establishments subject to the Federal Property and Administrative Services Act, 40 U.S.C. § 102(4)(A) ensure that any contract, or "contract-like" instruments, include a clause that the contractor and any subcontractor shall comply with all Safer Federal Workforce Task Force guidance for contractor and subcontractor workplace locations. The clause must include application to lower-tier subcontractors. The government intends to use the clause to ensure that federal contractors abide by the federal government present safety protocols to combat Covid-19, including mandating vaccination of its workers, even if they work outdoors at the work locations or work remotely. (Evidence Attachment E, Safer Federal Workforce Task Force, COVID-19 Workplace Safety: Guidance for Federal Contractors and Subcontractors.)

Considering its complexity and interrelated requirements, contractors may not realize that this mandate only covers certain contractors who conduct business with the federal government. The executive order exempts certain contracts such as those with a value below "the simplified acquisition threshold," which is typically $250,000. 86 Fed. Reg. at 50,986–87; FAR § 2.101. The executive order applies to contracts entered into, renewed, or with an option to be exercised on or after October 15, 2021. 86 Fed. Reg. at 50,987.

In short, the Federal Contractor Vaccination Mandate: 1) does not cover all federal contractors and subcontractors subject to EO 11246, etc.; 2) only applies to employers with certain contracts for services plus construction, concessions, and leased real estate—including services provided at or in connection with federal property or land; 3) does not cover most supply contracts providing goods to the Federal Government (and similar subcontracts to federal Prime contractors). (Information obtained from *See* McGuire Woods power point slides/video presentation: COVID-19 Employee Vaccine and Testing Mandates New Requirements for Large Employers, Federal Contractors and Healthcare Organizations https://www.mcguirewoods.com/events/firm-events/2021/9/covid-19-employee-vaccine-and-testing-mandates

Some details may change as additions are made to procurement and agency regulations and standards adjusted. Most importantly, though, this mandate should not apply until a company's contract comes up for renewal, company enters into a new contract or company chooses to agree to mutual modification. At that time, the contractor may negotiate the inclusion of the vaccine mandate clause.

Many requirements are quite restrictive and expansive. The Federal Contractor Vaccine Mandate requires the individual contractor to evaluate medical and religious exemptions. Like the Federal Employee Vaccine Mandate, the Federal Contractor Mandate limits accommodations because contractors will not be able to offer remote work or weekly testing. Additionally, employee exemptions are unclear. The mandate assures the states that the mandate will preempt any conflicting state or local law, but more restricted state or local laws are valid. Contract employers are left with potential legal challenges since ADA disability, Section 503 disability, RFRA and Title VII religious exemptions and rules requiring accommodations still apply.

In a recent stay of the Biden Administration's vaccine mandate for businesses with more than 100 employees, the Fifth Circuit properly raised grave concerns over the Federal Government reaching out across the United States to mandate certain actions by small and large businesses. *BST Holdings, LLC, et. al. v. OSHA*, No. 21-60845 (5th Cir. Nov. 5, 2021). The same concerns are raised with the Administration's vaccine mandate in EO 14042 against businesses merely because they have a direct, or even indirect, connection to a contract with the United States.[16]

Ten states have already expressed their concerns about this unlawful usurpation of power by filing a complaint in federal court. (Evidence Attachment F, *State of Missouri, et. al. v. President Biden*, et. al., Case 4:21-cv-01300 (E.D. Mo., filed Oct. 29, 2021).) The Complaint asserts ten claims for relief. The Attorney Generals from these states first claim violations of the Procurement Act, 40 U.S.C. §§ 101 and 121, which is the federal government's cited authority for its mandate. The other counts include violations of: the Procurement Policy Act, 41 U.S.C. § 1707; States' policy powers, Anti-commandeering doctrine under the Tenth Amendment of

---

16. See EO 14042, https://www.whitehouse.gov/briefing-room/presidential-actions/2021/09/09/executive-order-on-ensuring-adequate-covid-safety-protocols-for-federal-contractors/.

the United States Constitution, Procedures of the Administrative Procedures Act (APA) (OMB conclusion), Substantive sections of the APA, APA Agency action not in accordance with law and in excess of authority (OMB and FAR guidance-two counts), APA Notice requirements constituting arbitrary and capricious agency action, and Separation of Powers. First Amendment Free Exercise infringements are obviously included within those claims. Certainly, EO 14042 cannot waive or preempt contractors' or employees' constitutional rights.

"A law that operates so as to make the practice of religious beliefs more expensive in the context of business activities imposes a burden on the exercise of religion." *Burwell v. Hobby Lobby Stores, Inc.*, 573 U.S. 682, 134 S. Ct. 2751, 189 L. Ed. 2d 675 (2014). Clearly, RFRA provides one legal remedy for the above-covered contractors, subcontractors, and their employees who religiously object to the vaccine to seek injunctive relief against enforcement of the Federal Contractor Vaccination Mandate. Standing to assert a claim or defense under RFRA is governed by the general rules of standing under article III of the Constitution. 42 U.S.C.A. § 2000bb-1. "Out-of-pocket cost to a business of obeying a new rule of government can be sufficient to constitute an injury in fact, as element for Article III standing, and cost need not be large; all that is required is some concrete and particularized injury." *Little Sisters of the Poor Home for the Aged v. Sebelius*, 6 F. Supp. 3d 1225 (D. Colo. 2013), aff'd sub nom. *Little Sisters of the Poor Home for the Aged, Denver, Colo. v. Burwell*, 794 F.3d 1151 (10th Cir. 2015), vacated and remanded sub nom. *Zubik v. Burwell*, 578 U.S. 403, 136 S. Ct. 1557, 194 L. Ed. 2d 696 (2016). Thus, once these contractors and subcontractors suffer under this mandate, they have a case. The *Hobby Lobby* and the *Little Sisters of the Poor* cases support such a claim. As discussed previously, in Section IIB, RFRA imposes the pre-Smith strict scrutiny standard to any federal law—a standard this mandate cannot meet.

Plainly, a preliminary or temporary injunction is an "extraordinary remedy that may only be awarded upon a clear showing that the plaintiff is entitled to such relief." *Winter v. Nat. Res. Def.*

Council, 555 U.S. 7, 22 (2008). An extraordinary mandate from the federal government against individuals which harms their lives and infringes on their constitutional right to practice their faith demands an extraordinary remedy.

"The first step in a Rule 65(a) situation is for the court to balance the 'likelihood' of irreparable harm to the plaintiff against the 'likelihood' of harm to the defendant." *Direx Israel, Ltd. v. Breakthrough Med. Corp.*, 952 F.2d 802, 813–14 (4th Cir. 1991). Deprivation of constitutional rights unquestionably constitutes irreparable injury when determining whether to issue a permanent injunction. *Grimm v. Gloucester Cty. Sch. Bd.*, 400 F. Supp. 3d 444, 462 (E.D. Va. 2019), aff'd, 972 F.3d 586 (4th Cir. 2020), as amended (Aug. 28, 2020), cert. denied, 141 S. Ct. 2878 (2021); *Planned Parenthood S. Atl. v. Wilson*, 520 F. Supp. 3d 823 (D.S.C. 2021); *Berean Baptist Church v. Cooper*, 460 F. Supp. 3d 651 (E.D.N.C. 2020). Even more critically, the loss of First Amendment rights even for minimal periods of time warrants action. *Garden District Book Shop, Inc. v. Stewart*, M.D.La.184 F. Supp. 3d 331 (2016); *Field Day, LLC v. County of Suffolk*, 463 F.3d 167. (2d Cir., NY 2006) (emphasis added).

Some courts may deny injunctive relief because a plaintiff can obtain money damages for an unlawful loss of a job; however, those "monetary damages are inadequate to compensate for the loss of those First Amendment freedoms." *Hum. Rts. Def. Ctr. v. Sw. Virginia Reg'l Jail Auth.*, 448 F. Supp. 3d 581, 585 (W.D. Va. 2020).

EO 14042 mandates COVID-19 vaccinations to only certain contractors and subcontractors, and their employees, to promote economy and efficiency in federal procurement. There can be no economy or efficiency with complex rules and uncertain terms in which they must hire lawyers and other specialists to decipher or keep them updated on more changes from the Federal Government. There can be no efficiency or economy when only some are coerced to comply. There certainly can be no efficiency in the contractor's business as they deal with medical and religious exemptions and continually having to validate employee compliance and face potential lawsuits. There certainly can be no efficiency or economy as these contractors and subcontractors lose more and more employees who cannot comply. The Federal Government can call in the Military and the National Guard to fill in missing staff if too many people leave. The contractors do not have such options.

The Federal Government holds a hammer waiting to strike contractors and their employees into submission with whatever enforcement tools they care to use. Contractors and subcontractors, however, have all the responsibilities and risk. The government's alleged interest fails in the real world. Even if the compelling interest test is met, the Federal Government Contractor Vaccine Mandate falls far short from being the least restrictive means to achieve that interest. No weekly testing and no remote work are allowed. Only vaccinations are approved. The mandate ties the contractors' and subcontractors' hands on accommodations for religious objectors to vaccines especially. There are no choices within constitutional boundaries or the RFRA requirements. Irreparable harm to the contractors and subcontractors clearly outweighs the harm to the government if there is noncompliance.

Next in a case for injunctive relief, the plaintiffs must establish likely success on the merits of their claim. *Toure v. Hott*, 458 F. Supp. 3d 387 (E.D. Va. 2020), appeal dismissed, No. 20-6695, 2020 WL 9596387 (4th Cir. Oct. 6, 2020). This does not mean, however, that the plaintiffs need to prove certain success. *Id*. All preceding arguments will likely lead to success once a contractor or employee demonstrates the sincerity of their religious belief and how this mandate forces them to violate it.

In the final analysis, the court balances equities and the public interest. In fact, when one party is the government, the "balance of equities" and "public interest" factors for preliminary injunction merge and are properly considered together. *Am. Coll. of Obstetricians & Gynecologists v. United States Food & Drug Admin.*, 472 F. Supp. 3d 183 (D. Md. 2020), order clarified sub nom. *Am. Coll. of Obstetricians & Gynecologists on behalf of Council of Univ. Chairs of Obstetrics & Gynecology v. United States Food & Drug Admin.*,

LAW *CONTRA* FEDERAL COVID VACCINE MANDATE(S)

No. CV TDC-20-1320, 2020 WL 8167535 (D. Md. Aug. 19, 2020), and appeal dismissed sub nom. *Am. Coll. of Obstetricians & Gynecologists v. Indiana*, No. 20-1784, 2021 WL 3276054 (4th Cir. May 19, 2021).

The court serves the public interest when it protects constitutional rights, especially First Amendment freedoms. This case would be no different. A different result would invite great imbalances of power. In such a situation, the government wins with brute force and the mighty pen scribing clauses of confusing edicts against Americans. Considering so many individuals around this country are fighting vaccine mandates, the public interest undoubtedly tips the scales of justice towards Plaintiffs—actual or forthcoming.

DIGEST OF SOUTH CAROLINA LAW ON RELIGION-RELATED MATTERS

I. SOUTH CAROLINA CONSTITUTIONAL AND STATUTORY PROVISIONS

The following provisions relate to religious rights and principles, especially the free exercise of religion and the prohibition against the establishment of a religion:

S.C. Const. art. I, § 2 ("The General Assembly shall make no law respecting an establishment of religion or prohibiting the free exercise thereof.");

S.C. Const. art. XI, § 4 ("No money shall be paid from public funds nor shall the credit of the State or any of its political subdivisions be used for the direct benefit of any religious or other private educational institution.");

S.C. Code Ann. § 1 1380 (South Carolina Human Affairs Law prohibition on employment discrimination based on race, *religion*, color, sex, age, national origin, or disability);

S.C. Code Ann. §§ 13210 to -60 (South Carolina Religious Freedom Act; restores the compelling interest test as set forth in *Wisconsin v. Yoder*, 406 U.S. 205 (1972), and *Sherbert v. Verner*, 374 U.S. 398 (1963), guarantees that a test of compelling state interest will be imposed on all state and local laws and ordinances in all cases in which the free exercise of religion is substantially burdened, and provides a claim or defense to persons whose exercise of religion is substantially burdened by the State);

S.C. Code Ann. § 811230(3) (the Department of Administration is authorized and directed to "[a]fter coordinating with agencies served, develop fair employment policies to assure that appointments to position in the State classified service are made on the basis of merit and fitness without regard to race, sex, age, *religion*, political affiliation or national origin" (emphasis added));

S.C. Code Ann. § 312170(D) (South Carolina Fair Housing Law; "Nothing in this chapter prohibits a religious organization, association, or society, or any nonprofit institution or organization operated, supervised, or controlled by or in conjunction with a religious organization, association, or society, from limiting the sale, rental, or occupancy of any dwelling which it owns or operates for other than a commercial purpose to persons of the same religion or from giving preference to those persons, unless membership in the religion is restricted because of race, color, or national origin.");

S.C. Code Ann. § 335620(1)(b)(i) (South Carolina Solicitation of Charitable Funds Act, among other things, places limitations on the liability of charitable organizations to a person sustaining an injury or dying by reason of the tortious act of commission or omission of an employee of a charitable organization; "Charitable organization" does not include "a church, synagogue, mosque, or other congregation organized for the purpose of divine worship, and integrated auxiliaries of them, or a religious organization determined by the Internal Revenue Service to be a tax exempt organization that is not required to file Internal Revenue Service Form 990, Form 990EZ, or Form 990N based on its religious classification. 'Integrated auxiliaries,' as used in this subsection, include men's or women's organizations, seminaries, mission societies, and youth groups affiliated with a church, synagogue, mosque, or other congregation organized for the purpose of divine worship.");

S.C. Code Ann. § 45910(A) ("All persons shall be entitled to the full and equal enjoyment of the goods, services, facilities, privileges, advantages, and accommodations of any place of public accommodation, as defined in Article 1 of this chapter, without discrimination or segregation on the ground of race, color, *religion*, or national origin." (emphasis added));

S.C. Code Ann. §§ 531100, -110 ("No person shall be required to work on Sunday who is conscientiously opposed to Sunday work. If any person refuses to work on Sunday because of conscientious or physical objections, he shall not jeopardize his seniority rights by such refusal or be discriminated against in any manner. Sunday work shall be compensated at a rate no less than that required by the Fair Labor Standards Act.");

S.C. Code Ann. § 531150(C) ("Any employee of any business which operates on Sunday under the provisions of this section has the option of refusing to work in accordance with Section 531100. Any employer who dismisses or demotes an employee because he is a conscientious objector to Sunday work is subject to a civil penalty of treble the damages found by the court or the jury plus court costs and the employee's attorney's fees. The court may order the employer to rehire or reinstate the employee in the same position he was in prior to dismissal or demotion without forfeiture of compensation, rank, or grade. No proprietor of a retail establishment who is opposed to working on Sunday may be forced by his lessor or franchisor to open his establishment on Sunday nor may there be discrimination against persons whose regular day of worship is Saturday.");

S.C. Code Ann. § 591435 (Religious Viewpoints Antidiscrimination Act; school districts must not discriminate against students based on a religious viewpoint expressed by a student on an otherwise permissible subject, or penalize or reward a student based on the religious content of his work, or discriminate against student groups that meet for prayer or other religious speech);

S.C. Code Ann. § 5917140 (each school district during annual inservice training shall provide a program of instruction for teachers and administrators in the essentials of constitutional protections and prohibitions as they relate to religion and public-school operations, and such instruction shall include, but not be limited to, 19 topics set forth in the statute).

DIGEST OF SOUTH CAROLINA LAW ON RELIGION-RELATED MATTERS

II. RELIGION-RELATED TORTS

The following cases involve one or more tort claims brought against churches, religious entities, or individuals associated with such churches or entities:

Goodwin v. Kennedy, 347 S.C. 30, 552 S.E.2d 319 (Ct. App. 2001) (jury question was presented as to whether AfricanAmerican minister's public references to AfricanAmerican high school assistant principal as "house nigger" were slander per se, as imputing unfitness in assistant principal's profession; statements were made in connection with assistant principal's role in discipline of AfricanAmerican student, minister testified that he meant assistant principal was puppet of principal and traitor to AfricanAmerican student who was disciplined, and assistant principal testified that students did not respond as well to his discipline after incidents in question and that he retired because of these continuing difficulties);

Smith v. Smith, 194 S.C. 247, 9 S.E.2d 584 (1940) (in action for slander arising out of minister's statement during course of a sermon that he did not blame plaintiff's husband for not living with her, as she had attempted to poison him, the alleged defamatory words would be held to have charged a crime under laws of North Carolina, in which state defamatory words were uttered, since the unlawful infliction of an injury by administering poison is a crime at common law in South Carolina and it would be presumed that the common law is in force in North Carolina);

Banks v. St. Matthew Baptist Church, 406 S.C. 156, 750 S.E.2d 605 (2013) (allegedly defamatory statements of church pastor at a congregational meeting were independent of religious doctrine or governance, and thus the issue of whether the statements constituted defamation of church trustees could be decided in a civil court of law, without violation of the First Amendment's Free Exercise Clause; the statements, including an allegation that trustees failed to inform pastor of a mortgage on church property, were all simple declarative statements about the actions of trustees, the truth or falsity of the statements could be easily ascertained by a

43

court without any consideration of religious issues or doctrines, and the setting in which the statements were made, i.e., at a church meeting, did not itself defeat a civil court's jurisdiction), *cert. denied*, 135 S. Ct. 48 (2014);

Brown v. Pearson, 326 S.C. 409, 483 S.E.2d 477 (Ct. App. 1997) (alleged victims of sexual harassment or abuse by pastor did not establish cause of action against church and its district superintendent for claims arising out of harassment and abuse; church's actions in responding to complaint against pastor represented attempts to further legitimate interests of all parties involved; mere expectation by parishioners that church and its superintendent would take action on their complaints regarding alleged sexual harassment and abuse by their pastor did not create any fiduciary relationship between them; actions by church and its superintendent in responding to parishioners' allegations of sexual harassment and abuse by their pastor were not extreme and outrageous, as to permit recovery in action for intentional infliction of emotional distress; parishioners' mere disappointment with level of response of church and its superintendent to their allegations of sexual harassment and abuse by their pastor is not legally actionable fraud);

Doe v. Bishop of Charleston, 407 S.C. 128, 754 S.E.2d 494 (2014) (terms of settlement agreement reached in class action against diocese with respect to claims of sexual abuse by priests did not waive res judicata effect of settlement as to all future claims or waive statute-of-limitations defense as to future claimants who failed to come forward within claims period provided in settlement; plaintiffs' claims against diocese arising out of alleged sexual abuse by priest, which claims were based upon theory of negligent supervision, were not barred by threeyear statute of limitations, where plaintiffs alleged diocese's systematic practice of secrecy and concealment of knowledge of sexual abuse by priests, including priest who allegedly committed abuse at issue);

Goode v. St. Stephens United Methodist Church, 329 S.C. 433, 494 S.E.2d 827 (Ct. App. 1997) (owner of apartment complex, a church, did not have knowledge that tenant at complex was violent person who had been in numerous fights, or that tenant had been involved in altercation with individual, who was assaulted by tenant and others when he visited premises as social guest, earlier in day of assault, and, thus, even assuming that guest was business invitee, owner did not owe duty to protect individual from assault; any negligence on part of owner of apartment complex was not proximate cause of criminal assault of social guest at complex, as owner had no reason to foresee that breach of any duty guest sought to impose against it would have natural and probable consequence of resulting in intentional attack on guest by third parties);

Joiner v. Fort, 226 S.C. 249, 84 S.E.2d 719 (1954) (in action for injuries sustained by invitee in a church who stepped into a vent left open without placing guard or warning over vent, by contractor engaged in cleaning heating system, whether contractor, in reasonable anticipation that it was probable that the annex would be used in conjunction with the main auditorium of the church, could anticipate that one would open sliding doors and enter therein, and whether a light was left by the open vent, were properly submitted to the jury; judgment for plaintiff for $7,500 affirmed);

Ex parte Doe, 393 S.C. 147, 711 S.E.2d 892 (2011) (releases of liability contained in settlement agreement between victims of childhood sexual abuse and religious organization released all of members' claims against organization, including claims for interest; members waived any right to interest when they signed releases discharging the organization from liability for all "actions, causes of action, claims, demands and compensation, up to and including the date of the release," and the releases did not reserve any rights as to any pending motions; rather, by their plain language, the releases resolved all of the members' claims);

Crocker v. Barr, 305 S.C. 406, 409 S.E.2d 368 (1991) (church, an unincorporated charitable association, could be held liable to member for injuries sustained while performing voluntary labor at church, caused by negligence of fellow members);

Morison v. Rawlinson, 193 S.C. 25, 7 S.E.2d 635 (1940) (church services carried on daily in thickly populated residential area until early hours of the morning, wherein worshippers gave forth weird and unearthly outcries, engaged in loud shouting, clapping of hands, stamping of feet, and incessant use of drums, timbrels, trombones, horns, scrubbing boards, and washtubs, so that tumult could be heard for many city blocks, and disorderly throngs congregated in adjoining streets, with frequent fights and disorders, constituted a "public nuisance" which municipal authorities could abate; where religious services constituted a public nuisance, abatement of such nuisance does not constitute "prohibiting the free exercise of religious worship" in any constitutional sense);

DeBorde v. St. Michael & All Angels Episcopal Church, 272 S.C. 490, 252 S.E.2d 876 (1979) (creation and operation of church's proposed cemetery on large wooded undeveloped area of 6.2acre tract, which would not be visible from lands of any surrounding property owners, was an appropriate and proper utilization of its premises that would not constitute a "private nuisance" as to any surrounding property owners, particularly in light of facts that addition of such cemetery would not cause any more or less funerals to be conducted at the church, that the visual activities attendant therewith would be unchanged from conditions existing prior to construction of cemetery, and that church had had an average of less than two funerals per year conducted on its premises since its founding);

Powell v. Immanuel Baptist Church, 261 S.C. 219, 199 S.E.2d 60 (1973) (where, according to complaint, excavation was made on adjoining church property, thus depriving plaintiff's property of lateral support, prior to commencement of action, and if plaintiff prevailed on merits, mandatory injunction requiring restoration of lateral support would be an appropriate remedy, temporary injunctive relief against construction of allegedly inadequate retaining wall on church's property would have had no tendency to protect plaintiff's property from feared erosion during pendency of action and was properly denied, notwithstanding that church might be subjected to added expense if it was required to reconstruct wall after judgment on merits).

III. SPLITTING DENOMINATIONS OR CONGREGATIONS

Civil courts have no jurisdiction of ecclesiastical questions and controversies, but they do have jurisdiction to adjudicate civil, contract, and property rights involved in a church controversy. *Bramlett v. Young*, 229 S.C. 519, 93 S.E.2d 873 (1956). When a division occurs in a church congregation, the question as to which faction is entitled to the church property is answered by determining which of the factions is the representative and successor to the church as it existed prior to the division or schism, and such question is determined by which of the two factions adhere to, or is sanctioned by, the appropriate governing body of the denomination. *Id.* at 538, 93 S.E.2d at 883. The court in *Bramlett* summed up the issue as "a question of identity." In *Bramlett*, a majority of a local Presbyterian church conveyed church realty to another corporation and later withdrew from the presbytery of which the local Presbyterian church was affiliated, and from the Presbyterian church in the United States, to continue as an independent Presbyterian church. The minority who remained loyal to the parent church organizations were entitled to have the deed reformed to the local Presbyterian church as the true owner, to have the realty impressed with a trust for the benefit of the local Presbyterian church and its members, and to have the majority enjoined from interfering with the church property.

The following are additional South Carolina cases on the subject of schisms or divisions within church denominations or congregations, including related disputes about the ownership of church property:

Fire Baptized Holiness Church of God of Americas v. Greater Fuller Tabernacle Fire Baptized Holiness Church, 323 S.C. 418, 475 S.E.2d 767 (Ct. App. 1996) (when entire congregation withdraws from hierarchical church, title to church property remains in church and does not follow congregation; evidence supported finding that local congregation was part of national church's organizational structure, for purposes of determining ownership of local church building and acreage; national church was hierarchical, local congregation had always operated as part of national church, national church contributed $5,000 to local congregation to help construct church building, minister of local church was appointed by bishop of national body at its annual convention, and entire local congregation had submitted its resignation from national church; even if court were to construe deed from standpoint of whether its language was sufficient to convey title to national church, court would conclude that national church did hold title, despite local congregation's claim of ownership; there was no independent local church entity to receive title to property);

Dillard v. Jackson, 304 S.C. 79, 403 S.E.2d 136 (Ct. App. 1991) (when entire congregation of a hierarchical church withdraws from the church, title to church property remains in the church and does not follow the congregation; evidence in action to quiet title supported special referee's conclusion that local church was a hierarchical church owned by national body of the denomination, notwithstanding that national body had not met in the last 30 or 40 years);

Seldon v. Singletary, 284 S.C. 148, 326 S.E.2d 147 (1985) (a majority of members control decisions of a congregational church; in action by corporate religious society against officials of individual church to determine ownership of church property, evidence established that individual church was "hierarchical" rather than "congregational" such that property was controlled by corporate organization rather than by majority of individual church members; action by church officials loyal to corporate religious organization against other church officials asserting independence, brought to determine ownership of church property, was moot, where evidence in earlier action established that church was hierarchical and that church property was thus controlled by corporate organization);

All Saints Parish, Waccamaw v. Protestant Episcopal Church in the Diocese of S.C., 358 S.C. 209, 595 S.E.2d 253 (Ct. App. 2004) (parish filed suit seeking removal from deed book of notice filed by bishop of diocese, stating diocese and national church held interest in certain property by means of church canons, and seeking declaration that parish was sole owner of real and personal property; diocese and national church counterclaimed, alleging property was owned by parish subject to canons of diocese and national church; guardian *ad litem* was appointed to represent interests of representatives of descendants to original trustees of trust deed; finding that settlor's intent was to ensure property was used for divine worship, rather than specific denomination, was error; genuine issue of material fact as to whether trust deed failed when the Church of England ceased to exist in the United States precluded summary judgment; genuine issue of material fact as to whether parish had adversely possessed property in excess of 40 years precluded summary judgment; circuit court had subject-matter jurisdiction to determine ownership of personal property);

All Saints Parish Waccamaw v. Protestant Episcopal Church in Diocese of S.C., 385 S.C. 428, 685 S.E.2d 163 (2009) (trust of land created by a 1745 trust was executed by the Statute of Uses, vesting title in the intended beneficiary, the congregation of the parish, at the time the Church Act of 1767 formed the parish; trustees had no duties, but were mere appointees of colony given authority to accept land to establish parishes, under colonial practice in which settlor placed property in trust for congregation until government recognized the church, while beneficiary of 1745 was capable of taking title according to the express terms of the original Church Act of 1706, by which a colonial parish could hold title to land; articles of amendment of corporate entity of parish congregation were lawfully adopted, which effectively severed the corporation's legal ties to denomination's national religious organization and state diocese, such that its vestry members were the true officers of the entity; articles were approved by board of directors while still in good standing with the diocese, with the majority vestry acting as corporation's board, more than ninetenths of votes cast by congregation were in favor of amendments, exceeding twothirds statutorily required, and nothing in parish bylaws or constitutions and canons of national organization or state diocese required thirdparty approval for amendments to a congregation's charter);

S.C. Dist. Council of Assemblies of God v. River of Life Int'l Worship Ctr., 372 S.C. 581, 643 S.E.2d 104 (Ct. App. 2007) (under provision of denomination's district council's constitution and bylaws for districtaffiliated churches, stating that property of disaffiliated churches became property of the district council, when congregation voted to disaffiliate from the denomination, the property became the property of the district council; under bylaws of denomination's general governing body, providing that if minimal requirements for affiliation with general governing body were not attained church would revert to district affiliation, after local church no longer had a credentialed minister in good standing with the denomination, the church status changed from that of affiliation with the general governing body to that of a districtaffiliated church, and thus church was required to conduct its business in accordance with rules for districtaffiliated churches, as provided in the bylaws);

Adickes v. Adkins, 264 S.C. 394, 215 S.E.2d 442 (1975) (where majority of local Presbyterian church by resolution severed connection with the Bethel Presbytery and the Presbyterian church in the United States, the minority, who did not vote to secede but remained loyal to parent church organizations, were entitled to take over and control properties of church, and court order so holding did not violate majority's rights guaranteed by Establishment and Due Process Clauses of federal or state Constitution); the minority, who did not vote to secede but remained loyal to parent church organizations, could bring action against majority of local Presbyterian church, who by resolution severed connection with parent church organizations, to settle dispute as to right to take over and control property of church, without joining eleemosynary corporation, in which title was vested, or the parent church organizations);

McCain v. Brightharp, 399 S.C. 240, 730 S.E.2d 916 (Ct. App. 2012) (former church trustees and deacons brought action seeking to enjoin pastor from continuing to act as church pastor and to reinstate plaintiffs to their former positions; the circuit court found pastor to be in contempt, declared any actions taken by church following board meeting in which 12 board members voted to terminate pastor's contract to be null and void, and ordered him to reinstate plaintiffs to their former positions; pastor appealed; the court of appeals held that the circuit court had subject-matter jurisdiction to restore the status quo prevailing before church's unauthorized action of removing and silencing church trustees and deacons, and the action by church to remove and silence trustees and deacons was a nullity);

Bowen v. Green, 275 S.C. 431, 272 S.E.2d 433 (1980) (since minister of congregational church failed to demonstrate source of authority whereby boards of trustees and deacons, rather than church members, exercised power of excommunication, supreme court would restore status quo, entitling excommunicated members to reinstatement and to congregational meeting to review pastoral office);

Jeffery v. Ehrhardt, 210 S.C. 519, 43 S.E.2d 483 (1947) (where church that had allowed its incorporation to lapse had continued to exist as an unincorporated association or society, and realty was conveyed to the church, the fee simple deed to the church was effective to convey good title to its members organized as the church, and title was vested in the present members; where members of unincorporated religious society contracted to convey realty belonging to society and members authorized minister to convey premises by fee simple deed by resolution that was unanimously adopted at duly called meeting of members at which quorum was present, conveyance by minister would bind church and its members and vest in purchaser fee simple title to premises);

Epstin v. Berman, 78 S.C. 327, 58 S.E. 1013 (1907) (a complaint alleged that the plaintiffs, as members and trustees of a religious corporation, were entitled to the custody and control of a certain lot with a synagogue thereon, the property of the corporation, and that defendants, wrongfully claiming to be the trustees, were assuming to act as such, and were wrongfully exercising control and custody over the lot and synagogue to the plaintiffs' damage, wherefore they prayed, besides other relief, for a certain sum in damages; held, that the wrongful acts alleged did not necessarily import substantial pecuniary damage to the plaintiffs and the court properly ordered the complaint amended by stating with particularity how and in what way the plaintiffs had been damaged);

First Baptist Church of Woodruff v. Turner, 248 S.C. 71, 149 S.E.2d 45 (1966) (church members had no right to compel perpetual maintenance of church property as place of worship, and no right to prevent church from conveying fee simple title to real property for purpose of using proceeds to pay part of indebtedness incurred in construction of new church where majority of members had approved the move and the property was not subject to any restrictions, reverters, reversions, or right of reentry under original conveyances to church);

Pringle v. Dorsey, 3 S.C. 502 (1872) (P., being seized in fee of a lot in Columbia, endorsed upon his title deed the following words and figures: "Received from P., in trust for the congregation of Christ Church, Columbia, November 18th, 1850;" this endorsement was signed by "C., for the vestry of Christ Church, Columbia," and the deed was delivered to him by P; Christ Church, Columbia, was an unincorporated religious association; they erected a church edifice upon the lot, and worshipped in it as a congregation until 1865, when it was destroyed by fire; the association was then broken up, and the congregation ceased to exist: held, that when the congregation ceased to exist, the trust resulted to P. and he could sell and make good title to the lot);

Hatcher v. S.C. Dist. Council of Assemblies of God, Inc., 267 S.C. 107, 226 S.E.2d 253 (1976) (in class action seeking, inter alia, a judgment declaring plaintiffs to be the members of named local church and either the legal or equitable owners of the church property, special master's finding, concurred in by the lower court, that the district presbytery acted arbitrarily in dissolving the entire membership of the church, was supported by the record, and the lower court therefore properly ordered the district council to restore to membership the expelled members of the church);

Hardin v. Horger, 252 S.C. 298, 166 S.E.2d 215 (1969) (where church property was acquired by deed containing trust clause requiring that the premises be used, kept, maintained, and disposed of as place of divine worship for use of ministry and membership of particular church that had a connectional organization with centralized form of government, the beneficiaries of trust were the ministry and membership of the particular church, and local congregation was beneficiary only so long as it retained membership in the particular church; under provision of deed stating that church property shall be used, kept, maintained, and disposed of as a place of divine worship for the use of ministry and membership of particular church that had a centralized form of government, even assuming that complaints of local congregation to district superintendents were not handled properly and in strict accord with provisions of discipline of church, local congregation was not entitled to secede from church and to continue to use property for their own purposes while no longer members of the particular church);

Whitmire v. Adams, 273 S.C. 453, 257 S.E.2d 160 (1979) (where present congregation had its genesis in the "Joanna Revival Center," but had been active and expanding body since that time, where no separate rolls had ever been kept segregating original charter members from those who later joined church, and no distinction ever made as between them, church was substantially unified and continuing body since its inception, and, thus, name and charter of "Joanna Revival Center" was not property of congregation represented by defendants);

St. Andrews Evangelical Lutheran Church, of Columbia, S.C. v. St. Andrews Evangelical Lutheran Church of Columbia, S.C., Inc., 223 S.C. 9, 73 S.E.2d 845 (1952) (validity of incorporation of congregation of Lutheran church was not subject to collateral attack in action by certain members to enjoin sale of old church building and parsonage when congregation voted to relocate church; where minutes of congregational meeting of Lutheran church showed that 53 members in good standing voted for relocation of church and 16 members against relocation, and there was no question as to accuracy of minutes, sufficient number of members voted for relocation);

Middleton v. Ellison, 95 S.C. 158, 78 S.E. 739 (1913) (where there is a schism in a church, the courts will not undertake to inquire into the ecclesiastical acts of the several parties, but will determine the property rights in favor of the party or division maintaining the church organization as it previously existed; where defendants originally took their pulpits under the authority of the plaintiff bishop, they cannot subsequently question his authority, and a temporary injunction will be issued to restrain them from interference in all cases except where the congregation practically unanimously adopted the theories of defendants);

Turbeville v. Morris, 203 S.C. 287, 26 S.E.2d 821 (1943) (in suit to determine property rights of factions of a congregation, wherein plaintiffs represented the faction of the unified church and defendants opposed it, evidence justified the award of the property to plaintiffs on ground that the union of the churches had been adopted by the branches thereof);

Brock v. Bennett, 313 S.C. 513, 443 S.E.2d 409 (Ct. App. 1994) (plaintiffs who were not members of church lacked standing to bring action addressing issue of church property and conduct of its services; former trustee of church lost his standing to maintain action addressing issue of church property and conduct of its services when church was incorporated and new trustees appointed and also when he gave up his membership in church and joined another one);

Wilson v. Presbyterian Church of John's Is., 19 S.C. Eq. (2 Rich. Eq.) 192 (1846) (in 1735, funds were bequeathed to certain persons in trust to apply the interest "to the sole use and behoof, and for the maintenance of a minister of the Gospel, according to the Presbyterian profession, who is, or shall be, from time to time, regularly called and settled on John's Island, and who shall acknowledge and subscribe the Westminster confession of faith, as the confession of his faith, and shall firmly believe and preach the same to the people there committed, or which shall hereafter be committed to his care and pastoral inspection"; the church on John's Island, for the benefit of which the trust was created, was in regular connexion with a Presbytery until 1838, when, by resolution of its members, adopted by a majority of twelve to three, it was declared an "Independent Presbyterian Church, absolved from all connection with the Presbytery and every other ecclesiastical body"; the majority remained in possession of the funds of the church, and retained the minister who had been before in charge of the church, and who was a regularly ordained minister of the Gospel, according to the Presbyterian profession, had signed the Westminster confession of faith, as the confession of his faith, and had been regularly called and ordained minister of the John's Island Church; the minority organized themselves as a church by the election of officers, and were recognized by the presbytery, by the synod and General Assembly of the United States, as the Presbyterian Church of John's Island; held, on bill filed, that the minority, the complainants, were the persons who, under the terms of the bequest, constituted the church for whose benefit the trust was created; in 1754, property was conveyed to trustees for the use of the minister or pastor, for the time being, of the John's Island Church, "during the time he shall so be and continue minister or pastor of said congregation, according to the rules and discipline of Presbyterian Church government, and no longer"; held, that the minority, through their pastor, were also entitled to the use of this property);

Harmon v. Dreher, 17 S.C. Eq. (Speers Eq.) 87 (1843) (in this country, no ecclesiastical body has any power to enforce its decisions by temporal sanctions; such decisions are, in this sense, advisory—they are addressed to the conscience of those who have voluntarily subjected themselves to their spiritual sway and, except where civil rights are dependent upon them, can have no influence beyond the tribunal from which they emanate; where a civil right depends upon an ecclesiastical matter, it is the civil court, and not the ecclesiastical, that is to decide; the civil tribunal tries the civil right, and no more; taking the ecclesiastical decisions out of which the right arises, as it finds them; this court cannot look into the regularity of the process by which an ecclesiastical body proceeds to its judgment; every competent tribunal must, of necessity, regulate its own formulas; where, as well from the testimony, as from the terms of a charter incorporating a church, it is apparent that it was in full connection with a synodical body, and not independent of it as a congregation, if a portion of it secede, the rest, however small their number, secure their corporate existence, and are entitled to all the privileges and property of the corporation—but before corporators can forfeit their membership, they must be proved to have seceded from the corporation of which they are members; it seems that if a portion of corporators are guilty of such misconduct towards a body on which the corporation depends as tends to forfeit the connexion, while another portion still acknowledges the connexion and fulfils its duties, the faithful party will be entitled to stand for the corporation, and claim such remedies as may be necessary to avert the forfeiture);

Bethel Presbyterian Church v. Donnom's Ex'r, 1 S.C. Eq. (1 Des. Eq.) 154, 154-55 (1788) (a congregation with funds, becoming incorporated, has a right to the funds; "This was a bill filed by complainants to have an account of the estate and of the profits arising from the personal estate formerly in the hands of Mr. James Donnom, as a trustee for a Presbyterian church then unincorporated. The congregation had been formed of persons residing in St. Bartholomews parish, on the west bank of Ponpon river, and its vicinity; and the funds collected by voluntary subscription to uphold a church and parsonage for the use of the congregation and minister, *near* Ponpon river. The trustees were to be residents; and if they removed out of the parish, or declined acting, their places were to be supplied. James Donnom, the surviving trustee, had possession of the estate for a considerable time; and directed by his last will, that the property should go to certain persons whom he names, to be held in trust; and twothirds of the income to be applied to support a minister at the church near Ponpon river; the other onethird to be applied to *support a minister at the Saltcatcher church*, (within the parish of St. Bartholomew, but above twenty miles from the church on Ponpon river), to which place he, Donnom, had removed. The other facts and points in the case related merely to an account. The congregation became incorporated by the name of the Presbyterian church of Bethel in St. Bartholomew's parish. Their bill is to recover the whole property from defendant's representatives. On hearing the arguments of counsel, the court was of opinion, 'that Donnom had no right to divert the funds of the society to different purposes than what they were originally intended for, viz. for the meetinghouse and parsonage at that time established on the west side of Ponpon river: And whatever part of said society chose to move to another place (although in the same parish) it was a dereliction of their share of the funds of the society.'" (court's emphasis)).

IV. FREE EXERCISE

The following cases deal with the right to free exercise of one's religion:

Pearson v. Church of God, 318 S.C. 417, 458 S.E.2d 68 (Ct. App. 1995) (both state and federal Constitutions assure religious freedom, without secular interference; whether church's revocation of minister's license was equivalent to revocation of his ministry, for purposes of pension contract providing that minister would lose pension rights upon revocation of ministry, was "ecclesiastical matter," which was outside trial court's constitutional authority to decide), *aff'd*, 325 S.C. 45, 478 S.E.2d 849 (1996);

State v. Bing, 272 S.C. 544, 253 S.E.2d 101 (1979) (defendant's religion which forbade defendant from testifying against another member of the religion did not relieve him from his political responsibilities, and he was properly found guilty of contempt upon refusing to so testify; effective operation of court of justice is compelling state interest such as will warrant requiring witness to violate his own religious convictions by testifying);

City of Gaffney v. Putnam, 197 S.C. 237, 15 S.E.2d 130 (1941) (evidence that defendant was attempting to sell a magazine that was one of the propagandic mediums of Jehovah's Witnesses, that to call attention to the magazine he would call out "Religion is ruining the nations; Christianity will save the people," that a passerby took exception to statements of defendant, who was given a severe beating, and that the passerby was the aggressor, did not sustain conviction for violating ordinance providing that any person creating any disturbance or creating or engaging in any brawl, affray, fighting or indulging in profane, obscene, abusive, or vulgar language shall be subject to a fine);

Town of McCormick v. Follett, 204 S.C. 337, 29 S.E.2d 539 (1943) (a municipal ordinance prescribing an occupational license tax of $1 per day or $15 per year for agents selling books, as applied to a resident representative of Jehovah's Witnesses earning his living by selling religious books within the municipality, does not violate constitutional guaranty of "free exercise of religion"), *rev'd sub nom. Follett v. Town of McCormick, S.C.*, 321 U.S. 573 (1944);

Holley v. Mount Vernon Mills, Inc., 312 S.C. 320, 440 S.E.2d 373 (1994) (clear and unambiguous language of statute exempted textile manufacturer from another statutory provision that prohibited discrimination against employees whose regular day of worship was Saturday (citing Code 1976 §§ 53-1-110, -150));

Alton Newton Evangelistic Ass'n v. S.C. Employment Sec. Comm'n, 284 S.C. 302, 326 S.E.2d 165 (Ct. App. 1985) (one's freedom to hold whatever religious belief he believes in is absolute, and no state definition of religion that discriminates on its face against a particular religious doctrine will satisfy constitutional requirements; evangelistic association was not a "church," for purposes of exemption from required contribution to unemployment insurance fund, because its primary purpose was operating nursing home, a secular activity, rather than conducting worship services, particularly since nursing home catered to persons of all faiths, even though minister who was president of the association conducted regular worship services at the home);

In re White, 391 S.C. 581, 707 S.E.2d 411 (First Amendment rights to freedom of speech and freedom of religion do not prevent disciplinary action for an attorney's misconduct that is violative of the professional standards set by the courts; First Amendment did not protect attorney's failure to respect rights of third persons, in violation of professional conduct rule, when he sent to client church's landlords and to town manager a letter that questioned whether town manager had a soul, stated that manager had no brain, and called leadership of the town "pagans," "insane," and "pigheaded"), *reinstatement granted*, 393 S.C. 227, 712 S.E.2d 436 (2011);

Silverman v. Campbell, 326 S.C. 208, 486 S.E.2d 1 (1997) (provisions of state constitution barring persons who deny existence of "Supreme Being" from holding public office violate First Amendment religion clauses and Religious Test Clause of federal Constitution);

Williams v. Wilson, 349 S.C. 336, 563 S.E.2d 320 (2002) (determination that church was a "congregational" church, in which the congregation rather than the trustees had authority over church matters, did not infringe upon the church's ability to choose its own form of government or infringe the church's right to the free exercise of religion; the church bylaws supported the finding that the church was in fact a congregational church);

S.C. Dep't of Soc. Servs. v. Father & Mother, 294 S.C. 518, 366 S.E.2d 40 (Ct. App. 1988) (child abuse statute prohibiting intentional or excessive corporal punishment by parent was not unconstitutional, on theory that it denied parent's right to religious liberty under First Amendment);

Bessinger v. BiLo, Inc., 366 S.C. 426, 622 S.E.2d 564 (Ct. App. 2005) (retail grocers and store managers did not violate First Amendment free speech rights of manufacturer of barbecue sauce, even if they terminated their relationship with manufacturer based solely on manufacturer's political and religious views, which included manufacturer's use of Confederate flag on barbecue sauce labels and distribution of religious literature at his restaurants; such termination of relationship did not involve state action restricting expression in public forum);

Knotts v. Williams, 319 S.C. 473, 462 S.E.2d 288 (1995) (under Free Exercise Clause, supreme court lacked subject-matter jurisdiction to dictate procedures for church to follow in terminating its pastor, as church was governed congregationally, such that court had jurisdiction only to review actions taken by congregation, and no action had been taken by congregation; neither congregation nor church was named as party to suit, and congregation never approved agreement to have court determine percentage vote necessary to terminate its pastor and who would be eligible to vote, but, rather, parties that consented to agreement were board of deacons and group of members of church, who were not church's governing authority);

Sherbert v. Verner, 240 S.C. 286, 125 S.E.2d 737 (1962) (by restricting her availability for employment through her refusal to work from sundown Friday until sundown Saturday because of her religious convictions, textile mill employee was not "available for work" within Unemployment Compensation Law), *rev'd*, 374 U.S. 398 (1963) (South Carolina could not constitutionally apply eligibility provisions of its unemployment compensation statutes so as to deny benefits to claimant who refused Saturday employment because of her religious beliefs);

State v. Meredith, 197 S.C. 351, 15 S.E.2d 678 (1941) (a minister who, as a member of the religious society called Jehovah's Witnesses was engaged in going from house to house through the rural districts in order to preach and teach principles drawn from the Bible, in accordance with his faith, and who, as incidental to his work of evangelism, sold religious books and pamphlets for a consideration that was devoted to publication of other religious literature, was not guilty of violating the statute declaring that no person shall as "hawker" or "peddler" expose for sale or sell any goods, wares, and merchandise without having first obtained a license; it was not necessary for court to reach issue of whether prosecution also violated freedom to worship);

City of Darlington v. Thompson, 234 S.C. 89, 106 S.E.2d 918 (1959) (preaching, teaching, distributing, and taking subscriptions for religious magazines and literature by members of religious sect is not such business, trade, or profession as is contemplated by Darlington licensing ordinance; and where the "sale" of such literature by defendants was merely collateral to their main purpose of preaching and teaching tenets of their religion, and there was no profit motive involved, they should not have been convicted for violating ordinance).

V. ESTABLISHMENT CLAUSE AND SEPARATION OF CHURCH AND STATE

The following cases deal with issues concerning the prohibition against government establishment of religion and the separation of church and state:

Thayer v. S.C. Tax Comm'n, 307 S.C. 6, 413 S.E.2d 810 (1992) (statute granting exemption from use tax to religious publications violated Establishment Clause of the First Amendment; exemption did not have a secular objective, and its primary effect was to advance religion);

Magee v. O'Neill, 19 S.C. 170 (1883) (the constitutional provisions that prohibit the establishment of any one denomination of Christians protect each and all in the peaceable enjoyment of their own mode of worship; instead of renouncing all religious denominations, they protect all; a testator bequeathed a fund to trustees, the income whereof was to be appropriated to the maintenance and education of his granddaughter, then an infant, "provided she is educated in some Roman Catholic female seminary, or school, and is raised as a Roman Catholic, in the faith and communion of her deceased father," the whole amount to be paid to her at her majority or marriage, freed from all trusts; but, if she "is not educated in a Catholic seminary or school, or raised as a Roman Catholic, in the faith of the Roman Catholic Church, then" to testator's daughters; held, that the granddaughter not having been educated in a Roman Catholic school, or raised as a Roman Catholic, in the faith of the Roman Catholic Church, the fund, at her majority, became vested in testator's daughters, under the terms of his will);

Durham v. McLeod, 259 S.C. 409, 192 S.E.2d 202 (1972) (act authorizing state agency to make, insure, or guarantee loans to students at any institution of higher learning did not violate constitutional provision that prohibits the use of property or credit of the state directly or indirectly in aid of any church-controlled college or school since the loan fund was a trust fund, established by issuance of bonds payable solely from repayment of loans, grants, and revenues earned by the agency, and thus did not constitute "public money or credit" within meaning of the constitutional provision, and since all institutions of higher education, public or private and sectarian or secular, were eligible; act did not violate the Establishment Clauses of the state and federal Constitutions since it was scrupulously neutral between religion and irreligion and as between various religions, making students at all institutions of higher learning eligible to receive such loans);

Hunt v. McNair, 258 S.C. 97, 187 S.E.2d 645 (1972) (Educational Facilities Authority Act, under which private religious college would deed portions of its property to State, taking lease back, and State would give college proceeds of revenue bonds, to be paid with lease proceeds, for facilities and structures, property to be returned to college on retirement of bonds, with prohibition on use of property involved for sectarian instruction or religious worship, did not violate Establishment or Free Exercise of Religion Clauses), *aff'd*, 413 U.S. 734 (1973);

Hartness v. Patterson, 255 S.C. 503, 179 S.E.2d 907 (1971) (use of public funds, under statute making such funds available to provide financial aid for students attending independent institutions of higher learning, to provide tuition grants to students attending participating religious institutions, constituted "aid" to such institutions within meaning of, and prohibited by, article of constitution prohibiting use of public money, directly or indirectly, to aid institutions of higher learning controlled by sectarian groups);

State v. Solomon, 245 S.C. 550, 141 S.E.2d 818 (1965) (purpose of Sunday closing law was not religious but was to provide uniform day of rest for all citizens, permitting only work of necessity or charity, and the law thus did not violate federal and state constitutional provisions regarding establishment of religion and free exercise thereof; Sunday closing law provision that any employee working in retail store where there are more than three employees shall be granted time off to attend church services upon request abridged no right of retailer to free exercise of his religious beliefs);

Carolina Amusement Co. v. Martin, 236 S.C. 558, 115 S.E.2d 273 (1960) (statute prohibiting public sports or pastimes and construed to prohibit showing of motion pictures on Sunday is not unconstitutional as violative of prohibition against establishment of religion);

Xepapas v. Richardson, 149 S.C. 52, 146 S.E. 686 (1929) (law authorizing confiscation of goods offered or exposed for sale on Sunday held not unconstitutional);

State v. Hondros, 100 S.C. 242, 84 S.E. 781 (1915) (statute providing for the forfeiture of goods exposed for sale on Sunday does not violate constitutional provision declaring that the General Assembly shall make no law respecting an establishment of religion);

Parker v. Bates, 216 S.C. 52, 56 S.E.2d 723 (1949) (act authorizing allocation of state tax funds to counties for construction of health centers and hospitals would not be held invalid on ground that it contained provision permitting money to be used for privately owned eleemosynary hospitals in violation of constitutional provision prohibiting grant of public funds for a sectarian purpose, in absence of showing of any attempted or intended violation of constitutional provision by governing board of any county in application of the funds);

Mullis v. Celanese Corp. of Am., 234 S.C. 380, 108 S.E.2d 547 (1959) (General Assembly may, in its discretion, classify pursuits, occupations, or businesses for inclusion in, or exemption from, statutes requiring observance of Sunday and such classification, if based upon pertinent and substantial differences rationally justifying the diversity; this does not offend Equal Protection Clause, nor does it render the statute special legislation repugnant to constitutional provision forbidding enactment of special laws if a general law can be made applicable);

State v. Smith, 271 S.C. 317, 247 S.E.2d 331 (1978) (statute making it unlawful to sell any goods, wares, or merchandise on Sunday is not violative of equal protection as discriminatory, because it exempts from prohibition grocery stores that can be operated with three or fewer employees, as legislature could reasonably find that health and welfare of populace require that items normally sold by small grocery stores be made available and that at same time, a day of rest be extended to maximum number of citizens);

Banks v. St. Matthew Baptist Church, 406 S.C. 156, 750 S.E.2d 605 (2013) (in accordance with the constitutional freedom of religion and corresponding separation of church and state enshrined in the First Amendment, religious organizations must be given an independence from secular control or manipulation, in short, power to decide for themselves, free from state interference, matters of church government as well as those of faith and doctrine; allegedly defamatory statements of church pastor at a congregational meeting were independent of religious doctrine or governance, and thus the issue of whether the statements constituted defamation of church trustees could be decided in a civil court of law), *cert. denied*, 135 S. Ct. 48 (2014);

State v. Floyd, 353 S.C. 55, 577 S.E.2d 215 (2003) (juror was permitted to make an affirmation, rather than swear a religious oath ["so help you God"], and, thus, trial court erred in dismissing juror who was unwilling to take religious oath because he was not religious and thought the oath violated the requirement of separation of church and state, in prosecution for taking a hostage and carrying a weapon while an inmate);

Young v. County of Charleston, No. 97CP103491, 1999 WL 33530383, at *6 (S.C. Com. Pl. Jan. 21, 1999) (unpublished opinion) (resolution of County Council authorizing the display of the Ten Commandments in the County Council Chambers, and the subsequent display, were in violation of the Establishment Clauses of the U.S. and South Carolina Constitutions);

Gilbert v. Bath, 267 S.C. 171, 227 S.E.2d 177 (1976) (basic intent of provision of lease agreement, entered into by regional health services district, owner of certain land conveyed to it by city as site for proposed hospital and proposed recipient of county funds for construction thereof, for lease of entire tract, with improvements to be erected thereon, to private, nonprofit corporation which was to operate new hospital and contribute bulk of construction costs thereof, was to permit training of nurses and interns, a universally accepted function of 300bed hospital; those educational functions are positive factors in treating sick, and such functions would not convert facility into private educational institution, so as to fall within constitutional prohibition of expending any public funds for direct benefit of any religious or other private educational institution).

EVIDENCE ATTACHMENT A

Church Complaint

IN THE UNITED STATES DISTRICT COURT
FOR THE DISTRICT OF COLUMBIA
Civil Action No.: 1:21-cv-xxxx
VERIFIED COMPLAINT FOR
DECLARATORY AND
INJUNCTIVE RELIEF
JURY TRIAL DEMANDED
October 24, 2021

Plaintiffs[1] Steven Church, Lesley Church, Alma Gonzalez, Dynika Barnwell, Douglas Czerwinski, Jason Coffey, Joshua Schmidt, Melina Royer, Tamika Walls, Jaime Espitia, Somer Stephens, Alex Berne, Alan Camp, Stephanie Perrotta, Christopher Axtell, Grace Brown, Kristofor Hallfrisch, Dorothy Morgan, Andrew Soto, and Christopher Hall (collectively, "Plaintiffs"), by and through undersigned counsel, file this action against Defendants Joseph R. Biden, in his official capacity as President of the United States, Lloyd J. Austin III, in his official capacity as Secretary of the Department of Defense, Antony J. Blinken, in his official capacity as Secretary of State, Janet Yellen, in her official capacity as Secretary of Treasury, Merrick B. Garland, in his official capacity as Attorney General of the United States, Thomas J. Vilsack, in his

---

1. Plaintiffs contemporaneously file a Motion to Proceed under Pseudonym to Omit Home Addresses from the Complaint. *See* LCvR 5.1(c)(1).

official capacity as Secretary of Agriculture, Gina M. Raimondo, in her official capacity as Secretary of Commerce, Martin J. Walsh, in his official capacity as Secretary of Labor, Xavier Becerra, in his official capacity as Secretary of the Department of Health and Human Services, Marcia L. Fudge, in her official capacity as Secretary of Housing and Urban Development, Peter Buttigieg, in his official capacity as Secretary of Transportation, Jennifer N. Granholm, in her official capacity as Secretary of Energy, Miguel Cardona, in his official capacity as Secretary of Education, Denis McDonough, in his official capacity as Secretary of Veteran Affairs, Alejandro Mayorkas, in his official capacity as Secretary of Homeland Security, Clarence W. Nelson II, in his official capacity as Administrator of the National Aeronautics and Space Administration, Kilolo Kihakazi, in her official capacity as Acting Commissioner of the Social Security Administration, and Robin Carnahan, in her official capacity as Administrator of General Services Administration (collectively, "Defendants" or "federal government") on the grounds and in the amount set forth as follows:

URGENCY OF THIS ACTION REQUIRES EMERGENCY RELIEF

Plaintiffs are federal employees of the United States government and active-duty military members with sincerely held religious beliefs that prohibit them from complying with the vaccine mandate imposed by President Biden by signing Executive Order 14043 on September 9, 2021 ("E.O. 14043") or Secretary of Defense Lloyd Austin III's Order issued on August 24, 2021. ("DoD Order") (collectively, "Vaccine Mandates"). Absent the relief requested, Plaintiffs, along with hundreds of thousands of other federal employees and active-duty service members will be terminated, discharged or separated on or before November 22, 2021.[2]

---

2. To be "fully vaccinated" by the deadline of November 22, 2021, Plaintiffs (and all other federal employees) must receive (1) the second dose of the two-dose BioNTech and Moderna vaccine series; or (2) the J&J single-dose vaccine no less than two weeks prior to November 22; thus, **the salient date relevant for the**

EVIDENCE ATTACHMENT A

While reasonable minds can disagree as to the magnitude of the COVID-19 pandemic, the Supreme Court reminds us that "even in a pandemic, the Constitution cannot be put away and forgotten." Roman Catholic Diocese of Brooklyn v. Cuomo, 141 S. Ct. 63, 68 (2021) (emphasis added). Contemporaneous with the commencement of this action Plaintiffs have filed an Application for a Temporary Restraining Order ("TRO") and Preliminary Injunction to maintain the status quo of our federal governmental operations and to put an end to this involuntary game of Monty Hall millions of Americans have been compelled to involuntary play. And while the currency of this game is not exclusively money but also the rights to life, liberty, and property, it would be imprudent to not address the magnitude of the economic impact of this case.

Absent the injunctive relief Plaintiffs request herein, Plaintiffs will suffer irreparable harm as their fundamental rights are trampled and they lose their jobs for no reason beyond their sincerely held religious beliefs. If Defendants are not enjoined from enforcing the Vaccine Mandates, hundreds of thousands of federal workers and military personnel will be forcibly removed from our government and Armed Forces, thrusting our nation into a state more vulnerable than the United States has experienced in a quarter of a millennium. Allowing Defendants to continue enforcing the Vaccine Mandate that was issued to save lives will only cause more lives to be lost, or at the very minimum, subject 360 million American lives to dangers far greater than COVID-19. To do so would be unfathomable.

JURISDICTION & VENUE

This action arises under the Free Exercise Clause of the First Amendment, the Religious Freedom Restoration Act, 42 U.S.C. §§ 2000bb to 2000bb-4, ("RFRA"), the Equal Protection Clause of the

---

emergency relief requested is November 8, 2021. As of the date of this filing, the Johnson & Johnson ("J&J") shot is the only vaccine available to Plaintiffs that satisfies the rapidly approaching November 22 deadline. The J&J vaccine is not FDA-approved.

Fifth Amendment to the United States Constitution, and under the Emergency Use Authorization provisions of the Federal Food Drug and Cosmetic Act, 21 U.S.C. § 360bbb-3 ("FDCA").

This Court has jurisdiction over this action pursuant to 28 U.S.C. §§ 1331 1343(a).

Venue is properly laid in this district pursuant to 28 U.S.C. § 1391(b)(2) because a substantial part of the events or omissions giving rise to Plaintiffs' claims occurred in this district.

This Court is authorized to grant declaratory relief under the Declaratory Judgment Act, 28 U.S.C. §§ 2201–2202, implemented through Fed. R. Civ. P. 57.

PARTIES

I. PLAINTIFFS

Plaintiff Steven D. Church ("Mr. Church") is an adult resident of Virginia and a federal employee within the meaning intended pursuant to E.O. 14043. Specifically, Mr. Church serves as the Staffing Recruitment and Operations Center ("SROC") Director under the Assistant Secretary of Administration for the Department of Health and Human Services ("HHS"). Prior to serving in this capacity, Mr. Church has served our government for twenty-five (25) years, first as an active-duty service member in the 101st Airborne Division of the United States Army followed by more than two decades of service as a civilian federal employee. Mr. Church is also an ordained minister and a devout Christian who cannot in morality receive the vaccine without compromising his closely held religious beliefs. Mr. Church lodges all counts in this four (4) count Verified Complaint against Defendants Joseph R. Biden, in his official capacity as President of the United States and Xavier Becerra, in his official capacity as Secretary of the Department Health and Human Services.

Plaintiff Lesley Church ("Mrs. Church") is an adult resident of Virginia and a federal employee within the meaning intended pursuant to E.O. 14043. Specifically, Mrs. Church serves as the

EVIDENCE ATTACHMENT A

Director of Operational Support for the Office of the Inspector General ("OIG") for the United States Department of Defense ("DoD"). Mrs. Church also serves as the DoD OIG COVID-19 coordinator and is responsible for inter alia coronavirus case reporting and tracking and coordinated and scheduled vaccinations for DOD OIG employees. Following up on behalf of employees' inquiries about COMIRNATY availability, Mrs. Church was informed that the Pentagon does not have COMIRNATY and does not know when COMIRNATY will be available. Additionally, Mrs. Church is a devout Christian who cannot in morality receive the vaccine without compromising her closely held religious beliefs. Mrs. Church lodges all counts in this four (4) count Verified Complaint against Defendants Joseph R. Biden, in his official capacity as President of the United States and Lloyd J. Austin III, in his official capacity as Secretary of the Department of Defense.

Plaintiff Alma Gonzalez is an adult resident of Georgia and a federal employee within the meaning intended pursuant to E.O. 14043. Specifically, Ms. Gonzalez is a Contact Representative for the U.S. Department of Treasury ("USDT"). Ms. Gonzalez is also a devout Christian who cannot in morality receive the vaccine without compromising her closely held religious beliefs. Ms. Gonzalez lodges all counts in this four (4) count Verified Complaint against defendants Joseph R. Biden, in his official capacity as President of the United States and Janet Yellen, in her official capacity as Secretary of Treasury.

Plaintiff Dynika Barnwell is an adult resident of Maryland and a federal employee within the meaning intended pursuant to E.O. 14043. Specifically, Ms. Barnwell is a Budget Analyst for the U.S. Department of Commerce ("DoC"). Ms. Barnwell is also a devout Christian who cannot in morality receive the vaccine without compromising her closely held religious beliefs. Ms. Barnwell lodges all counts in this four (4) count Verified Complaint against Defendants Joseph R. Biden, in his official capacity as President of the United States and Gina M. Raimondo, in her official capacity as Secretary of Commerce.

Plaintiff Douglas Czerwinski is an adult resident of Florida and a federal employee within the meaning intended pursuant to E.O. 14043. Specifically, Mr. Czerwinski is an AST in Experimental Facility Development for the U.S. National Aeronautics and Space Administration ("NASA"). Mr. Czerwinski is also a devout Christian who cannot in morality receive the vaccine without compromising his closely held religious beliefs. Mr. Czerwinski lodges all counts in this four (4) count Verified Complaint against Defendants Joseph R. Biden, in his official capacity as President of the United States and Clarence W. Nelson II, in his official capacity as Administrator of the National Aeronautics and Space Administration.

Plaintiff Jason Coffey is an adult resident of California and a federal employee within the meaning intended pursuant to E.O. 14043. Specifically, Mr. Coffey is a Special Agent for the Federal Bureau of Investigation ("FBI"), an agency within the U.S. Department of Justice ("DOJ"). Special Agent Coffey is also a devout Christian who cannot in morality receive the vaccine without compromising his closely held religious beliefs. Special Agent Coffey lodges all counts in this four (4) count Verified Complaint against Defendants Joseph R. Biden, in his official capacity as President of the United States and Merrick B. Garland, in his official capacity as Attorney General of the United States.

Plaintiff Joshua Schmidt is an adult resident of Illinois and a federal employee within the meaning intended pursuant to E.O. 14043. Specifically, Mr. Schmidt is a Customs and Border Protection Agent for the U.S. Department of Homeland Security ("DHS"). Mr. Schmidt is also a devout Christian who cannot in morality receive the vaccine without compromising his closely held religious beliefs. Mr. Schmidt lodges all counts in this four (4) count Verified Complaint against Defendants Joseph R. Biden, in his official capacity as President of the United States and Alejandro Mayorkas, is his official capacity as the Secretary of the Department of Homeland Security.

Plaintiff Melina Royer is an adult resident of Louisiana and a federal employee within the meaning intended pursuant to E.O.

EVIDENCE ATTACHMENT A

14043. Specifically, Ms. Royer is a Conservationist for the U.S. Department of Agriculture ("USDA"). Ms. Royer is also a devout Christian who cannot in morality receive the vaccine without compromising her closely held religious beliefs. Ms. Royer lodges all counts in this four (4) count Verified Complaint against Defendants Joseph R. Biden, in his official capacity as President of the United States and Thomas J. Vilsack, in his official capacity as Secretary of Agriculture.

Plaintiff Tamika Walls is an adult resident of Maryland and a federal employee within the meaning intended pursuant to E.O. 14043. Specifically, Ms. Walls is a Senior Program Analyst for the U.S. Department of Housing and Urban Development ("HUD"). Ms. Walls is also a devout Christian who cannot in morality receive the vaccine without compromising her closely held religious beliefs. Ms. Walls lodges all counts in this four (4) count Verified Complaint against Defendants Joseph R. Biden, in his official capacity as President of the United States and Marcia Fudge, in her official capacity as Secretary of Housing and Urban Development.

Plaintiff Jaime Espitia is an adult resident of Illinois and a federal employee within the meaning intended pursuant to E.O. 14043. Specifically, Mr. Espitia is an Investigator for the Occupational Safety and Health Administration ("OSHA"), an agency within the U.S. Department of Labor ("DOL"). Mr. Espitia is also a devout Christian who cannot in morality receive the vaccine without compromising his closely held religious beliefs. Mr. Espitia lodges all counts in this four (4) count Verified Complaint against Defendants Joseph R. Biden, in his official capacity as President of the United States and Martin J. Walsh, in his official capacity as Secretary of Labor.

Plaintiff Somer Stephens is an adult resident of Tennessee and a federal employee within the meaning intended pursuant to E.O. 14043. Specifically, Ms. Stephens is a General Engineer for the U.S. Department of Energy ("DOE"). Ms. Stephens is also a devout Christian who cannot in morality receive the vaccine without compromising her closely held religious beliefs. Ms. Stephens lodges all counts in this four (4) count Verified Complaint against

Defendants Joseph R. Biden, in his official capacity as President of the United States and Jennifer N. Granholm, in her official capacity as Secretary of Energy.

Plaintiff Alex Berne is an adult resident of Florida and a federal employee within the meaning intended pursuant to E.O. 14043. Specifically, Mr. Berne is a Claims Specialist for the U.S. Social Security Administration ("SSA"). Mr. Berne is also a devout Christian who cannot in morality receive the vaccine without compromising his closely held religious beliefs. Mr. Berne lodges all counts in this four (4) count Verified Complaint against Defendants Joseph R. Biden, in his official capacity as President of the United States and Kilolo Kijakazi is the Acting Commissioner of the Social Security Administration.

Plaintiff Alan Camp is an adult resident of Colorado and a federal employee within the meaning intended pursuant to E.O. 14043. Specifically, Mr. Camp is a Project Manager for the U.S. General Services Administration ("GSA"). Mr. Camp is also a devout Christian who cannot in morality receive the vaccine without compromising his closely held religious beliefs. Mr. Camp lodges all counts in this four (4) count Verified Complaint against Defendants Joseph R. Biden, in his official capacity as President of the United States and Robin Carnahan, in her official capacity as Administrator of General Services Administration.

Plaintiff Stephanie Perrotta is an adult resident of New York and a federal employee within the meaning intended pursuant to E.O. 14043. Specifically, Ms. Perrotta is a Veterans and Military Crisis Line Social Science Assistant for the U.S. Department of Veterans Affairs ("VA"). Ms. Perrotta is also a devout Christian who cannot in morality receive the vaccine without compromising her closely held religious beliefs. Ms. Perrotta lodges all counts in this four (4) count Verified Complaint against Defendants Joseph R. Biden, in his official capacity as President of the United States and Denis McDonough, in his official capacity as Secretary of Veteran Affairs

Plaintiff Christopher Axtell is an adult resident of Iowa and a federal employee within the meaning intended pursuant to E.O.

14043. Specifically, Mr. Axtell is an Operations Supervisor for Air Traffic Control within the U.S. Department of Transportation ("DOT"). Mr. Axtell is also a devout Christian who cannot in morality receive the vaccine without compromising his closely held religious beliefs. Mr. Axtell lodges all counts in this four (4) count Verified Complaint against Defendants Joseph R. Biden, in his official capacity as President of the United States and Peter Buttigieg,, in his official capacity as Secretary of Transportation.

Plaintiff Grace Brown is an adult resident of Maryland and a federal employee within the meaning intended pursuant to E.O. 14043. Specifically, Ms. Brown is a Management Analyst for the U.S. Department of Education ("DoED"). Additionally, Ms. Brown is also a devout Christian who cannot in morality receive the vaccine without compromising her closely held religious beliefs. Ms. Brown lodges all counts in this four (4) count Verified Complaint against Defendants Joseph R. Biden, in his official capacity as President of the United States and Miguel Cardona, in his official capacity as Secretary of Education.

Plaintiff Kristofor Hallfrisch is an adult citizen of the United States domiciled in the State of Texas and a federal employee within the meaning intended pursuant to E.O. 14043. Specifically, Mr. Hallfrisch is a Special Agent for the U.S. Department of State ("DOS"). Mr. Hallfrisch is also a devout Christian who cannot in morality receive the vaccine without compromising his closely held religious beliefs. Because of his sincerely held religious beliefs, DOS granted Special Agent Hallfrisch a religious exemption and accommodation in accord with constitutional and federal statutory law and the provisions of E.O. 14043. Special Agent Hallfrisch's accommodation does not change his work environment, it does not impact his ability to dutifully perform the functions of his job, and otherwise impose no burden or undue hardship on his employer. DOS merely stated Special Agent Hallfrisch is to abide by CDC guidance. Despite this, however, President Biden and Secretary Blinken, by and through their officers, agents, or subordinates, have continued to engage in a relentless barrage of demands that Special Agent Hallfrisch provide information about his religion. by and through his officers, However, on October 11, 2021, the Department of State attempted to revoke the exemption and accommodation to which he is lawfully entitled on the basis that he did not submit the right form to GMT, the personnel office within the Department of State. Special Agent Hallfrisch lodges Count IV of this four (4) count Verified Complaint against Defendant Joseph R. Biden, in his official capacity as President of the United States and Secretary Blinken, in his official capacity as Secretary of State.

Plaintiff Dorothy Morgan is an adult resident of Maryland and a federal employee within the meaning intended pursuant to E.O. 14043. Specifically, Ms. Morgan is a Training Administrator for the Bureau of Land Management, an agency within the U.S. Department of Interior ("DOI"). Ms. Morgan is also a devout Christian who cannot morally receive the vaccine without compromising her closely held religious beliefs. Ms. Morgan lodges all counts in this four(4) count Verified Complaint against Defendants Joseph R. Biden, in his official capacity as President of the United States and Debra Ann Haaland, in her official capacity as Secretary of the Interior.

Plaintiff Andrew Soto is an adult resident of North Carolina and an active-duty service member within the meaning of the Vaccine Mandate Secretary Austin issued on August 24, 2021. Specifically, Mr. Soto is a First Lieutenant in the United States Marine Corps and a devout Christian who cannot morally receive the vaccine without compromising his closely held religious beliefs. In light of his religious beliefs, First Lieutenant Soto submitted a request for a religious exemption four days later, on August 28, 2021; however, on September 29, 2021, the Department of the Navy denied First Lieutenant Soto's request. As such, First Lieutenant Soto lodges all counts in this four (4) count Verified Complaint against Defendants Joseph R. Biden, in his official capacity as President of the United States and Lloyd J. Austin III, in his official capacity as Secretary of Defense.

Plaintiff Christopher Hall is an adult resident of Illinois and an active-duty service member within the meaning of the Vaccine

EVIDENCE ATTACHMENT A

Mandate Secretary Austin issued on August 24, 2021. Specifically, Mr. Hall is a Corporal in the United States Marine Corps and a devout Christian who cannot morally receive the vaccine without compromising his closely held religious beliefs. In light of his religious beliefs, Corporal Hall submitted a request for a religious exemption four days later, on August 28, 2021; however, on September 29, 2021, the Department of the Navy denied Corporal Hall's request. As such, Corporal Hall lodges all counts in this four (4) count Verified Complaint against Defendants Joseph R. Biden, in his official capacity as President of the United States and Lloyd J. Austin III, in his official capacity as Secretary of Defense.

II. DEFENDANTS

Defendant Joseph R. Biden is the President of the United States, and he is sued in his official capacity. As President, Defendant Biden is the head of the federal government and Commander-in-Chief of the United States Armed Forces, and is responsible for enacting, implementing, and enforcing the Vaccine Mandates. On his first day in office, President Biden signed Executive Order 13991 ("E.O. 13991") and created the Safter Federal Workforce Task Force ("Task Force") which, under Defendant Biden's authority, promulgates and issues all policy-related guidance to the varies heads of the agencies defined by 5 U.S.C. § 105.

Defendant Lloyd J. Austin III is the Secretary of the Department of Defense ("DoD") and he is sued in his official capacity. On or about August 24, 2021, Secretary Austin issued a DoD Order that operates as a blanket vaccination mandate for all active-duty service members and is responsible for overseeing and ensuring that his order complies with the United States Constitution and federal statutory law, including requirements that inter alia all active-duty military personnel are afforded their constitutional rights, including the right to freely exercise their religion. Defendant Austin is also responsible for supervising all civilian DoD employees and the branches of the U.S. Armed Forces concerning the promulgation, implementation, and enforcement of the policies and regulations that govern military service in all branches of the U.S. Armed Services and Departments, including the Department of the Army, Department of the Navy,[3] and Department of the Air Force;[4] and for ensuring the legality of these policies and regulations. In this role, he is responsible for the maintenance and enforcement of the Departments of the Military, including all medical and records departments related to the Pentagon, DiLorenzo Clinic, or TRICARE program.

Defendant Antony J. Blinken is the Secretary of State ("DOS") and he is sued in his official capacity. Secretary Blinken is responsible for implementing and enforcing the Vaccine Mandate for inter alia all federal employees of DOS. In this capacity, Secretary Blinken issued a directive, in accordance with E.O 14043, mandating that all DOS employees be inoculated against COVID-19 or before November 22, 2021. As part of that directive, and in whole, in part, or in conjunction with the Task Force's acts, omissions pressures, instructions, directions, suggestions, or guidance, Defendant Blinken has taken steps to ensure that no DOS employee receives an exemption from the Vaccine Mandate for lawful reasons, whether religious, medical, or otherwise.

Defendant Janet Yellen is the Secretary of Treasury ("USDT") and she is sued in her official capacity. Defendant Yellen is responsible for implementing and enforcing the Vaccine Mandate for inter alia all federal employees of USDT. In this capacity, Defendant Yellen issued a directive, in accordance with E.O 14043, mandating that all USDT employees be inoculated against COVID-19 or before November 22, 2021. As part of that directive, and in whole, in part, or in conjunction with the Task Force's acts, omissions pressures, instructions, directions, suggestions, or guidance, Defendant Yellen has taken steps to ensure that no USDT employee receives an exemption from the Vaccine Mandate for lawful reasons, whether religious, medical, or otherwise.

---

3. The Department of the Navy has jurisdiction over the United States Marines Corps.

4. The Department of the Air Force has jurisdiction over the United States Air Force and United States Space Force.

EVIDENCE ATTACHMENT A

Defendant Merrick B. Garland is the Attorney General of the United States and the head of the Department of Justice ("DOJ") and he is sued in his official capacity. Defendant Garland is responsible for implementing and enforcing the Vaccine Mandate for inter alia all federal employees of DOJ. In this capacity, Defendant Garland issued a directive, in accordance with E.O 14043, mandating that all DOJ employees be inoculated against COVID-19 or before November 22, 2021. As part of that directive, and in whole, in part, or in conjunction with the Task Force's acts, omissions pressures, instructions, directions, suggestions, or guidance, Defendant Garland has taken steps to ensure that no DOJ employee receives an exemption from the Vaccine Mandate for lawful reasons, whether religious, medical, or otherwise.

Defendant Debra Ann Haaland is the Secretary of the Interior ("DOI") and she is sued in her official capacity. Defendant Haaland is responsible for implementing and enforcing the Vaccine Mandate for inter alia all federal employees of DOI. In this capacity, Defendant Haaland issued a directive, in accordance with E.O 14043, mandating that all DOI employees be inoculated against COVID-19 or before November 22, 2021. As part of that directive, and in whole, in part, or in conjunction with the Task Force's acts, omissions pressures, instructions, directions, suggestions, or guidance, Defendant Haaland has taken steps to ensure that no DOI employee receives an exemption from the Vaccine Mandate for lawful reasons, whether religious, medical, or otherwise.

Defendant Thomas J. Vilsack is the Secretary of the Department of Agriculture ("USDA") and he is sued in his official capacity. Defendant Vilsack is responsible for implementing and enforcing the Vaccine Mandate for inter alia all federal employees of USDA. In this capacity, Defendant Vilsack issued a directive, in accordance with E.O 14043, mandating that all USDA employees be inoculated against COVID-19 or before November 22, 2021. As part of that directive, and in whole, in part, or in conjunction with the Task Force's acts, omissions pressures, instructions, directions, suggestions, or guidance, Defendant Vilsack has taken steps to ensure that no USDA employee receives an exemption from the

Vaccine Mandate for lawful reasons, whether religious, medical, or otherwise.

Defendant Gina Raimondo is the Secretary of the Department of Commerce ("DOC") and she is sued in her official capacity. Defendant Raimondo is responsible for implementing and enforcing the Vaccine Mandate for inter alia all federal employees of DOC. In this capacity, Defendant Raimondo issued a directive, in accordance with E.O 14043, mandating that all DOC employees be inoculated against COVID-19 or before November 22, 2021. As part of that directive, and in whole, in part, or in conjunction with the Task Force's acts, omissions pressures, instructions, directions, suggestions, or guidance, Defendant Raimondo has taken steps to ensure that no DOC employee receives an exemption from the Vaccine Mandate for lawful reasons, whether religious, medical, or otherwise.

Defendant Martin J. Walsh is the Secretary of the Department of Labor ("DOL") and he is sued in his official capacity. Defendant Walsh is responsible for implementing and enforcing the Vaccine Mandate for inter alia all federal employees of DOL. In this capacity, Defendant Walsh issued a directive, in accordance with E.O 14043, mandating that all DOL employees be inoculated against COVID-19 or before November 22, 2021. As part of that directive, and in whole, in part, or in conjunction with the Task Force's acts, omissions pressures, instructions, directions, suggestions, or guidance, Defendant Walsh has taken steps to ensure that no DOL employee receives an exemption from the Vaccine Mandate for lawful reasons, whether religious, medical, or otherwise.

Defendant Xavier Becerra is the Secretary of the Department of Health and Human Services ("HHS") and he is sued in his official capacity. Defendant Becerra is responsible for implementing and enforcing the Vaccine Mandate for inter alia all federal employees of HHS. In this capacity, Defendant Becerra issued a directive, in accordance with E.O 14043, mandating that all HHS employees be inoculated against COVID-19 or before November 22, 2021. As part of that directive, and in whole, in part, or in conjunction with the Task Force's acts, omissions pressures, instructions, directions,

EVIDENCE ATTACHMENT A

suggestions, or guidance, Defendant Becerra has taken steps to ensure that no HHS employee receives an exemption from the Vaccine Mandate for lawful reasons, whether religious, medical, or otherwise.

Defendant Marcia L. Fudge is the Secretary of the Department of Housing and Urban Development ("HUD") and she is sued in her official capacity. Defendant Fudge is responsible for implementing and enforcing the Vaccine Mandate for inter alia all federal employees of HUD. In this capacity, Defendant Fudge issued a directive, in accordance with E.O 14043, mandating that all HUD employees be inoculated against COVID-19 or before November 22, 2021. As part of that directive, and in whole, in part, or in conjunction with the Task Force's acts, omissions pressures, instructions, directions, suggestions, or guidance, Defendant Fudge has taken steps to ensure that no HUD employee receives an exemption from the Vaccine Mandate for lawful reasons, whether religious, medical, or otherwise.

Defendant Peter Buttigieg is the Secretary of the Department of Transportation ("DOT") and he is sued in his official capacity. Defendant Buttigieg is responsible for implementing and enforcing the Vaccine Mandate for inter alia all federal employees of DOT. In this capacity, Defendant Buttigieg issued a directive, in accordance with E.O 14043, mandating that all DOT employees be inoculated against COVID-19 or before November 22, 2021. As part of that directive, and in whole, in part, or in conjunction with the Task Force's acts, omissions pressures, instructions, directions, suggestions, or guidance, Defendant Buttigieg has taken steps to ensure that no DOT employee receives an exemption from the Vaccine Mandate for lawful reasons, whether religious, medical, or otherwise.

Defendant Jennifer M. Granholm is the Secretary of the Department of Energy ("DOE") and she is sued in her official capacity. Defendant Granholm is responsible for implementing and enforcing the Vaccine Mandate for inter alia all federal employees of DOE. In this capacity, Defendant Granholm issued a directive, in accordance with E.O 14043, mandating that all DOE employees be inoculated against COVID-19 or before November 22, 2021. As part of that directive, and in whole, in part, or in conjunction with the Task Force's acts, omissions pressures, instructions, directions, suggestions, or guidance, Defendant Granholm has taken steps to ensure that no DOE employee receives an exemption from the Vaccine Mandate for lawful reasons, whether religious, medical, or otherwise.

Defendant Miguel Cardona is the Secretary of the Department of Education ("DoED") and he is sued in his official capacity. Defendant Cardona is responsible for implementing and enforcing the Vaccine Mandate for inter alia all federal employees of DoED. In this capacity, Defendant Cardona issued a directive, in accordance with E.O 14043, mandating that all DoED employees be inoculated against COVID-19 or before November 22, 2021. As part of that directive, and in whole, in part, or in conjunction with the Task Force's acts, omissions pressures, instructions, directions, suggestions, or guidance, Defendant Cardona has taken steps to ensure that no DoED employee receives an exemption from the Vaccine Mandate for lawful reasons, whether religious, medical, or otherwise.

Defendant Denis McDonough is the Secretary of the Department of Veterans Affairs ("V.A.") and he is sued in his official capacity. Defendant McDonough is responsible for implementing and enforcing the Vaccine Mandate for inter alia all federal employees of V.A. In this capacity, Defendant McDonough issued a directive, in accordance with E.O 14043, mandating that all V.A. employees be inoculated against COVID-19 or before November 22, 2021. As part of that directive, and in whole, in part, or in conjunction with the Task Force's acts, omissions pressures, instructions, directions, suggestions, or guidance, Defendant McDonough has taken steps to ensure that no V.A. employee receives an exemption from the Vaccine Mandate for lawful reasons, whether religious, medical, or otherwise.

Defendant Alejandro Mayorkas is the Secretary of the Department of Homeland Security ("DHS") and he is sued in his official capacity. Defendant Mayorkas is responsible for implementing and

EVIDENCE ATTACHMENT A

enforcing the Vaccine Mandate for inter alia all federal employees of DHS. In this capacity, Defendant Mayorkas issued a directive, in accordance with E.O 14043, mandating that all DHS employees be inoculated against COVID-19 or before November 22, 2021. As part of that directive, and in whole, in part, or in conjunction with the Task Force's acts, omissions pressures, instructions, directions, suggestions, or guidance, Defendant Mayorkas has taken steps to ensure that no DHS employee receives an exemption from the Vaccine Mandate for lawful reasons, whether religious, medical, or otherwise.

Defendant Clarence W. Nelson II is the Administrator of the National Aeronautics and Space Administration ("NASA") and he is sued in his official capacity. Defendant Nelson is responsible for implementing and enforcing the Vaccine Mandate for inter alia all federal employees of NASA. In this capacity, Defendant Nelson issued a directive, in accordance with E.O 14043, mandating that all NASA employees be inoculated against COVID-19 or before November 22, 2021. As part of that directive, and in whole, in part, or in conjunction with the Task Force's acts, omissions pressures, instructions, directions, suggestions, or guidance, Defendant Nelson has taken steps to ensure that no NASA employee receives an exemption from the Vaccine mandate for lawful reasons, whether religious, medical, or otherwise.

Defendant Kilolo Kijakazi is the Acting Commissioner of the Social Security Administration ("SSA") and she is sued in her official capacity. Defendant Kijakazi is responsible for implementing and enforcing the Vaccine Mandate for inter alia all federal employees of SSA. In this capacity, Defendant Kijakazi issued a directive, in accordance with E.O 14043, mandating that all SSA employees be inoculated against COVID-19 or before November 22, 2021. As part of that directive, and in whole, in part, or in conjunction with the Task Force's acts, omissions pressures, instructions, directions, suggestions, or guidance, Defendant Kijakazi has taken steps to ensure that no SSA employee receives an exemption from the Vaccine Mandate for lawful reasons, whether religious, medical, or otherwise.

Defendant Robin Carhahan is the Administrator of the General Services Administration ("GSA") and she is sued in her official capacity. Defendant Carhahan is responsible for implementing and enforcing the Vaccine Mandate for inter alia all federal employees of GSA. In this capacity, Defendant Carhahan issued a directive, in accordance with E.O 14043, mandating that all GSA employees be inoculated against COVID-19 or before November 22, 2021. As part of that directive, and in whole, in part, or in conjunction with the Task Force's acts, omissions pressures, instructions, directions, suggestions, or guidance, Defendant Carhahan has taken steps to ensure that no GSA employee receives an exemption from the Vaccine Mandate for lawful reasons, whether religious, medical, or otherwise.

STATEMENT OF FACTS

A. THE FEDERAL VACCINE MANDATES

On January 20, 2021, President Biden issued Executive Order No. 13991[5] ("E.O. 13991"), which inter alia established the Safer Federal Workforce Task Force ("Task Force") Among other things, E.O. 13991 states the Task Force "shall provide ongoing guidance to heads of agencies on the operation of the Federal Government . . . and shall address . . . vaccine administration [and] . . . circumstances under which exemptions might appropriately be made to agency policies in accordance with CDC guidelines, such as for mission-critical purposes." Id. § 4(e)(ix), (xii).

From his first day in office, as demonstrated in E.O. 13991, President Biden has revered CDC guidelines as the holy grail of not only medical authority—but legal authority, too. Indeed, the exemptions to agency policy should be promulgated in accordance with the United States Constitution, or at a minimum, federal statutory law.

On August 24, 2021, the day after the FDA-approved the COMIRNATY COVID- 19 vaccine (as discussed further below),

---

5. Exec. Order 13991, *see* Exhibit 1.

EVIDENCE ATTACHMENT A

Secretary Austin issued a DoD Order[6] requiring all active- duty servicemembers to be vaccinated against COVID-19 or face adverse employment action, up to and including dishonorable discharge.

On September 9, 2021, President Biden signed Executive Order No. 14043[7] ("E.O. 14043"), which inter alia ordered all agencies to implement a program "requiring COVID-19 vaccination for all of its federal employees, with exceptions only as required by law"[8] (the "Vaccine Mandate"). In addition to making vaccination against COVID-19 a condition of employment for federal employees, E.O. 14043 also states, "the Task Force shall issue guidance within 7 days of the date of this order on agency implementation of this requirement for all agencies covered by this order."[9]

On September 13, 2021, the Task Force published Guidance titled "COVID-19 Workplace Safety: Agency Model Safety Principles."[10] The Guidance, entirely devoid of any information as to religious exemptions: (1) sets a deadline of November 22 federal employees to be "fully vaccinated"; (2) reiterates the Biden Administration's policy for a "safer" federal workforce; and (3) delegates significant decision-making authority to the heads of each respective agency.[11]

Indeed, the Task Force violated E.O. 14043 on its face by not including guidance as to exceptions as provided by law–but the

6. Sec. Austin, *Memorandum for SeniorPentagon Leadership Commanders of the Combatant Commands Defense Agency and DoD Field Activity Directors*, (Aug. 24, 2021); *see* Exhibit 2.

7. Exec. Order 14043; *see* Exhibit 3.

8. "Vaccine Mandate" shall mean "requiring COVID-19 vaccination for all of its federal employees, with exceptions only as required by law." Exec. Order No. 14043, § 2, 88 F.R. 175 (Sept. 9, 2021).

9. "Requirement" shall mean the directive that "the Task Force shall issue guidance within 7 days of the date of [E.O. 14043] on agency implementation of programs "requiring COVID-19 vaccination for all of its federal employees, with exceptions only as required by law." *Id.*

10. Safer Federal Workforce, *COVID-19 Workplace Safety: Agency Model Safety Principles*, WHITE HOUSE (Sept. 13, 2021); *see* Exhibit 4.

11. The term "agency" means an Executive agency as defined in 5 U.S.C. § 105 (excluding the Government Accountability Office). *Id.* at § 3.

egregiousness as to why the Task Force refused to give the agencies guidance is conscious shocking.

B. THE TASK FORCE'S SCHEME TO CIRCUMVENT THE FIRST AMENDMENT AND DEPRIVE PLAINTIFF'S OF THEIR FREE EXERCISE OF RELIGION

Since the day President Biden issued the Vaccine Mandate, hundreds of thousands of federal government employees have been in complete disarray. Federal employees with serious, life-threatening conditions and others with sincerely held religious beliefs, such as Plaintiffs, have frantically sought guidance on how to obtain reasonable accommodations.

Due to the rapidly approaching deadline and Defendants' full awareness that Plaintiffs have the fundamental right to engage in the free exercise of religion, Defendants concocted a scheme that imposes a "deadline" to submit religious exemption requests to help "evaluate the scope" of how many federal employees have sincerely held religious beliefs prohibiting compliance with the vaccine requirement. After determining the scope, the Task Force instructed the agencies to "collect information" through a questionnaire calculated to elicit information the agencies can then use as the basis for denying a respondent's exemption request.

Video Footage from an October 8, 2021 Task Force Zoom call[12] involving over 400 high-level officials from varies agencies reveals Samuel Berger, a former Senior Advisor in the Obama Administration and the former Vice President of Democracy for John Podesta's Center for American Progress ("CAP") discussing the methodical approach each agency is to take when dealing with religious exemptions.

The Task Force advised each agency[13] to establish a deadline which the agencies are not to enforce – because there is no deadline

12. Samuel Berger, *COVID-19 Guidance Zoom Meeting*, SAFER FEDERAL WORKFORCE TASK FORCE (Oct. 8, 2021);

see Exhibit 5.

13. The term "agency" means an Executive agency as defined in 5 U.S.C. §

EVIDENCE ATTACHMENT A

imposed on the fundamental right to freely exercise religion – but rather, to use as a "forcing function" that will induce all or nearly all federal employees with sincerely held religious beliefs to submit their requests.

Once all or nearly all federal employees have submitted their religious exemption requests, the agencies, individually or in conjunction with the Task Force, can then "evaluate the scope" of how many federal employees wish to exercise their fundamental right to freely exercise their religion.

The Task Force then directed the agencies to refrain from issuing any decisions, because "**once you grant an exemption to an individual in a job category, it is very hard to say that you're not going to grant [an exemption] to a similarly situated person**."

The Task Force further instructed the agencies to "**take their time**" and the agencies "**should not feel rushed that they have to take steps immediately**" because it is important to "**collect information**" on federal employees, such as Plaintiffs, whose sincerely held religious beliefs prohibit them from complying with the vaccine requirement.

To collect this information, the Task Force advised it provided the agencies with a religious exemption form with questions that are intended to elicit information from federal employees seeking religious exemptions. The Task Force directed the agencies to "work bearing in mind that **a fair bit of thought went into the range of questions and the kind of information that [the questions] would provide**." The Task Force then gives the agencies authority to refuse to provide accommodations under whatever circumstances each agency so chooses.

Rather than advising the agencies under what circumstances the refusal to provide an accommodation would constitute a violation of federal law or deprivation of fundamental rights, the Task Force merely emphasized how important it is for the agencies to "figure[e] it out as quickly as possible . . . because [the agencies

---

105 (excluding the Government Accountability Office). *See* Exec. Order No. 14043 at § 3. It does not include the White House ("WH"), Centers for Disease Control and Prevention ("CDC"), the National Institute of Health ("NIH").

are] not going to run an accommodation in those places–and that's totally fine."

As a result, Defendants have either failed to implement a process by which Plaintiffs and other federal employees are able to submit religious exemptions or implemented a process that Plaintiffs to provide information to Defendants to which they are not entitled in violation of current EEOC Guidance, federal statutory law, and Plaintiffs' fundamental First Amendment right to engage in the free exercise of religion.

C. PLAINTIFFS' RELIGIOUS EXEMPTION REQUESTS

On October 12, 2021, Mr. Church submitted to HHS a request for religious exemption from the Vaccine Mandate as an accommodation of his sincerely held beliefs. Mr. Church articulated that he has exercised and continues to exercise sincerely held religious beliefs that compel him to abstain from receiving any of the currently available COVID-19 vaccines. Mr. Church has never exhibited or demonstrated any behavior, and no factors exist, that give rise to an objective basis for HHS or any entity within the federal government to question either the nature or the sincerity of his religious beliefs, observances, or practices. Mr. Church is amenable to continuing to work with the reasonable accommodations in place and within which he has worked for nearly two years since the outset of the pandemic without incident, including working from home just as he has for the last 584 consecutive days. With such accommodations, Mr. Church remains fully capable of performing the essential functions and duties of his job without compromising the safety of the federal workforce or his productivity, and the aforesaid reasonable accommodation does not pose an undue hardship on his employer. Despite this, Mr. Church's request for a religious exemption and accommodation has not been approved, and he imminently faces severe adverse employment action including without limitation, reprimand, loss of benefits, loss of promotional opportunity, termination of employment, and other life-altering disciplinary measures for exercising and seeking

EVIDENCE ATTACHMENT A

accommodation of his sincerely held religious beliefs prohibiting him from complying with Executive Order 14043.

On October 12, 2021, Mrs. Church submitted to the DoD a request for religious exemption from the Vaccine Mandate as an accommodation of her sincerely held beliefs. Mrs. Church articulated that she has exercised and continues to exercise sincerely held religious beliefs that compel her to abstain from receiving any of the currently available COVID-19 vaccines. Mrs. Church has never exhibited or demonstrated any behavior, and no factors exist, that give rise to an objective basis for the DoD or any entity within the federal government to question either the nature or the sincerity of her religious beliefs, observances, or practices. Mrs. Church is amenable to continuing to work with the reasonable accommodations in place and within which she has worked for nearly two years since the outset of the pandemic without incident, including working from home just as she has for the last 584 consecutive days. With such accommodations, Mrs. Church remains fully capable of performing the essential functions and duties of her job without compromising the safety of the federal workforce or her productivity and the reasonable accommodation she has requested does not pose an undue hardship on her employer. Despite this, Mrs. Church's request for a religious exemption and accommodation has not been approved, and she imminently faces severe adverse employment action including without limitation, reprimand, loss of benefits, loss of promotional opportunity, termination of employment, and other life- altering disciplinary measures for exercising and seeking accommodation of her sincerely held religious beliefs prohibiting her from complying with Executive Order 14043.

On September 29, 2021, Special Agent Hallfrisch submitted to the Deputy Chief of Mission of his assigned post at the U.S. Embassy in Djibouti a request for religious exemption from the Vaccine Mandate as an accommodation of his sincerely held beliefs. Mr. Hallfrisch articulated that he has exercised and continues to exercise sincerely held religious beliefs that compel him to abstain from receiving any of the currently available COVID-19 vaccines. Mr. Hallfrisch has never exhibited or demonstrated any behavior, and no factors exist, that give rise to an objective basis for DOS or any entity within the federal government to question either the nature or the sincerity of his religious beliefs, observances, or practices. Special Agent Hallfrisch is amenable to continuing to work in the environment he has worked since the outset of the pandemic, which he has done for nearly two years without incident. In fact, in July 2020, DOS even relocated Special Agent Hallfrisch and his family to Addis Ababa, Ethiopia on a commercial flight and then transported them to Djibouti on a private flight because the Djibouti airport remained closed due to the pandemic. Being that DOS went so far as to fund and utilize private air travel into a closed airport to accommodate Special Agent Hallfrisch, it is without a doubt that DOS can easily accommodate Special Agent Hallfrisch now–and indeed, DOS has done so. On September 29, 2021, the Deputy Chief of Mission at the U.S. Embassy in Djibouti informed Special Agent Hallfrisch that his religious exemption request had been approved:

> **From:** Tomaszewicz, Andrea J (Djibouti)
> **To:** Hallfrisch, Kristofor R (Djibouti)
> **Subject:** RE: Request for Reasonable Accommodation
> **Date:** Wednesday, September 29, 2021 4:47:13 PM
>
> Dear Kris,
>
> I approve your request for an exemption to the vaccine requirement. As part of this reasonable accommodation, I request that you follow CDC guidance for unvaccinated individuals. Should there be a situation where post guidance differs from CDC guidance, you and I will discuss on a case-by-case basis.
>
> Please let me know if you have any questions or concerns.
>
> Andrea
>
> *Andrea J. Tomaszewicz*
> *Deputy Chief of Mission*
> *U.S. Embassy Djibouti*
> tomaszewiczaj@state.gov
> +253 ▮▮▮ (office)
> +253 ▮▮▮ (mobile)
> ▮▮▮ (IVG)

Special Agent Hallfrisch is fully capable of performing the essential functions and duties of his job without compromising the safety of the federal workforce or his productivity and the

EVIDENCE ATTACHMENT A

reasonable accommodation he has received clearly does not pose an undue hardship on his employer. Since October 11, 2021, however, President Biden and Secretary Blinken, by and through their directors, officers, agents, or subordinates, have engaged in a series of retaliatory and harassing behavior demanding to obtain irrelevant medical and religious information to which they are not lawfully entitled. As a result, and despite having a religious exemption that accommodates his religious beliefs, Special Agent Hallfrisch, imminently faces severe adverse employment action including without limitation, reprimand, loss of benefits, loss of promotional opportunity, termination of employment, and other life-altering disciplinary measures for exercising his sincerely held religious beliefs.

On October 8, 2021, Ms. Brown submitted to the DoED a request for religious exemption from the Vaccine Mandate as an accommodation of her sincerely held beliefs. Ms. Brown articulated that she has exercised and continues to exercise sincerely held religious beliefs that compel her to abstain from receiving any of the currently available COVID-19 vaccines. Ms. Brown has never exhibited or demonstrated any behavior, and no factors exist, that give rise to an objective basis for the DoED or any entity within the federal government to question either the nature or the sincerity of her religious beliefs, observances, or practices. Ms. Brown is amenable to continuing to work with the reasonable accommodations in place and within which she has worked for nearly two years since the outset of the pandemic without incident. Ms. Brown rarely if ever interacts with others in person and if necessary, would be willing to self-check symptoms, wear a mask and social distance. With such accommodations, Ms. Brown remains fully capable of performing the essential functions and duties of her job without compromising the safety of the federal workforce or her productivity and the reasonable accommodation she has requested does not pose an undue hardship on her employer. Despite this, Ms. Brown's request for a religious exemption and accommodation has not been approved, and she imminently faces severe adverse employment action including without limitation, reprimand, loss of benefits, loss of promotional opportunity, termination of employment, and other life-altering disciplinary measures for exercising and seeking accommodation of her sincerely held religious beliefs prohibiting her from complying with Executive Order 14043.

Following the issuance of President Biden's Vaccine Mandate, Ms. Gonzalez submitted to the USDT a request for religious exemption from the Vaccine Mandate as an accommodation of her sincerely held beliefs. Ms. Gonzalez articulated that she has exercised and continues to exercise sincerely held religious beliefs that compel her to abstain from receiving any of the currently available COVID-19 vaccines. Ms. Gonzalez has never exhibited or demonstrated any behavior, and no factors exist, that give rise to an objective basis for the USDT or any entity within the federal government to question either the nature or the sincerity of her religious beliefs, observances, or practices. Ms. Gonzalez is amenable to continuing to work with the reasonable accommodations in place and within which she has worked for nearly two years since the outset of the pandemic without incident. With such accommodations, Ms. Gonzalez remains fully capable of performing the essential functions and duties of her job without compromising the safety of the federal workforce or her productivity and the reasonable accommodation she has requested does not pose an undue hardship on her employer. Despite this, Ms. Gonzalez's request for a religious exemption and accommodation has not been approved, and she imminently faces severe adverse employment action including without limitation, reprimand, loss of benefits, loss of promotional opportunity, termination of employment, and other life-altering disciplinary measures for exercising and seeking accommodation of her sincerely held religious beliefs prohibiting her from complying with Executive Order 14043.

On October 7, 2021, Ms. Barnwell submitted to the DOC a request for religious exemption from the Vaccine Mandate as an accommodation of her sincerely held beliefs. Ms. Barnwell articulated that she has exercised and continues to exercise sincerely held religious beliefs that compel her to abstain from receiving any of the currently available COVID-19 vaccines. Ms. Barnwell has

EVIDENCE ATTACHMENT A

never exhibited or demonstrated any behavior, and no factors exist, that give rise to an objective basis for the DOC or any entity within the federal government to question either the nature or the sincerity of her religious beliefs, observances, or practices. Ms. Barnwell is amenable to continuing to work with the reasonable accommodations in place and within which she has worked for nearly two years since the outset of the pandemic without incident. With such accommodations, Ms. Barnwell remains fully capable of performing the essential functions and duties of her job without compromising the safety of the federal workforce or her productivity and the reasonable accommodation she has requested does not pose an undue hardship on her employer. Despite this, Ms. Barnwell's request for a religious exemption and accommodation has not been approved, and she imminently faces severe adverse employment action including without limitation, reprimand, loss of benefits, loss of promotional opportunity, termination of employment, and other life-altering disciplinary measures for exercising and seeking accommodation of her sincerely held religious beliefs prohibiting her from complying with Executive Order 14043.

On October 14, 2021, Mr. Czerwinski submitted to NASA a request for religious exemption from the Vaccine Mandate as an accommodation of his sincerely held beliefs. Mr. Czerwinski articulated that he has exercised and continues to exercise sincerely held religious beliefs that compel him to abstain from receiving any of the currently available COVID-19 vaccines. Mr. Czerwinski has never exhibited or demonstrated any behavior, and no factors exist, that give rise to an objective basis for NASA or any entity within the federal government to question either the nature or the sincerity of his religious beliefs, observances, or practices. Mr. Czerwinski is amenable to continuing to work with the reasonable accommodations in place and within which he has worked for nearly two years since the outset of the pandemic without incident. Since March 2020, Mr. Czerwinski has worked from home. When he is required to go on-site, Mr. Czerwinski has worn a mask, socially distanced, and wash his hands frequently. With such accommodations, Mr. Czerwinski remains fully capable of performing the essential functions and duties of his job without compromising the safety of the federal workforce or his productivity, and the aforesaid reasonable accommodation does not pose an undue hardship on his employer. Despite this, Mr. Czerwinski's request for a religious exemption and accommodation has not been approved, and he imminently faces severe adverse employment action including without limitation, reprimand, loss of benefits, loss of promotional opportunity, termination of employment, and other life-altering disciplinary measures for exercising and seeking accommodation of his sincerely held religious beliefs prohibiting him from complying with Executive Order 14043.

On September 24, 2021, Special Agent Coffey submitted to the DOJ a request for religious exemption from the Vaccine Mandate as an accommodation of his sincerely held beliefs. Special Agent Coffey articulated that he has exercised and continues to exercise sincerely held religious beliefs that compel him to abstain from receiving any of the currently available COVID-19 vaccines. Special Agent Coffey has never exhibited or demonstrated any behavior, and no factors exist, that give rise to an objective basis for the DOJ or any entity within the federal government to question either the nature or the sincerity of his religious beliefs, observances, or practices. Special Agent Coffey is amenable to continuing to work with the reasonable accommodations in place and within which he has worked for nearly two years since the outset of the pandemic without incident. With such accommodations, Special Agent Coffey remains fully capable of performing the essential functions and duties of his job without compromising the safety of the federal workforce or his productivity and the reasonable accommodation he has requested does not pose an undue hardship on his employer. Despite this, Special Agent Coffey's request for a religious exemption and accommodation has not been approved, and he imminently faces severe adverse employment action including without limitation, reprimand, loss of benefits, loss of promotional opportunity, termination of employment, and other life-altering disciplinary measures for exercising and seeking

EVIDENCE ATTACHMENT A

accommodation of his sincerely held religious beliefs prohibiting him from complying with Executive Order 14043.

Following the issuance of President Biden's Vaccine Mandate, Mr. Schmidt submitted to DHS a request for religious exemption from the Vaccine Mandate as an accommodation of his sincerely held beliefs. Mr. Schmidt articulated that he has exercised and continues to exercise sincerely held religious beliefs that compel him to abstain from receiving any of the currently available COVID-19 vaccines. Mr. Schmidt has never exhibited or demonstrated any behavior, and no factors exist, that give rise to an objective basis for DHS or any entity within the federal government to question either the nature or the sincerity of his religious beliefs, observances, or practices. Mr. Schmidt is amenable to continuing to work with the reasonable accommodations in place and within which he has worked for nearly two years since the outset of the pandemic without incident. With such accommodations, Mr. Schmidt remains fully capable of performing the essential functions and duties of his job without compromising the safety of the federal workforce or his productivity and the reasonable accommodation he has requested does not pose an undue hardship on his employer. Despite this, Mr. Schmidt's request for a religious exemption and accommodation has not been approved, and he imminently faces severe adverse employment action including without limitation, reprimand, loss of benefits, loss of promotional opportunity, termination of employment, and other life- altering disciplinary measures for exercising and seeking accommodation of his sincerely held religious beliefs prohibiting him from complying with Executive Order 14043.

Following the issuance of President Biden's Vaccine Mandate, Ms. Royer submitted to the USDA a request for religious exemption from the Vaccine Mandate as an accommodation of her sincerely held beliefs. Ms. Royer articulated that she has exercised and continues to exercise sincerely held religious beliefs that compel her to abstain from receiving any of the currently available COVID-19 vaccines. Ms. Royer has never exhibited or demonstrated any behavior, and no factors exist, that give rise to an objective basis for the USDA or any entity within the federal government to question either the nature or the sincerity of her religious beliefs, observances, or practices. Ms. Royer is amenable to continuing to work with the reasonable accommodations in place and within which she has worked for nearly two years since the outset of the pandemic without incident. With such accommodations, Ms. Royer remains fully capable of performing the essential functions and duties of her job without compromising the safety of the federal workforce or her productivity and the reasonable accommodation she has requested does not pose an undue hardship on her employer. Despite this, Ms. Royer's request for a religious exemption and accommodation has not been approved, and she imminently faces severe adverse employment action including without limitation, reprimand, loss of benefits, loss of promotional opportunity, termination of employment, and other life-altering disciplinary measures for exercising and seeking accommodation of her sincerely held religious beliefs prohibiting her from complying with Executive Order 14043.

Following the issuance of President Biden's Vaccine Mandate, Ms. Walls submitted to HUD a request for religious exemption from the Vaccine Mandate as an accommodation of her sincerely held beliefs. Ms. Walls articulated that she has exercised and continues to exercise sincerely held religious beliefs that compel her to abstain from receiving any of the currently available COVID-19 vaccines. Ms. Walls has never exhibited or demonstrated any behavior, and no factors exist, that give rise to an objective basis for HUD or any entity within the federal government to question either the nature or the sincerity of her religious beliefs, observances, or practices. Ms. Walls is amenable to continuing to work with the reasonable accommodations in place and within which she has worked for nearly two years since the outset of the pandemic without incident. With such accommodations, Ms. Walls remains fully capable of performing the essential functions and duties of her job without compromising the safety of the federal workforce or her productivity and the reasonable accommodation she has requested does not pose an undue hardship on her employer. Despite this, Ms. Walls' request for a religious exemption and accommodation has not been approved, and she imminently faces severe adverse employment action including without limitation, reprimand, loss of benefits, loss of promotional opportunity, termination of employment, and other life-altering disciplinary measures for exercising and seeking accommodation of her sincerely held religious beliefs prohibiting her from complying with Executive Order 14043.

Following the issuance of President Biden's Vaccine Mandate, Mr. Espitia submitted to DOL a request for religious exemption from the Vaccine Mandate as an accommodation of his sincerely held beliefs. Mr. Espitia articulated that he has exercised and continues to exercise sincerely held religious beliefs that compel him to abstain from receiving any of the currently available COVID-19 vaccines. Mr. Espitia has never exhibited or demonstrated any behavior, and no factors exist, that give rise to an objective basis for DOL or any entity within the federal government to question either the nature or the sincerity of his religious beliefs, observances, or practices. Mr. Espitia is amenable to continuing to work with the reasonable accommodations in place and within which he has worked for nearly two years since the outset of the pandemic without incident. With such accommodations, Mr. Espitia remains fully capable of performing the essential functions and duties of his job without compromising the safety of the federal workforce or his productivity and the reasonable accommodation he has requested does not pose an undue hardship on his employer. Despite this, Mr. Espitia's request for a religious exemption and accommodation has not been approved, and he imminently faces severe adverse employment action including without limitation, reprimand, loss of benefits, loss of promotional opportunity, termination of employment, and other life-altering disciplinary measures for exercising and seeking accommodation of his sincerely held religious beliefs prohibiting him from complying with Executive Order 14043.

Following the issuance of President Biden's Vaccine Mandate, Ms. Stephens submitted to DOE a request for religious exemption from the Vaccine Mandate as an accommodation of her sincerely held beliefs. Ms. Stephens articulated that she has exercised and continues to exercise sincerely held religious beliefs that compel her to abstain from receiving any of the currently available COVID-19 vaccines. Ms. Stephens has never exhibited or demonstrated any behavior, and no factors exist, that give rise to an objective basis for DOE or any entity within the federal government to question either the nature or the sincerity of her religious beliefs, observances, or practices. Ms. Stephens is amenable to continuing to work with the reasonable accommodations in place and within which she has worked for nearly two years since the outset of the pandemic without incident. With such accommodations, Ms. Stephens remains fully capable of performing the essential functions and duties of her job without compromising the safety of the federal workforce or her productivity and the reasonable accommodation she has requested does not pose an undue hardship on her employer. Despite this, Ms. Stephens' request for a religious exemption and accommodation has not been approved, and she imminently faces severe adverse employment action including without limitation, reprimand, loss of benefits, loss of promotional opportunity, termination of employment, and other life-altering disciplinary measures for exercising and seeking accommodation of her sincerely held religious beliefs prohibiting her from complying with Executive Order 14043.

Following the issuance of President Biden's Vaccine Mandate, Mr. Berne submitted to SSA a request for religious exemption from the Vaccine Mandate as an accommodation of his sincerely held beliefs. Mr. Berne articulated that he has exercised and continues to exercise sincerely held religious beliefs that compel him to abstain from receiving any of the currently available COVID-19 vaccines. Mr. Berne has never exhibited or demonstrated any behavior, and no factors exist, that give rise to an objective basis for SSA or any entity within the federal government to question either the nature or the sincerity of his religious beliefs, observances, or practices. Mr. Berne is amenable to continuing to work with the reasonable accommodations in place and within which he has

EVIDENCE ATTACHMENT A

worked for nearly two years since the outset of the pandemic without incident. With such accommodations, Mr. Berne remains fully capable of performing the essential functions and duties of his job without compromising the safety of the federal workforce or his productivity and the reasonable accommodation he has requested does not pose an undue hardship on his employer. Despite this, Mr. Berne's request for a religious exemption and accommodation has not been approved, and he imminently faces severe adverse employment action including without limitation, reprimand, loss of benefits, loss of promotional opportunity, termination of employment, and other life-altering disciplinary measures for exercising and seeking accommodation of his sincerely held religious beliefs prohibiting him from complying with Executive Order 14043.

Following the issuance of President Biden's Vaccine Mandate, Mr. Camp submitted to the GSA a request for religious exemption from the Vaccine Mandate as an accommodation of his sincerely held beliefs. Mr. Camp articulated that he has exercised and continues to exercise sincerely held religious beliefs that compel him to abstain from receiving any of the currently available COVID-19 vaccines. Mr. Camp has never exhibited or demonstrated any behavior, and no factors exist, that give rise to an objective basis for the GSA or any entity within the federal government to question either the nature or the sincerity of his religious beliefs, observances, or practices. Mr. Camp is amenable to continuing to work with the reasonable accommodations in place and within which he has worked for nearly two years since the outset of the pandemic without incident. With such accommodations, Mr. Camp remains fully capable of performing the essential functions and duties of his job without compromising the safety of the federal workforce or his productivity and the reasonable accommodation he has requested does not pose an undue hardship on his employer. Despite this, Mr. Camp's request for a religious exemption and accommodation has not been approved, and he imminently faces severe adverse employment action including without limitation, reprimand, loss of benefits, loss of promotional opportunity, termination of employment, and other life-altering disciplinary measures for exercising and seeking accommodation of his sincerely held religious beliefs prohibiting him from complying with Executive Order 14043.

Following the issuance of President Biden's Vaccine Mandate, Ms. Perrotta submitted to the VA a request for religious exemption from the Vaccine Mandate as an accommodation of her sincerely held beliefs. Ms. Perrotta articulated that she has exercised and continues to exercise sincerely held religious beliefs that compel her to abstain from receiving any of the currently available COVID-19 vaccines. Ms. Perrotta has never exhibited or demonstrated any behavior, and no factors exist, that give rise to an objective basis for the VA or any entity within the federal government to question either the nature or the sincerity of her religious beliefs, observances, or practices. Ms. Perrotta is amenable to continuing to work with the reasonable accommodations in place and within which she has worked for nearly two years since the outset of the pandemic without incident. With such accommodations, Ms. Perrotta remains fully capable of performing the essential functions and duties of her job without compromising the safety of the federal workforce or her productivity and the reasonable accommodation she has requested does not pose an undue hardship on her employer. Despite this, Ms. Perrotta's request for a religious exemption and accommodation has not been approved, and she imminently faces severe adverse employment action including without limitation, reprimand, loss of benefits, loss of promotional opportunity, termination of employment, and other life-altering disciplinary measures for exercising and seeking accommodation of her sincerely held religious beliefs prohibiting her from complying with Executive Order 14043.

Following the issuance of President Biden's Vaccine Mandate, Mr. Axtell submitted to DOT a request for religious exemption from the Vaccine Mandate as an accommodation of his sincerely held beliefs. Mr. Axtell articulated that he has exercised and continues to exercise sincerely held religious beliefs that compel him to abstain from receiving any of the currently available COVID-19 vaccines. Mr. Axtell has never exhibited or demonstrated any behavior, and no factors exist, that give rise to an objective basis for

DOT or any entity within the federal government to question either the nature or the sincerity of his religious beliefs, observances, or practices. Mr. Axtell is amenable to continuing to work with the reasonable accommodations in place and within which he has worked for nearly two years since the outset of the pandemic without incident. With such accommodations, Mr. Axtell remains fully capable of performing the essential functions and duties of his job without compromising the safety of the federal workforce or his productivity and the reasonable accommodation he has requested does not pose an undue hardship on his employer. Despite this, Mr. Axtell's request for a religious exemption and accommodation has not been approved, and he imminently faces severe adverse employment action including without limitation, reprimand, loss of benefits, loss of promotional opportunity, termination of employment, and other life-altering disciplinary measures for exercising and seeking accommodation of his sincerely held religious beliefs prohibiting him from complying with Executive Order 14043.

Following the issuance of President Biden's Vaccine Mandate, Ms. Morgan submitted to DOI a request for religious exemption from the Vaccine Mandate as an accommodation of her sincerely held beliefs. Ms. Morgan articulated that she has exercised and continues to exercise sincerely held religious beliefs that compel her to abstain from receiving any of the currently available COVID-19 vaccines. Ms. Morgan has never exhibited or demonstrated any behavior, and no factors exist, that give rise to an objective basis for the DOI or any entity within the federal government to question either the nature or the sincerity of her religious beliefs, observances, or practices. Ms. Morgan is amenable to continuing to work with the reasonable accommodations in place and within which she has worked for nearly two years since the outset of the pandemic without incident. With such accommodations, Ms. Morgan remains fully capable of performing the essential functions and duties of her job without compromising the safety of the federal workforce or her productivity and the reasonable accommodation she has requested does not pose an undue hardship on her employer. Despite this, Ms. Morgan's request for a religious exemption and accommodation has not been approved, and she imminently faces severe adverse employment action including without limitation, reprimand, loss of benefits, loss of promotional opportunity, termination of employment, and other life-altering disciplinary measures for exercising and seeking accommodation of her sincerely held religious beliefs prohibiting her from complying with Executive Order 14043.

Following the issuance of Secretary Austin's Vaccine Mandate, First Lieutenant Soto submitted to the Department of the Navy a request for religious exemption from the Vaccine Mandate as an accommodation of his sincerely held beliefs. First Lieutenant Soto articulated that he has exercised and continues to exercise sincerely held religious beliefs that compel her to abstain from receiving any of the currently available COVID-19 vaccines. First Lieutenant Soto has never exhibited or demonstrated any behavior, and no factors exist, that give rise to an objective basis for the Department of the Navy or any entity within the federal government to question either the nature or the sincerity of her religious beliefs, observances, or practices. First Lieutenant Soto is amenable to continuing to serving with the reasonable accommodations in place and within which she has worked for nearly two years since the outset of the pandemic without incident. With such accommodations, First Lieutenant Soto remains fully capable of performing the essential functions and duties of his job without compromising the safety or readiness of the U.S. Armed Forces and the reasonable accommodation he has requested does not pose an undue hardship on the Department of the Navy, Department of Defense, or United States Armed Forces. Despite this, on October 10, 2021, First Lieutenant Soto's request for a religious exemption was denied. As a result, First Lieutenant Soto has suffered, and continues to suffer irreparable harm as his fundamental rights have been deprived, or at a minimum, are imminently guaranteed to be deprived, resulting in severe adverse employment action being taken against him including without limitation, reprimand, loss of benefits, loss of promotional opportunity, termination of employment, and other life-altering disciplinary measures for exercising

EVIDENCE ATTACHMENT A

and seeking accommodation of his sincerely held religious beliefs prohibiting him from complying with Secretary Austin's August 24, DoD Order.

Following the issuance of Secretary Austin's Vaccine Mandate, Corporal Hall submitted to the Department of the Navy a request for religious exemption from the Vaccine Mandate as an accommodation of his sincerely held beliefs. Corporal Hall articulated that he has exercised and continues to exercise sincerely held religious beliefs that compel her to abstain from receiving any of the currently available COVID-19 vaccines. Corporal Hall has never exhibited or demonstrated any behavior, and no factors exist, that give rise to an objective basis for the Department of the Navy or any entity within the federal government to question either the nature or the sincerity of her religious beliefs, observances, or practices. Corporal Hall is amenable to continuing to serving with the reasonable accommodations in place and within which she has worked for nearly two years since the outset of the pandemic without incident. With such accommodations, Corporal Hall remains fully capable of performing the essential functions and duties of his job without compromising the safety or readiness of the U.S. Armed Forces and the reasonable accommodation he has requested does not pose an undue hardship on the Department of the Navy, Department of Defense, or United States Armed Forces. Despite this, on September 29, 2021, Corporal Hall's request for a religious exemption was denied. As a result, Corporal Hall has suffered, and continues to suffer irreparable harm as his fundamental rights have been deprived, or at a minimum, are imminently guaranteed to be deprived, resulting in severe adverse employment action being taken against him including without limitation, reprimand, loss of benefits, loss of promotional opportunity, termination of employment, and other life-altering disciplinary measures for exercising and seeking accommodation of his sincerely held religious beliefs prohibiting him from complying with Secretary Austin's August 24, DoD Order.

D. PLAINTIFFS' SINCERELY HELD RELIGIOUS BELIEFS

As stated above, all Plaintiffs have sincerely held religious beliefs, as rooted in Scripture, that preclude them from complying with the Vaccine Mandate because of the connections between the available COVID-19 vaccines and the cell lines of aborted fetuses, whether in the vaccines' origination, production, development, testing, or other inputs. Plaintiffs also have sincerely held religious beliefs, rooted in Scripture, that their bodies are temples of the Holy Spirit and that they cannot place anything into their Temples without confirmation and conviction from the Holy Spirit.

A fundamental component of Plaintiffs' sincerely held religious beliefs is that all life is sacred, from the moment of conception to natural death, and that abortion is the murder of an innocent life and a grave sin against God.

Plaintiffs' sincerely held religious beliefs are rooted in Scripture's teachings that "[a]ll Scripture is given by inspiration of God, and is profitable for doctrine, for reproof, for correction, [and] for instruction in righteousness." 2 Timothy 3:16 (KJV).

Because of that sincerely held religious belief, Plaintiffs believe that they must conform their lives, including their decisions relating to medical care, to the commands and teaching of Scripture.

Plaintiffs have sincerely held religious beliefs that God forms children in the womb and knows them prior to birth, and that because of this, life is sacred from the moment of conception to natural death. See Psalm 139:13–14 (ESV) ("For you formed my inward parts; you knitted me together in my mother's womb. I praise you, for I am fearfully and wonderfully made."); Psalm 139:16 (ESV) ("Your eyes saw my unformed substance; in your book were written, every one of them, the days that were formed for me, when as yet there was none of them"); Isaiah 44:2 (ESV) ("Thus says the LORD who made you, who formed you from the womb"); Isaiah 44:24 (ESV) ("Thus says the LORD, your Redeemer, who formed you from the womb: 'I am the Lord, who made all things '"); Isaiah 49:1b (ESV) ("The LORD called me from the womb, from the body of my mother he named my name.'"); Isaiah 49:5 (ESV) ("And now the LORD says, he who formed me from the womb to be his servant"); Jeremiah 1:5 (ESV) ("'Before I formed you in the womb I knew you, and before you were born I consecrated you; I appointed you a prophet to the nations.'")

Plaintiffs also have sincerely held religious beliefs that every child's life is sacred because each is made in the image of God. See Genesis 1:26–27 (ESV) ("Then God said, 'Let us make man in our image, after our likeness So God created man in his own image, in the image of God he created him; male and female he created them.'" (Footnote omitted)).

Plaintiffs have sincerely held religious beliefs that because life is sacred from the moment of conception, the killing of that innocent life is the murder of an innocent human in violation of Scripture. See, e.g., Exodus 20:13 (ESV) ("'You shall not murder.'"); Exodus 21:22– 23 (ESV) (imposing death penalty for killing of an unborn child); Exodus 23:7 (ESV) ("'[D]o not kill the innocent and righteous '"); Genesis 9:6 (ESV) ("'Whoever sheds the blood of man, by man shall his blood be shed, for God made man in his own image.'"); Deuteronomy 27:25 (ESV) ("Cursed be anyone who takes a bribe to shed innocent blood." (Internal quotation marks omitted)); Proverbs 6:16–17 (ESV) ("There are six things that the LORD hates, seven that are an abomination to him: . . . hands that shed innocent blood").

Abortion is the modern-day sacrifice of children made in the image of God. Plaintiffs do not want to be part of such an "abomination." They do not want indirectly or directly to be in any way associated with abortion. To do so is abhorrent, loathsome, detestable, abominable to God. In short, to require these employees to inject a substance into their bodies that has any association (no matter how near or remote to abortion) is a sin against their Creator, their Lord, and their Savior.

Plaintiffs also believe in the fundamental Christian teaching of therapeutic proportionality, which an assessment of whether the benefits of a medical intervention outweigh the undesirable side-effects and burdens in light of the integral good of the person, including, psychological, and spiritual bodily goods.

It can also extend to the good of others and the common good, which likewise entail spiritual and moral dimensions and are not reducible to public health.

The judgment of therapeutic proportionality must be made by the person who is the potential recipient of the intervention in the concrete circumstances, not by public health authorities or by other individuals who might judge differently in their own situations.

Plaintiffs' religious beliefs compel them to not condone, support, justify, or benefit (directly or indirectly) from the taking of innocent human life via abortion, and that to do so is sinning against God.

Plaintiffs' sincerely held religious beliefs preclude them from accepting any one of the three currently available COVID-19 vaccines derived from, produced or manufactured by, tested on, developed with, or otherwise connected to aborted fetal cell lines.

E. PFIZER'S COMIRNARY® & PFIZER-BIONTECH VACCINES

On August 23, 2021, the FDA approved Pfizer's COMIRNATY® (COVID-19 vaccine, mRNA) ("COMIRNATY"), which is legally distinguishable from the BioNTech vaccine as evidenced by the FDA's COMIRNATY approval announcement published on August 23, 2021.

The FDA approval letter, however, only states that COMIRNATY is FDA- approved. BioNTech, is not, nor has it ever been approved by the FDA.

The two Pfizer vaccines are legally distinct and include differences. For example, the two vaccines have different number of ingredients: COMIRNATY has ten (11) ingredients while BioNTech has just ten (10) ingredients.

It could not be clearer that BioNTech is not FDA-approved and therefore, the vaccine remains subject to the EUA provisions

EVIDENCE ATTACHMENT A

of the federal Food, Drug, and Cosmetic Act ("FDCA"). As a result, a mass misinformation campaign has construed the two legally distinct vaccines to be considered by the public at-large as a single "Pfizer vaccine" —this is not correct.

The approval announcement posted on the FDA's website reads, "On August 23, 2021, the FDA approved the first COVID-19 vaccine. The vaccine has been known as the Pfizer- BioNTech COVID-19 Vaccine, and will now be marketed as COMIRNATY, for the prevention of COVID-19 disease in individuals 16 years of age and older."[14]

Ingredients	Quantity after Dilution (per vial)	Function
SARS-CoV-2 spike glycoprotein mRNA (UNII: 5085ZFP6SJ)	225 μg	Active Ingredient
(b) (4) [4-hydroxybutyl]azanediyl]bis (hexane-6,1-diyl)bis(2-hexyldecanoate) (UNII: (b) (4))	3.23 mg	Lipid component
(b) (4) [2-(polyethylene glycol 2000)-N,N-ditetradecylacetamide] (UNII: (b) (4))	0.4 mg	Lipid component
DSPC [1,2-distearoyl-sn-glycero-3-phosphocholine] (UNII: 043IPI2M0K)	0.7 mg	Lipid component
Cholesterol (UNII: 97C5T2UQ7J)	1.4 mg	Lipid component
Potassium chloride (UNII: 660YQ98I10)	0.07 mg	Excipient
Monobasic potassium phosphate (UNII: 4J9FJ0HL51)	0.07 mg	Excipient
Sodium Chloride (UNII: 451W47IQ8X)	2.7 mg	Excipient
Dibasic sodium phosphate dihydrate (UNII: GR686LBA74)	0.49 mg	Excipient
Sucrose (UNII: C151H8M554)	46.0 mg	Excipient
(b) (4) (UNII: (b) (4))	0.450 mL	Excipient

Table 2. Composition of COMIRNATY Multiple Dose Vial
https://www.fda.gov/media/151755/download

As you can see in the above graph, 0.45mg of the 2.25mg (20%) of ingredients contained in a COMIRNATY vial has been sanitized.

While Pfizer's COMIRNATY approval letter states that its two vaccines share the same formulation, the FDA concedes that

---

14. The Food and Drug Administration, *Vaccine Information Fact Sheet for Recipients and Caregivers about COMIRNATY (COVID-19 Vaccine, mRNA) and Pfizer-BioNTech COVID-19 Vaccine to Prevent Coronavirus Disease 2019 (COVID-19)* (Aug. 23, 2021), available at: https://www.fda.gov/media/144414/download

"the products are legally distinct with certain differences . . ." Id. (emphasis added).

To date, no entity has revealed, nor have Plaintiffs been able to obtain, any evidence indicating what those "certain differences" may be. Despite this, the FDA asserts that the two formulations can be used interchangeably.

For example, in the FDA's fact sheet[15] for recipients and caregivers, for example, it reads, "The FDA-approved COMIRNATY (COVID-19 Vaccine, mRNA) and the FDA- authorized Pfizer-BioNTech COVID-19 Vaccine under Emergency Use Authorization (EUA) have the same formulation and can be used interchangeably to provide the COVID-19 vaccination series."

In a press release[16] announcing Pfizer's collaboration with Brazil's Eurofarma to manufacture COVID-19 vaccine doses, Pfizer wrote, "COMIRNATY® (COVID-19 Vaccine, mRNA) is an FDA-approved COVID-19 vaccine made by Pfizer for BioNTech" and "Pfizer- BioNTech COVID-19 Vaccine has received EUA from FDA." The press release continued, stating, "This emergency use of the product has not been approved or licensed by FDA, but has been authorized by FDA under an Emergency Use Authorization (EUA) to prevent Coronavirus Disease 2019 (COVID-19) . . .". Id.

Then, in a September 6, 2021 press release[17] announcing a submittal to a request by the European Medicines Agency (EMA) to update its Conditional Marketing Authorization (CMA) for a booster dose, BioNTech–Pfizer's co-partner in the production of the Pfizer-BioNTech COVID-19 vaccine–clearly states, "The

15. The Food and Drug Administration, *Vaccine Information Fact Sheet for Recipients and Caregivers about COMIRNATY (COVID-19 Vaccine, mRNA) and Pfizer-BioNTech COVID-19 Vaccine to Prevent Coronavirus Disease 2019 (COVID-19)* (Aug. 23, 2021), available at: https://www.fda.gov/media/144414/download.

16. Pfizer, *Pfizer and BioNTech Announce Collaboration with Brazil's Eurofarma to Manufacture COVID-19 Vaccine Doses for Latin America* (Aug. 26, 2021), available at: https://www.pfizer.com/news/press-release/press-release- detail/pfizer-and-biontech-announce-collaboration-brazils.

17. Press Release, *Pfizer and BioNTech Submit a Variation to EMA with the Data in Support of a Booster Dose of COMIRNATY®*, BIONTECH (Sept. 6, 2021), available at: https://investors.biontech.de/node/10581/pdf.

EVIDENCE ATTACHMENT A

Pfizer-BioNTech COVID-19 vaccine has not been approved or licensed by the U.S. Food and Drug Administration (FDA), but has been authorized for emergency use by FDA under an Emergency Use Authorization (EUA) to prevent Coronavirus Disease 2019 (COVID-19)...". Id.

The product's labeling is even indicative that the vaccines are distinguishable. In a letter addressed to Pfizer, the FDA stated, "The Pfizer-BioNTech COVID-19 Vaccine vial label and carton labels are clearly marked for 'Emergency Use Authorization.'"[18]

Mindful of this new marketing change, the FDA included specific language in its August 23 letter to Pfizer distinguishing the two vaccines, stating "the licensed vaccine (COMIRNATY) has the same formulation as the EUA-authorized vaccine (Pfizer-BioNTech) and the products can be used interchangeably to provide the vaccination series without presenting any safety or effectiveness concerns." Id. This is not true.

According to the CDC, "the FDA approved the licensure of COMIRNATY (COVID-19 Vaccine, mRNA), made by Pfizer for BioNTech."[19] The FDA did not approve the Pfizer-BioNTech vaccine. Despite full knowledge that the BioNTech vaccine is not FDA- approved, the CDC nevertheless stated that, because "[t]he FDA-approved Pfizer-BioNTech product COMIRNATY and the FDA-authorized Pfizer-BioNTech COVID-19 vaccine have the same formulation[,] [the two vaccines] can be used interchangeably to provide the COVID-19 vaccination series . . .". As a result, the CDC has advised:

> [V]accination providers can use doses distributed under EUA [(e.g., the non-FDA approved Pfizer-BioNTech

---

18. Food and Drug Administration, Pfizer-BioNTech COVID-19 EUA LOA reissued August 23, 2021, (Aug. 23, 2021), available at: https://www.fda.gov/media/150386/download.

19. Centers for Disease Control and Prevention, *Interim Clinical Considerations for Use of COVID-19 Vaccines Currently Approved or Authorized in the United States*, (last visited Sept. 15, 2021), available at: https://www.cdc.gov/vaccines/covid-19/clinical-considerations/covid-19-vaccines-us.html.

vaccine)] to administer the vaccination series as if the doses were the licensed vaccine.[20]

The CDC is wrong. The EUA statute, 21 U.S.C. § 360bbb-3, explicitly states that anyone to whom an EUA product is administered must be informed of the option to accept or to refuse it, as well as alternatives to the product and the risks and benefits of receiving it.

The CDC's erroneous assertion that "vaccination providers can use doses distributed under EUA to administer the vaccination series as if the doses were the licensed vaccine" fails to appreciate perhaps the most consequential difference between COMIRNATY and BioNTech: their current availability.

The FDA's COMIRNATY approval letter facially states, the CDC: (1) explicitly distinguishes the COMIRNATY and BioNTech vaccines; (2) expressly distinguishes that COMIRTNATY is approved and BioNTech is not FDA-approved but under EUA; (3) asserts that COMIRNATY and BioNTech have the same "formulation"; (4) alleges that BioNTech can be used interchangeably with COMIRNATY despite "certain differences" existing between the two different vaccines; and then with abject audacity, advises that "[a]lthough COMIRNATY is approved . . . there is not sufficient approved vaccine available for distribution to this population in its entirety at the time of reissuance of [the BioNTech] EUA."

In unequivocal terms, the FDA has made it expressly clear: "There is no adequate, approved, and available alternative to the emergency use of [the BioNTech] COVID-19 Vaccine to prevent COVID-19."

The only vaccine that has received FDA approval is COMIRNATY, yet COMIRNATY is unavailable. No FDA-approved COVID-19 vaccine is available.

---

20. *Id.*

EVIDENCE ATTACHMENT A

F. IRRESPECTIVE OF FDA APPROVAL, NONE OF THE CURRENTLY AVAILABLE COVID-19 VACCINES COULD EXIST BUT FOR THE USE OF FETAL CELL TISSUE FROM ABORTED FETUSES.

Use of tissue procured from aborted fetuses is not new. It has been adjudicated as that bioprocurement companies have, in fact, sold fetal tissue in violation of federal law.

On July 15, 2015, the United States House of Representatives Energy and Commerce Committee and House Judiciary Committee opened investigations into illegal fetal tissue procurement practices.[21] On August 14, 2015, the House Oversight and Government Reform Committee initiated a third investigation.[22] On October 7, 2015, and as a means to consolidate the three House investigations into one, the House created a Select Investigative Panel within the Energy and Commerce Committee.[23] The Senate Judiciary Committee also initiated its own investigation, which it conducted contemporaneously and independent of the consolidated House investigation.[24]

The two Congressional investigations concluded in December 2016[25] after both, the House and Senate independently concluded

21. Press Release, House Energy and Commerce Committee, Energy and Commerce Committee Launches Investigation Following "Abhorrent" Planned Parenthood Video (Jul. 15, 2015) *see also* Press Release, House Judiciary Committee, Chairman Goodlatte Announces House judiciary Committee Investigation into Horrific Abortion Practices (Jul. 15, 2015).

22. Letter from Jason Chaffetz, Chariman, Committee on Oversight and Government Reform, *et al.*, to Cecile Richards, President, Planned Parenthood Federation of America, Inc. (Aug. 14, 2015).

23 Wesley Lowery & Mike DeBonis, *Boehner: There will be no government shutdown; select committee will probe Planned Parenthood*, WASHINGTON POST (Sep. 27, 2015), available at: https://wapo.st/2QxxdDR.

23. 23Wesley Lowery & Mike DeBonis, *Boehner: There will be no government shutdown; select committee will probe Planned Parenthood*, WASHINGTON POST (Sep. 27, 2015), available at: https://wapo.st/2QxxdDR.

24. *Id.*

25. *Id.*

that many actors within the abortion industry had committed systemic violations of the law.[26] Due to these findings, the House Select Investigative Panel and Senate Judiciary Committee issued numerous criminal and regulatory referrals to federal, state, and local law enforcement entities, including for several abortion providers and fetal tissue procurement companies.

In October 2016, the Orange County, California, District Attorney initiated a civil prosecution against DV Biologics and DaVinci Biosciences for illegally re-selling fetal tissue the companies obtained from Planned Parenthood of Orange and San Bernardino Counties ("PP- Orange").[27] The successful prosecution resulted in a stipulated judgment in which both companies admitted to selling fetal body parts obtained from PP-Orange for profit. The parties also agreed to pay $7.8 million for violating state and federal laws.[28]

In December 2016, the Texas Health and Human Services Division ("Texas HHS") issued a Final Notice of Termination to Planned Parenthood Gulf Coast ("PP-Gulf Coast") based in Houston that terminated its enrollment in the Texas Medicaid program. According to Texas HHS, the termination was based on two factors: (1) footage of CMP's visit to the PP-Gulf Coast clinic revealing that PP-Houston would modify procedures in order to sell tissue; and (2) the U.S. House investigation's conclusion that PP-Houston had repeatedly lied to it.[29]

In January 2017, the Attorney General of Arizona initiated a civil prosecution against abortion provider, Jackrabbit Family

26. Select Investigative Panel of the Energy & Commerce Committee, FINAL REPORT (Dec. 30, 2016); *see also* Majority Staff Of S. Comm. On The Judiciary, 114TH CONG., Human Fetal Tissue Research: Context and Controversy, S. DOC. NO. 114-27 (2d Sess. 2016).

27. *See* Complaint, *The People of the State of California v. DV Biologics, LLC*, Orange Cnty. No. 30-2016-00880665- CU-BT-CJC (Cal. Super., Oct. 11, 2016).

28. *See* Judgment, *The People of the State of California v. DV Biologics, LLC*, Orange Cnty. No. 30-2016-00880665- CU-BT-CJC (Cal. Super., Dec. 19, 2017).

29. Letter from Stuart W. Bowen, Jr., Inspector General, Texas Health & Human Services Commission, to Planned Parenthood Gulf Coast, et al. (Dec. 20, 2016).

EVIDENCE ATTACHMENT A

Medicine, P.C. ("Camelback Family Planning") for illegally transferring fetal tissue to StemExpress, LLC, a California-based bioprocurement company.[30] The prosecution was successful, and the Arizona Attorney General determined that the consent formed used by StemExpress were deficient because:

> The consent forms did not state certain facts regarding StemExpress's business. The consent forms [] did not state that, under the agreement [Camelback Family Planning] had entered into with StemExpress in addition to supplying the collection tubes and paying the costs of shipping the samples to StemExpress, StemExpress would pay [Camelback Family Planning] set amounts from $75–250 for each blood and tissue sample provided.[31]

As part of the settlement, Camelback Family Planning was required to return all payments received it received from StemExpress and agree it would refrain from selling fetal tissue in the future.[32] Camelback Family Planning ultimately returned the money it received from StemExpress in exchange for inter alia fetal tissues.[33]

Fetal tissue has a long history of being procured and sold and it is not subject to dispute that HEK-293 and PER.C6 fetal cell lines were used in the development and testing of the three (3) available COVID-19 vaccines.

As reported by the North Dakota Department of Health, in its handout literature for those considering one of the COVID-19 vaccines, "[t]he non-replicating viral vector vaccine produced by Johnson & Johnson did require the use of fetal cell cultures, specifically PER.C6, in order to produce and manufacture the vaccine."[34]

---

30. See Complaint, *State of Arizona v. Jackrabbit Family Medicine, P.C.*, Maricopa Cnty. No. CV2017-000863 (Ariz. Super., Jan. 19, 2017).

31. See Assurance of Discontinuance, *State of Arizona v. Jackrabbit Family Medicine, P.C.*, Maricopa Cnty. No. CV2017-000863 (Ariz. Super., Jan. 19, 2017).

32. Id.

33. Id.

34. See North Dakota Health, COVID-19 Vaccines & Fetal Cell Lines (Apr.

The Louisiana Department of Health likewise confirms that the Johnson & Johnson COVID-19 vaccine used the PER.C6 fetal cell line, which "is a retinal cell line that was isolated from a terminated fetus in 1985."[35]

Scientists at the American Association for the Advancement of Science have likewise published research showing that the Johnson & Johnson vaccine used aborted fetal cell lines in the development and production phases of the vaccine.[36]

The same is true of the Moderna and Pfizer-BioNTech mRNA vaccines. The Louisiana Department of Health's publications again confirm that aborted fetal cells lines were used in the "proof of concept" phase of the development of their mRNA vaccines.[37]

The North Dakota Department of Health likewise confirms: "Early in the development of mRNA vaccine technology, fetal cells were used for 'proof of concept' (to demonstrate how a cell could take up mRNA and produce the SARS-CoV-2 spike protein) or to characterize the SARS-CoV-2 spike protein."[38]

The Chief Scientific Officer and Senior Director of Worldwide Research for Pfizer have also been reported to demonstrate that its COVID-19 vaccine is derived from aborted fetal cells and have made statements that they wanted to keep that information from the public.[39]

20, 2021), available at: https://www.health.nd.gov/sites/www/files/documents/COVID%20Vaccine%20Page/COVID- 19_Vaccine_Fetal_Cell_Handout.pdf.

35. La. Dep't of Public Health, You Have Questions, We Have Answers: COVID-19 Vaccine FAQ (Dec. 21, 2020), available at: https://ldh.la.gov/assets/oph/Center-PHCH/Center- PH/immunizations/You_Have_Qs_COVID19_Vaccine_FAQ.pdf. emphasis added).

36. Meredith Wadman, Vaccines that use human fetal cells draw fire, Science (June 12, 2020), available at: https://science.sciencemag.org/content/368/6496/1170.full.

37. *See* La. Dep't of Public Health, *supra* fn. 29.

38. N.D. Health, *supra* fn. 28 (emphasis added).

39. *See* PFIZER LEAKS: Whistleblower Goes On Record, Reveals Internal Emails from Chief Scientific Officer & Senior Director of Worldwide Research Discussing COVID Vaccine ... 'We Want to Avoid Having the Information on the Fetal Cells Floating Out There', ProjectVeritas (Oct. 6, 2021), available at: www.projectveritas.com/news/

Specifically, Vanessa Gelman, Pfizer Senior Director of Worldwide Research: "From the perspective of corporate affairs, we want to avoid having the information on fetal cells floating out there...The risk of communicating this right now outweighs any potential benefit we could see, particularly with general members of the public who may take this information and use it in ways we may not want out there. We have not received any questions from policy makers or media on this issue in the last few weeks, so we want to avoid raising this if possible." Id.

And, Philip Dormitzer, Pfizer's Chief Scientific Officer is reported as saying that he wanted to keep the information secret because of the objections that pro-life individuals, such as Plaintiffs in this action, would have: "HEK293T cells, used for the IVE assay, are ultimately derived from an aborted fetus. On the other hand, the Vatican doctrinal committee has confirmed that they consider it acceptable for Pro-Life believers to be immunized. Pfizer's official statement couches the answer well and is what should be provided in response to an outside inquiry." Id.

Because all three of the currently available COVID-19 vaccines are developed and produced from, tested with, researched on, or otherwise connected with the aborted fetal cell lines HEK-293 and PER.C6, Plaintiffs' sincerely held religious beliefs compel them to abstain from obtaining or injecting any of these products into their body, regardless of the perceived benefit or rationale.

G. PLAINTIFFS' AMENABILITY TO LESS RESTRICTIVE ALTERNATIVES THAT COMPORT WITH THEIR RELIGIOUS BELIEFS & ACHIEVE THE SAME GOAL SOUGHT TO BE ACHIEVED BY VACCINATION

Plaintiffs have offered, and are ready, willing, and able to comply with all reasonable health and safety requirements to facilitate their religious exemption and accommodation from the Vaccine Mandate.

---

pfizer-leaks-whistleblower-goes-on-record-reveals-internal-emails-from-chief/.

Plaintiffs have, and continue to, engage in a variety of mitigation strategies to stem, if not entirety prevent, the spread of COVID-19, which is the very objective of the Vaccine Mandate. While engaged in these accommodating mitigation strategies, Plaintiffs dutifully fulfilled their employment obligations to, at minimum, a satisfactory standard.

Mr. Church and Mrs. Church have worked from home for 584 consecutive days. Since the beginning of her employment, Ms. Morgan has only ever visited a physical federal office location on two occasions–once, to get a battery in her government-provided computer replaced, and then a second time to replace the entire computer itself. Mr. Czerwinski, who works from home the majority of the time, frequently washes his hands and wears a mask while socially distancing whenever on-site work is required. The number of reasonable accommodations that not impose an undue hardship and are less restrictive than the blanket Vaccine Mandate could be articulated at nauseum. Despite this, Plaintiffs continue to remain open to reasonable accommodations in lieu of being forced to which fundamental right is most important to them: (1) freely exercising their religion; (2) pursuing the careers of their choosing; or (3) succumb to the unwanted injection of a medication, such as a vaccine, into their nonconsenting bodies.

The accommodations which have been ongoing for nearly two years are certainly reasonable under the accumulating scientific evidence. Indeed, a preliminary study has shown that in the case of a breakthrough infection, the Delta variant is able to grow in the noses of vaccinated people just as if they were not vaccinated at all. The virus that grows is just as infectious as that in unvaccinated people, meaning vaccinated people can transmit the virus and infect others.[40]

40. Sanjay Mishra, Evidence mounts that people with breakthrough infections can spread Delta easily, National Geographic (Aug. 20, 2021), available at: https://www.nationalgeographic.com/science/article/evidence-mounts-that- people-with-breakthrough-infections-can-spread-delta-easily (emphasis added); *see also* Statement from CDC Director Rochelle P. Walensky, MD, MPH Statement from CDC on Today's MMWR (July 30, 2021), available at: https://www.cdc.gov/media/releases/2021/s0730-mmwr-covid-19.html (noting "the

EVIDENCE ATTACHMENT A

H. DEPT. OF DEFENSE MISREPRESENTATIONS, FALSIFICATION OF MEDICAL RECORDS, & BLANKET DENIALS OF RELIGIOUS EXEMPTION REQUESTS

On August 23, 2021, the FDA admitted that "[a]lthough COMIRNATY is approved . . . **there is not sufficient approved vaccine available for distribution . . .**."[41]

Despite this, on August 27, 2021, Captain Rylan Commins received an email[42] in which Marine Lieutenant Alys Jordan, a HMLA-267 Flight Surgeon at Camp Pendleton, advised "**[t]he orders are in for the Comirnaty vaccine and we should have them by early next week.**"

On October 15, 2021, Major Edwin Paz requested information from the DiLorenzo Clinic as to whether the clinic had any of the FDA-approved COMIRNATY available. The email indicates that the Director of the DiLorenzo Clinic, Dr. Seto, stated: "**Pfizer has not made any Comirnaty. There is no expected date when we will receive Comirnaty.**" [43] This was also corroborated, DoD OIG COVID-19 Coordinator, Plaintiff Lesley Church, who has been informed by DoD officials that the Pentagon does not have COMIRNATY and does not know when COMIRNATY will be available.

It is indisputable: The United States Department of Defense does not, nor has it ever had, one or more FDA-approved doses of COMIRNITY – the only COVID-19 vaccine that has received approval from the FDA. Despite this, (1) the FDA indicating just 96 hours earlier that COMIRNATY was unavailable, DoD personnel

---

Delta infection resulted in similarly high SARS-CoV-2 viral loads in vaccinated and unvaccinated people.").

41. Centers for Disease Control and Prevention, *Interim Clinical Considerations for Use of COVID-19 Vaccines Currently Approved or Authorized in the United States*, (last visited Sept. 15, 2021), available at: https://www.cdc.gov/vaccines/covid-19/clinical-considerations/covid-19-vaccines-us.html

42. Email to Rylan Commins, U.S. Marine Corps (Aug. 27, 2021, 4:02PM) (on file with author); *see* Exhibit 6.

43. Email to Major Edward Paz, U.S. Marine Corps (Oct. 15, 2021, 10:49 AM) (on file with author); *see* Exhibit 7.

advised active-duty servicemembers that Camp Pendleton was expected to receive COMIRNATY "early [the following] week."; (2) DoD personnel orally misinformed active-duty that the vaccine being administered was the "same fluid" yet COMIRNITY and BioNTech do not even have the same number of ingredients; and (3) perhaps most egregious of all, **the DoD has falsified active-duty personnel's medical records.**

Jacob Workman, a Chief Warrant Officer One in the Missouri National Guard has testified that his immunization records within the TRICARE medical portal reflect that he was inoculated on October 8, 2021.[44]

Jacob Workman		CONFIDENTIAL		Page 2 of 4
IMMUNIZATION HISTORY				
Date Range: All		Sorted By: Vaccine (Ascending)		
Filter: None Applied				
Immunization	COVID-19 Pfizer (COMIRNATY)			
Date Given	08 Oct 2021		Next Due Date	29 Oct 2021
Dosage	0.3 ml		Series	
Provider	Unknown, Provider		Facility	
Manufacturer Name	Pfizer, Inc		Lot Number	FF8839

Finally, notwithstanding the above, the U.S. Marine Corps, under the jurisdiction of Secretary of Defense Austin and President Biden, has begun processing 1st Lt. Soto and Cpl. Hall for administrative separation and subjected them to adverse administrative disciplinary action pursuant to the Marine Administrative Message (MARDAMIN) issued on October 23, 2021.

Cpl. Hall submitted his religious exemption request on August 28, 2021, but it was unlawfully denied by the Marines Corps on September 29, 2021.[45] Likewise, First Lieutenant Soto submitted his religious exemption request on September 22, 2021, but it was unlawfully denied by the Marines Corps on October 10, 2021.[46]

44. Immunization History, Medical Records of Jacob Workman, TRICARE MED. PORT., (Oct. 8, 2021); *see* Exhibit 8

45. Cpl. Hall Denial Letter, Req. for Religious Accom., DEPT. OF THE NAVY (Sept. 29, 2021); *see* Exhibit 9.

46. 1st Lt. Soto Denial Letter, Req. for Religious Accom. DEPT. OF THE

EVIDENCE ATTACHMENT A

Notably, the language used by the Department of the Navy is identical, inapplicable, and/or irrelevant. The "copy and paste" language written of the denial letters written by Deputy Commandant for Manpower and Reserve Affairs, David A Ottington, states inter alia that he: (1) "carefully considered" the requests for an immunization waiver; and that he (2) "considered your requests dated [DATE], the command endorsements and exhibits attached to it, advice from the Director, Health Services Headquarters, U.S. Marine Corps, and the recommendation of the Religious Accommodation Review Board . . ." and that he "consulted with legal counsel."[47]

As a preliminary concern, the date Deputy Commandant Ottington claims Cpl. Hall submitted his exemption request is incorrect. Cpl. Hall submitted his request on August 28, 2021; not August 25, 2021. This is hardly careful consideration. Rather, the copy & paste verbatim language vitiates the notion that at least Cpl. Hall's religious exemption request was not "carefully considered."

To the extent one letter is not carefully considered, 1st Lt. Soto likewise has reason to believe his letter, too, was not carefully considered. And whereas the only two (2) means by which Defendants can deprive Plaintiffs of their fundamental right to the free exercise of religion is if the belief is not "sincerely held" or accommodating one's religion poses an "undue hardship" on Defendants, this material discrepancy is hardly an ancillary matter.

Of course, it is impossible to determine whether one's religious belief is "sincerely held" absent review on an individualized case-by-case basis; thus, the relevancy as to the blanket form denial letter is of the highest important when dealing with a fundamental right at stake. Upon information and belief, and pursuant to the basis articulated above, 1st Lt. Soto and Corporal Hall have been unconstitutionally deprived of their First Amendment rights because Defendants cannot establish their religious beliefs are not sincerely held.

NAVY (Oct. 10, 2021); *see* Exhibit 10.
   47. *See infra*, fn.'s 48-49; *see also* Exhibits 9-10.

As to the "undue hardship" justification, it is spectacularly cavalier to assert that "there is no less-restrictive way of accommodating [Plaintiffs'] request[s] that ensures military readiness and the preservation of the health of the force."[48] First, vaccinated individuals have infected thousands of vaccinated individuals.[49] Yet according to the CDC, out of 120.2 million COVID-19 cases in the United States, there is not a single case in which a person has re-contracted COVID-19 and transmitted it to another person.[50] In fact, just 10 days ago, San Diego County reported a total of 2,925 positive COVID-19 cases: 1,591 cases involving vaccinated patients and 1,334 cases involving unvaccinated patients.[51]

To summarize:

First, no FDA-approved COVID-19 vaccine has ever been made available to the DoD; thus, the only available vaccines are under EUA;

Second, the EUA provisions of the FDCA require recipients of EUA-authorized medical products must "[be] informed . . . [of] the option to accept or refuse administration of the product." See FDCA § 564(e)(1)(A)(ii)(III);

Third, DoD personnel misinformed active-duty service members that they were to receive an FDA-approved COVID-19 vaccine during prior to September 3;

Fourth, when confronted about the difference between the EUA-authorized BioNTech and FDA-approved COMIRNATY, DoD personnel falsely stated, "It's the same fluid" and advised Captain Steele that "the reason you don't have to sign an EUA is

---

48. *Id.*

49. Patricia Kime, *DoD has Had 1,640 COVID 'Breakthrough' Cases Among Vaccinated Beneficiaries*, MILITARY.COM (May 21, 2021), available at: https://www.military.com/daily-news/2021/05/21/dod-has-had-1640-covid-breakthrough-cases-among-vaccinated-beneficiaries.html (last visited Oct. 24, 2021).

50. Case Updates, *Estimated COVID-19 Burden*, CENTERS FOR DISEASE CONTROL AND PREVENTION, (July 27, 2021), available at: https://www.cdc.gov/coronavirus/2019-ncov/cases-updates/burden.html (last visited Oct. 24, 2021).

51. San Diego County, *Weekly Coronavirus Disease 2019 (COVID-19) Surveillance Report*, Health and Human Serv. Agency, (Sept. 20, 2021), *see* Exhibit 11.

EVIDENCE ATTACHMENT A

that this is being legally treated as the same thing" despite both, the FDCA prohibiting such conduct and the FDA expressly stating the products are "legally distinct";

Fifth, the Director of the DiLorenzo Clinic confirmed that as of October 15, 2021, "Pfizer has not made any Comirnaty" "[t]here is no expected date when we will receive Comirnaty" and the DoD OIG COVID-19 Coordinator has confirmed that "at no time has the Department of Defense had in its possession, expected to have in its possession, or as October 23, 2021, is there any indication or reason to believe that it ever will have in its possession, one or more vials of the FDA-approved COMIRNATY COVID-19 vaccine";

Sixth, DoD official medical records reflect that COMIRNATY has been administered despite never being in the DoD's possession; and

Seventh, 1st Lt. Soto and Cpl. Hall have had their religious exemptions unlawfully denied, with the verbatim language giving rise to the reasonable inference of a blanket denial and thus, the reasonable inference that neither of their denial letters were even reviewed on case-by-case basis, and as of October 23, 2021, now face administrative separation and are subject to adverse administrative disciplinary action because of their closely held religious beliefs.

The federal government itself disposes of any question concerning Plaintiff's FDCA claim. In a Memorandum to the President, the DOJ confirms that administration of EUA- authorized vaccines (e.g., every single vaccine available) "requir[e] potential recipients to be informed of the option to accept or refuse administration of the product . . .".[52]

---

52. Dawn Johnson Memo., *Whether Section 564 of the Food, Drug, and Cosmetic Act Prohibits Entities from Requiring the Use of a Vaccine Subject to an Emergency Use Authorization*, DEPT. OF JUSTICE, (Jul. 6, 2021), *see* Exhibit 12

I. OTHER COURTS HAVE ISSUED TRO'S AGAINST VACCINE MANDATES

Other reasonable protocols beyond the mass vaccination remain sufficient to prevent the spread of COVID-19 among employees; all of which constitute less restrictive and reasonable alternatives to the mandatory, universal mass vaccination of the entire federal workforce.

For example, the United States District Court for the Western District of Louisiana recently issued a TRO against a medical school for the school's failure to grant religious exemptions when other reasonable accommodations were available and mandatory vaccination was not the least restrictive means of achieving the school's interest in protecting the school's student body.[53]

The United States District Court for the Western District of Michigan issued a TRO against a university for its failure to allow students with religious objections to vaccination to participate in athletics and other extracurricular activities when other reasonable alternatives were available as a reasonable accommodation for their religious beliefs.[54] The Sixth Circuit Court of Appeals affirmed that preliminary injunction in its order refusing to stay the preliminary injunction.[55]

The United States District Court for the Northern District of New York and the Second Circuit Court of Appeals have both entered injunctions against enforcement of New York's COVID-19 vaccine mandate on healthcare workers that expressly excluded any religious exemption. On October 12, 2021, the Northern District of New York entered a preliminary injunction enjoining state officials from enforcing the mandate.[56] The court had pre-

---

53. *Magliulo v. Edward Via Col. of Osteo. Med.*, No. 3:21-CV-2304, 2021 WL 36799227 (W.D. La. Aug. 17, 2021).

54. *Dahl v. Bd. of Trustees of W. Mich. Univ.*, No. 1:21-cv-757, 2021 WL 3891620, *2 (W.D. Mich. Aug. 31, 2021).

55. *Dahl v. Bd. of Trustees of W. Mich. Univ.*, No. 1:21-cv-757, 2021 WL 3891620, *2 (W.D. Mich. Aug. 31, 2021).

56. *See Dr. A. v. Hochul*, No. 1:21-CV-1009, 2021 WL 4734404 (N.D.N.Y. Oct. 12, 2021).

viously entered a TRO to the same effect.[57] On September 30, in between the Northern District's TRO and preliminary injunction, the Second Circuit gave its imprimatur to the Dr. A. TRO in We The Patriots USA, Inc. v. Hochul, No. 21-2179, dkt. 65 (2d Cir. Sept. 30, 2021).

In We The Patriots, the Second Circuit issued an injunction pending appeal against New York's mandate, enjoining state officials from enforcing it "in a manner that would violate the terms of the temporary restraining order issued in Dr. A v. Hochul."

Several Plaintiffs have been previously infected with COVID-19 and have serologic test results that demonstrate the natural antibodies and their immunity to COVID-19. To require these Plaintiffs to nevertheless submit to forcible vaccination is not only contrary to logic and science, but perhaps the height of what constitutes an arbitrary and capricious agency decision. Plaintiffs, however, have yet to even receive an exemption as demanded by the First Amendment.

The Task Force failed to comply with E.O. 14043 because the guidance it has issued is entirely devoid of information as to "exemptions as required by law." Specifically, the Requirement imposed on the Task Force by E.O. 14043 demands that the Task Force issue all agencies guidance on the implementation of: (1) a program to require COVID-19 vaccination for all of its federal employees; inclusive of (2) lawfully required exceptions to such a program.

The Guidance fails to provide agency heads with information as to: (1) what exemptions are required by law; (2) what criteria is required for federal employees, such as Plaintiffs, to obtain an exemption; (3) the process in which federal employees, such as Plaintiffs, may submit requests for an exemption; or (4) the timeframe within which agencies must respond to requests for an exemption submitted by federal employees, such as Plaintiffs.

Due to the Task Force's failure to comply with the Executive Orders: (1) agency heads remain without guidance for exemption requests and as a result, continue to delay in providing Plaintiffs a

---

57. *See* 2021 WL 4189533 (N.D.N.Y. Sept. 14, 2021).

mechanism to submit their requests despite the rapidly approaching November 22 deadline to be "fully vaccinated"; or (2) some agencies have promulgated their own mechanism to ask impermissible ask invasive questions of those who are religious – while others do not have to provide such information – and the Task Force does so not only in direct violation of EEOC Guidance published this year, but also, in a manner that infringes upon Plaintiffs' fundamental right to the free exercise of religion.

FIRST CLAIM FOR RELIEF

Violation of Free Exercise, U.S. Const. amend I.

Against All Defendants

Plaintiffs re-allege and incorporate by reference as if fully set forth herein the allegations in all preceding paragraphs.

The First Amendment's Free Exercise Clause provides that "Congress shall make no law respecting an establishment of religion, or prohibiting the free exercise thereof." U.S. Const. amend I. Where, as here, a law targets religious practice for disparate treatment and is neither neutral nor generally applicable, that law is assessed under the Supreme Court's strict scrutiny rubric.

Defendants, acting under color of State law, has deprived and will continue to deprive Plaintiffs of their First Amendment rights.

Specifically, Defendants have instituted a Vaccine Mandate that is plainly and unconstitutionally targets religious practice for at least three reasons. First, in its text E.O. 14043 limits the vaccination requirement to merely Executive Branch employees of the "agencies", such as Plaintiffs, as defined by 5 U.S.C § 105 while the same vaccination requirement does not apply to other Executive Branch employees (e.g., White House, EOP, CDC, NIH, the WHO, NIAID) not being subject to the same mandate. Second, the way E.O. 14043 operates in practice, including the numerous exceptions to the vaccination requirement and scheme to intentionally circumvent Plaintiffs' First Amendment protections, make clear the intent to deprive Plaintiffs of their fundamental right to freely exercise their religion. Third, Defendants' own words and conduct demonstrate the intent to violate Plaintiffs' First Amendment rights, in that no guidance has been issued as to what constitutes a valid religious exemption and high-level agency officials have been instructed to determine the bases—irrespective of their legality—upon which the agencies respond to religious exemption requests. The Task Force merely emphasized how important it is for the agencies to "figure[e] it out as quickly as possible . . . because [the agencies are] not going to run an accommodation in those places–and that's totally fine."

Defendants' promulgation of the Vaccine Mandate further infringes upon Plaintiffs' First Amendment right to free exercise in that it demands Plaintiffs respond to an invasive questionnaire without an objective basis giving rise to a bona fide doubt as to the sincerity of their closely held religious beliefs.

Defendants' have also implemented a "deadline" that is not in fact, a deadline, but a "forcing function" to induce Plaintiffs to submit religious exemption requests by an arbitrary date for the sole purpose of "collect[ing] information" about them.

Defendants have required Plaintiffs to work from home, in part or entirely, for nearly two years. Plaintiffs have done so and dutifully performed their work obligations in satisfaction of, at a minimum, expectations. Defendants have also implemented other accommodating risk mitigation strategies such as social distancing and masking with which Plaintiffs have complied and continue to comply.

The compelling interest articulated in E.O. 14043 is to "halt the spread of coronavirus disease" – it is not to eradicate the disease. To that end, it is indisputable that vaccination does not achieve this end as many individuals who have been "fully vaccinated" have contracted, and continue to contract COVID-19 from unvaccinated persons. To the contrary, there is no evidence that an unvaccinated individual with naturally acquired antibodies has re-contracted COVID-19 and transmitted it to another person.

Defendants can offer no evidence as to the basis upon which there is no alternative to halting the spread of COVID-19.

The offered mechanism, mass vaccination, has not worked, nor will it work, in achieving the interest it purports to satisfy.

Plaintiffs have offered numerous, less restrictive means to achieve the interest of stemming the spread of COVID-19.

Plaintiffs have faced, and continue to face, adverse employment action such as threats, harassment, and workplace hostility.

The Vaccine Mandate also seeks to stem the spread of COVID-19 for the interest of the health and safety of our federal workforce; however, if enforced, the safety and health of those who work in our federal government (and the federal government as a whole) would be harmed; not protected due to mass terminations and loss of a ready military and functioning government.

Plaintiffs seek declaratory and injunctive relief because they have no adequate remedy at law to prevent future injury caused by Defendants' violation of their First Amendment right to the free exercise of religion.

SECOND CLAIM FOR RELIEF

VIOLATION OF RFRA, 42 U.S.C. § 2000bbb, et seq.,

Against All Defendants

Plaintiffs re-allege and incorporate all preceding paragraphs as if fully set forth herein.

The Religious Freedom Restoration Act (RFRA) provides that "Government shall not substantially burden a person's exercise of religion even if the burden results from a rule of general applicability." 42 U.S.C. § 2000bb-1(a).

RFRA also demands that, should the government substantially burden a person's free exercise of religion, it bears the burden of demonstrating that its burden on religious exercise furthers a compelling government interest and is the least restrictive means of achieving that compelling government interest. 42 U.S.C. § 2000bb-1(b).

RFRA plainly applies to Defendants, as they constitute a "branch, department, agency, instrumentality, and official of the United States." 42 U.S.C. § 2000bb-2(1).

Congress enacted RFRA "to provide very broad protection for religious liberty," going "far beyond what [the Supreme Court] has held is constitutionally required" under the First Amendment. Hobby Lobby, 573 U.S. 682, 693, 706 (2014) (emphasis added). As such, RFRA encompasses a very broad definition of "exercise of religion," which includes "'any exercise of religion, whether or not compelled by, or central to, a system of religious belief.'" Hobby Lobby, 573 U.S. at 696 (quoting 42 U.S.C. § 2000bb—5(7)(A)).

RFRA mandated that the law "'be construed in favor of a broad protection of religious exercise, to the maximum extent permitted by the terms of this chapter and the Constitution.'" Hobby Lobby, 573 U.S. at 696 (quoting 42 U.S.C. § 2000cc—3(g)).

"RFRA operates as a kind of super statute, displacing the normal operation of other federal laws." Bostock v. Clayton Cnty., 140 S. Ct. 1731, 1754 (2020).

Plaintiffs have sincerely held religious beliefs that Scripture is the infallible, inerrant word of the Lord Jesus Christ, and that they are to follow its teachings.

Plaintiffs have and exercise sincerely held religious beliefs (see supra, Section D) which compel them to abstain from receiving or accepting any of the currently available COVID- 19 vaccines.

The Vaccine Mandates, on its face and as applied, target Plaintiffs' sincerely held religious beliefs by prohibiting Plaintiffs from seeking and receiving exemption and accommodation for their sincerely held religious beliefs against the COVID-19 vaccines.

THIRD CLAIM FOR RELIEF

VIOLATION OF EQUAL PROTECTION

For Declaratory and Injunctive Relief

Plaintiffs re-allege and incorporate by reference all preceding paragraphs as if fully set forth herein.

The Vaccine Mandates require Plaintiffs and all other active-duty service members, federal employees, and federal contractors to obtain vaccination against COVID-19.

The Vaccine Mandates, either implicitly or expressly, state that exceptions will be made for those who are subject to the order but are exempt based on sincerely held religious beliefs or the professional opinions of licensed physicians.

While the Vaccine Mandates appear to be facially neutral and in compliance with well-established legal principles, their application and the manner in which the Vaccine Mandates are being promulgated deny Plaintiffs and other active-duty service members, federal employees, and federal contractors of Equal Protection.

The Vaccine Mandates deny Plaintiffs, and all other service members, federal employees, or federal contractors who have closely held religious beliefs that prevent their ability to get vaccinated in good conscience, good faith, or good health.

Plaintiffs and other service members, federal employees, and federal contractors who are religious or disabled have suffered, and continue to suffer, significant stress and psychological harm caused by this impending threat to their military service or employment.

Service members, federal employees, or federal contractors who are religious or disabled are also immediately injured by the stigma created by the Vaccine Mandates. Even if some religious or disabled service members, federal employees, or federal contractors are permitted to remain exempt from the Vaccine Mandate, they now serve in a military or under employment where the Commander-in-Chief or employer has announced that their service or work is unwanted and unwelcome, and that their religion is not respected, or their medical care will be withheld. Any religious or disabled service members, federal employees, or federal contractors permitted to remain in their current positions will necessarily be treated as, and experience the harms associated with, a person with second-class status.

Plaintiffs, including other service members, federal employees, and federal contractors who require religious accommodations or medically necessary care to treat their respective recognized disability(ies) are entitled to care on an equal basis to what is provided to service members, federal employees, or federal contractors without religious limitations, without disabilities, or with disabilities that do not preclude getting vaccinated against COVID-19.

The Vaccine Mandates single out Plaintiffs based upon their religion.

The Vaccine Mandates single out Plaintiffs based upon their medical history.

The Vaccine Mandates single out Plaintiffs based upon the status as the mechanism Defendants use satisfy its alleged objective in preserving the public health.

As a result of being singled out by Defendants, Plaintiffs have been subjected different treatment.

The different treatment to which Plaintiffs are subjected is arbitrary.

The different treatment to which Plaintiffs are subjected is capricious.

The Vaccine Mandates discriminate against Plaintiffs and other active-duty service members, federal employees, and federal contractors because of their religion.

The Vaccine Mandates discriminate against Plaintiffs and other active-duty service members, federal employees, and federal contractors because of their medical condition.

The Vaccine Mandates put fundamental rights at issue and therefore, are subject to strict scrutiny.

Defendants' actions of adopting, implementing, promulgating, delegating, and enforcing the Vaccine Mandates have discriminated and continue to discriminate against Plaintiffs and other service members, federal employees, and federal contractors on the basis of their religion and such actions do not survive strict scrutiny.

Defendants' actions of adopting, implementing, promulgating, delegating, and enforcing the Vaccine Mandates have discriminated and continue to discriminate against Plaintiffs and other service members, federal employees, and federal contractors on the basis of their medical condition and such actions do not survive strict scrutiny.

Defendants' actions of adopting, implementing, promulgating, delegating, and enforcing the Vaccine Mandates have discriminated and continue to discriminate against Plaintiffs and other service members, federal employees, and federal contractors on the basis of invidious stereotypes, irrational fears, and moral disapproval, which are not permissible bases for differential treatment under any standard of review.

Plaintiffs seek declaratory and injunctive relief because they have no adequate remedy at law to prevent future injury caused by Defendants' violation of their Fifth Amendment rights to equal protection.

FOURTH CLAIM FOR RELIEF

VIOLATION OF THE FDCA, 21 U.S.C. § 360bbb-3, et seq.

For Declaratory and Injunctive Relief

Plaintiffs incorporate by reference all preceding paragraphs as if fully set forth herein.

Federal law generally prohibits anyone from introducing or delivering for introduction into interstate commerce any "new drug" or "biological product" unless and until FDA has approved the drug or product as safe and effective for its intended uses. See,

EVIDENCE ATTACHMENT A

e.g., Food, Drug, and Cosmetic Act ("FDCA") §§ 301(a), 505(a), 21 U.S.C. §§ 331(a), 355(a); 42 U.S.C § 262(a). A vaccine is both a drug and a biological product. See FDCA § 201(g), 21 U.S.C § 321(g); 42 U.S.C. § 262(i)(1); FDCA § 564(a)(4)(C) (defining "product" to mean "a drug, device, or biological product"). However, an exception exists whereas the FDCA authorizes the FDA to issue EUAs for medical products (e.g., non-FDA-approved vaccines such as BioNTech) under certain emergency circumstances. 21 U.S.C. § 360bbb-3,

Once a product receives an EUA, the product may be introduced into interstate commerce and administered to individuals despite the medical product not yet having received full-FDA approval. Such administration is only permitted "[t]o the extent practicable" given the emergency circumstances, and "as the [agency] finds necessary or appropriate to protect the public health." As a result, "[a]ppropriate" conditions are imposed on each EUA the FDA issues. Id. § 564(e)(1)(A).

Perhaps the most critical condition imposed is ensuring all recipients have given "informed consent" prior to receiving the non-FDA-approved medical product. Under FDCA § 564(e)(1)(A)(ii)(III), recipients of a EUA-authorized medical products must "[be] informed" of inter alia **the option to accept or refuse administration of the product."** Id.

The FDCA also requires medical products that have not been fully approved by the FDA–such as the BioNTech vaccine– satisfy certain conditions "to ensure that individuals to whom the product is administered are informed . . . of the option to accept or refuse administration of the product, of the consequences, if any, of refusing administration of the product, and of the alternatives to the product that are available and of their benefits and risks." 21 U.S.C. 360bbb– 3(e)(ii).

Since December 2020, the FDA has issued an EUA for the BioNTech vaccine. As part of the BioNTech EUA, the FDA imposed a condition stating that all recipients must have the "option to accept or refuse" the non-FDA-approved vaccine. To effectuate this, the EUA requires all recipients to receive a Fact Sheet ("BioNTech

Fact Sheet") stating: "It is your choice to receive or not receive [the vaccine]."

Concerning the military, Congress enacted 10 U.S.C. § 1107a as a specific condition that expressly refers to the "option to accept or refuse" the medical product; the same condition requirement that applies to the public at-large and non-military personnel set forth in FDCA § 564(e)(1)(A)(ii)(III). See Pub. L. No. 108-136, sec. 1603(b)(1), § 1107a, 117 Stat. at 1690.

When an EUA product is administered to members of the armed forces, "the condition described in section 564(e)(1)(A)(ii)(III)", (e.g., the "option to accept or refuse"), is **required** pursuant to § 564(e)(1)(A), (2)(A). FDCA § 564 et seq.

On July 6, 2021, Acting Assistant Attorney General Dawn Johnsen ("DOJ") submitted a Memorandum Opinion to the Deputy Counsel for the President in response to the question: "Whether the 'option to accept or refuse' condition in section 564 prohibits entities from imposing such vaccination requirements while the only available vaccines for COVID-19 remain subject to EUAs."

The DOJ concluded that "FDCA § 564(e)(1)(A)(ii)(III) [requires] . . . potential vaccine recipients be "informed" of . . . "the option to accept or refuse administration of the product." Id. at 6–7. The DOJ's conclusion is also corroborated by both, the FDA and Pfizer. Specifically, Pfizer's EUA Letter, Pfizer's Fact Sheet, and the FDA's Fact Sheet, all state "that recipients 'have a choice to receive or not receive' the vaccine."

Because the only FDA-approved vaccine is COMIRNATY, and in light of the fact that COMIRNATY is unavailable, the only vaccines that can conceivably be administered are non- FDA-approved vaccines only available under EUA; therefore, because such vaccines are not fully- FDA-approved, and based upon the requirements of FDCA § 564(e) et seq., the DOJ's Memorandum Opinion, Pfizer's EUA Letter, Pfizer's Fact Sheet, and the FDA's Fact Sheet, it is not subject to dispute that **any recipient of the non-FDA-approved BioNTech vaccine made available exclusively under an EUA must receive the option to accept or refuse administration of the product."**

EVIDENCE ATTACHMENT A

The EUA is "final agency action for which there is no other adequate remedy." 5 U.S.C. § 704. Further, the EUA was a decision from which rights or obligations were determined and from which legal consequences (e.g., vitiating Plaintiffs' **statutorily provided "option to accept or refuse administration of the product"**, FDCA § 564(e)(1)(A)(ii)(III)) flowed.

Plaintiffs have no adequate or available administrative remedy.

In the alternative, any effort to obtain an administrative remedy would be futile.

Plaintiff has no adequate remedy at law.

As a direct and proximate result of Defendants' actions, Plaintiffs have suffered, and will continue to suffer, irreparable harm and their rights will be continued to be violated absent the injunctive relief requested.

As a direct and proximate result of E.O. 14042, the Federal Contractor Plaintiffs and respective Federal Contractor Class and Subclass Members have suffered, and will continue to suffer, irreparable harm and their rights will be continued to be violated absent the injunctive relief requested.

As a direct and proximate result of E.O. 14043, the Federal Employee Plaintiffs and respective Federal Employee Class and Subclass Members have suffered, and will continue to suffer, irreparable harm and their rights will be continued to be violated absent the injunctive relief requested.

PRAYER FOR RELIEF

WHEREFORE, Plaintiffs, on behalf of themselves and all others similarly situated, respectfully pray for relief as follows:

That the Court issue a temporary restraining order restraining and enjoining Defendants and their officers, agents, employees, and attorneys, and all other persons in active concert or participation with them, from enforcing, threatening to enforce, attempting to enforce, or otherwise requiring compliance with the Vaccine Mandate such that:

Defendants will immediately comply with the EUA Provisions of the FDCA so that each individual has the "option to accept or refuse" administration of all currently available COVID-19 vaccines as currently there is no FDA- approved COVID-19 vaccine is available to the population;

Defendants will immediately cease in their refusal to consider, evaluate, or accept Plaintiffs' requests for exemption and accommodation for their sincerely held religious beliefs;

Defendants' will immediately grant Plaintiffs' requests for religious exemption from the Vaccine Mandate to accommodate their sincerely held religious beliefs;

Defendants will immediately cease any actions arising from or connected to the Department of Defense, as to both, the civilian and servicemember Plaintiffs' religious exemption and accommodation requests, including current and ongoing punishment and threatening to dishonorably discharge, court martial, and impose other life-altering disciplinary actions on Plaintiffs for failure to accept a COVID-19 vaccine that violates their sincerely held religious beliefs;

That the Court issue a preliminary injunction pending trial, and a permanent injunction upon judgment, restraining and enjoining Defendants and their officers, agents, employees, and attorneys, and all other persons in active concert or participation with them, from enforcing, threatening to enforce, attempting to enforce, or otherwise requiring compliance with the Vaccine Mandates such that:

Defendants will immediately comply with the Emergency Use Authorization Statute so that each individual has the "option to accept or refuse" administration of the COVID-19 vaccines as there is currently no FDA approved COVID-19 vaccine available to the population;

Defendants will immediately cease in their refusal to consider, evaluate, or accept Plaintiffs' requests for exemption and accommodation for their sincerely held religious beliefs;

EVIDENCE ATTACHMENT A

Defendants' will immediately grant Plaintiffs' requests for religious exemption and accommodation from the Vaccine Mandate; and Defendants will immediately cease any actions arising from or connected to the Department of Defense, as to both, the civilian and servicemember Plaintiffs' religious exemption and accommodation requests, including current and ongoing punishment and threatening to dishonorably discharge, court martial, and impose other life-altering disciplinary actions on Plaintiffs for failure to accept a COVID-19 vaccine that violates their sincerely held religious beliefs; and

Defendants will immediately cease any actions arising from or connected to the military servicemember Plaintiffs' religious exemption and accommodation requests, including current and ongoing punishment and threatening to dishonorably discharge, court martial, and impose other life- altering disciplinary actions on Plaintiffs for failure to accept a COVID-19 vaccine that violates their sincerely held religious beliefs;

That this Court render a declaratory judgment declaring that the Vaccine Mandate, both on its face and as applied by Defendants, is illegal and unlawful in that it purports to remove federal civil rights and constitutional protections from federal employees and military servicemembers and further declare—

the Vaccine Mandate violates the EUA Provisions of the FDCA by imposing a mandatory COVID-19 vaccination condition upon Plaintiffs' employment and ability to remain free from adverse employment while depriving Plaintiffs of their statutorily provided "option to accept or refuse" all EUA products;

the Vaccine Mandate, without sufficient provision for exemption or accommodation for sincerely held religious beliefs, violates the First Amendment to the United States Constitution by imposing a substantial burden on Plaintiffs' sincerely held religious beliefs;

the Vaccine Mandate, without sufficient provision for exemption or accommodation for sincerely held religious beliefs, violates the federal Religious Freedom Restoration Act by imposing a substantial burden on Plaintiffs' sincerely held religious beliefs;

That this Court adjudge, decree, and declare the rights and other legal obligations and relations within the subject matter here in controversy so that such declaration shall have the full force and effect of final judgment;

That this Court retain jurisdiction over for purposes of issuing Order;

That this Court grant such other and further relief as the Court deems equitable and just under the circumstances.

Dated: October 24, 2021.
Respectfully submitted,
By: /S/ MICHAEL A. YODER
Michael A. Yoder [1600519]
THE LAW OFFICE OF MICHAEL A. YODER, PLLC
2300 Wilson Blvd., Suite 700
Arlington, VA 22202
Tel: (571) 234-5594
Fax: (571) 327-5554
michael@yoderesq.com

EVIDENCE ATTACHMENT B

Religious Request Form

TEMPLATE

REQUEST FOR A RELIGIOUS EXCEPTION TO THE COVID-19 VACCINATION REQUIREMENT

Government-wide policy requires all Federal employees as defined in 5 U.S.C. § 2105 to be vaccinated against COVID-19, with exceptions only as required by law. In certain circumstances, Federal law may entitle a Federal employee who has a religious objection to the COVID-19 vaccination requirement to an exception from that requirement, in which case the employee would instead comply with alternative health and safety protocols. The Federal Government is committed to respecting the important legal protections for religious liberty.

In order to request a religious exception, please fill out this form. The purpose of this form is to start the accommodation process and help your agency determine whether you may be eligible for a religious exception. You do not need to answer every question on the form to be considered for a religious exception, but we encourage you to provide as much information as possible to enable the agency to evaluate your request.

Where there is an objective basis to do so, the agency may ask you for additional information as needed to determine if you are legally entitled to an exception. Objections to COVID-19 vaccinations that are based on non-religious reasons, including personal preferences or non-religious concerns about the vaccine, do not qualify for a religious exception.

Agencies may consider several factors in assessing whether a request for an exception is based on a sincerely held religious belief, including whether the employee has acted in a manner inconsistent with their professed belief. But no one factor is determinative. An individual's beliefs—or degree of adherence—may change over time and, therefore, an employee's newly adopted or inconsistently observed practices may nevertheless be based on a sincerely held religious belief. All requests for a religious exception will be evaluated on an individual basis.

Signing this form constitutes a declaration that the information you provide is, to the best of your knowledge and ability, true and correct. Any intentional misrepresentation to the Federal Government may result in legal consequences, including termination or removal from Federal Service.

QUESTIONS:

1. Please describe the nature of your objection to the COVID-19 vaccination requirement.

2. Would complying with the COVID-19 vaccination requirement substantially burden your religious exercise or conflict with your sincerely held religious beliefs, practices, or observances? If so, please explain how.

3. Please provide any additional information that you think may be helpful in reviewing your request. For example:
    - How long you have held the religious belief underlying your objection
    - Whether your religious objection is to the use of all vaccines, COVID-19 vaccines, a specific type of COVID-19 vaccine, or some other subset of vaccines

EVIDENCE ATTACHMENT B

- Whether you have received vaccines as an adult against any other diseases (such as a flu vaccine or a tetanus vaccine)

I declare to the best of my knowledge and ability that the foregoing is true and correct.

_____   _____   _____
         Print Name   Signature   Date

EVIDENCE ATTACHMENT C
Pope Letter

11/8/21

CONGREGATION FOR THE DOCTRINE OF THE FAITH
Note on the morality of using some anti-Covid-19 vaccines

The question of the use of vaccines, in general, is often at the center of controversy in the forum of public opinion. In recent months, this Congregation has received several requests for guidance regarding the use of vaccines against the SARS-CoV-2 virus that causes Covid-19, which, in the course of research and production, employed cell lines drawn from tissue obtained from two abortions that occurred in the last century. At the same time, diverse and sometimes conflicting pronouncements in the mass media by bishops, Catholic associations, and experts have raised questions about the morality of the use of these vaccines.

There is already an important pronouncement of the Pontifical Academy for Life on this issue, entitled "Moral reflections on vaccines prepared from cells derived from aborted human fetuses" (5 June 2005). Further, this Congregation expressed itself on the matter with the Instruction Dignitas Personae (September 8, 2008, cf. nn. 34 and 35). In 2017, the Pontifical Academy for Life returned to the topic with a Note. These documents already offer some general directive criteria.

Since the first vaccines against Covid-19 are already available for distribution and administration in various countries, this Congregation desires to offer some indications for clarification of this matter. We do not intend to judge the safety and efficacy of these vaccines, although ethically relevant and necessary, as this evaluation is the responsibility of biomedical researchers and drug agencies. Here, our objective is only to consider the moral aspects of the use of the vaccines against Covid-19 that have been developed from cell lines derived from tissues obtained from two fetuses that were not spontaneously aborted.

As the Instruction Dignitas Personae states, in cases where cells from aborted fetuses are employed to create cell lines for use in scientific research, "there exist differing degrees of responsibility"[1] of cooperation in evil. For example, "in organizations where cell lines of illicit origin are being utilized, the responsibility of those who make the decision to use them is not the same as that of those who have no voice in such a decision".[2]

In this sense, when ethically irreproachable Covid-19 vaccines are not available (e.g. in countries where vaccines without ethical problems are not made available to physicians and patients, or where their distribution is more difficult due to special storage and transport conditions, or when various types of vaccines are distributed in the same country but health authorities do not allow citizens to choose the vaccine with which to be inoculated) it is morally acceptable to receive Covid-19 vaccines that have used cell lines from aborted fetuses in their research and production process.

The fundamental reason for considering the use of these vaccines morally licit is that the kind of cooperation in evil (passive material cooperation) in the procured abortion from which

---

1. Congregation for the Doctrine of the Faith, Instruction *Dignitas Personae* (8th December 2008), n. 35;
AAS (100), 884.
2. *Ibid*, 885.

these cell lines originate is, on the part of those making use of the resulting vaccines, remote. The moral duty to avoid such passive material cooperation is not obligatory if there is a grave danger, such as the otherwise uncontainable spread of a serious pathological agent[3]—in this case, the pandemic spread of the SARS-CoV-2 virus that causes Covid-19. It must therefore be considered that, in such a case, all vaccinations recognized as clinically safe and effective can be used in good conscience with the certain knowledge that the use of such vaccines does not constitute formal cooperation with the abortion from which the cells used in production of the vaccines derive. It should be emphasized, however, that the morally licit use of these types of vaccines, in the particular conditions that make it so, does not in itself constitute a legitimation, even indirect, of the practice of abortion, and necessarily assumes the opposition to this practice by those who make use of these vaccines.

In fact, the licit use of such vaccines does not and should not in any way imply that there is a moral endorsement of the use of cell lines proceeding from aborted fetuses.[4] Both pharmaceutical companies and governmental health agencies are therefore encouraged to produce, approve, distribute and offer ethically acceptable vaccines that do not create problems of conscience for either health care providers or the people to be vaccinated.

At the same time, practical reason makes evident that vaccination is not, as a rule, a moral obligation and that, therefore, it must be voluntary. In any case, from the ethical point of view, the

---

3. Cfr. Pontifical Academy for Life, "Moral reflections on vaccines prepared from cells derived from aborted human foetuses." 5th June 2005.

4. Congregation for the Doctrine of the Faith, Instruct. *Dignitas Personae*, n. 35: "When the illicit action is endorsed by the laws which regulate healthcare and scientific research, it is necessary to distance oneself
from the evil aspects of that system in order not to give the impression of a certain toleration or tacit acceptance of actions which are gravely unjust. Any appearance of acceptance would in fact contribute to the growing indifference to, if not approval of, such actions in certain medical and political circles.

morality of vaccination depends not only on the duty to protect one's own health, but also on the duty to pursue the common good. In the absence of other means to stop or even prevent the epidemic, the common good may recommend vaccination, especially to protect the weakest and most exposed. Those who, however, for reasons of conscience, refuse vaccines produced with cell lines from aborted fetuses, must do their utmost to avoid, by other prophylactic means and appropriate behavior, becoming vehicles for the transmission of the infectious agent. In particular, they must avoid any risk to the health of those who cannot be vaccinated for medical or other reasons, and who are the most vulnerable.

Finally, there is also a moral imperative for the pharmaceutical industry, governments and international organizations to ensure that vaccines, which are effective and safe from a medical point of view, as well as ethically acceptable, are also accessible to the poorest countries in a manner that is not costly for them. The lack of access to vaccines, otherwise, would become another sign of discrimination and injustice that condemns poor countries to continue living in health, economic and social poverty.[5]

The Sovereign Pontiff Francis, at the Audience granted to the undersigned Prefect of the Congregation for the Doctrine of the Faith, on 17 December 2020, examined the present Note and ordered its publication.

Rome, from the Offices of the Congregation for the Doctrine of the Faith, on 21 December 2020, Liturgical Memorial of Saint Peter Canisius.

Luis F. Card. Ladaria, S.I., *Prefect*

+ S.E. Mons. Giacomo Morandi, *Titular Archbishop of Cerveteri Secretary*

---

5. Cfr. Francis, Address to the members of the "Banco Farmaceutico" foundation. 19 September 2020.

EVIDENCE ATTACHMENT D

Catholic Exemption Template

[DATE]

To Whom It May Concern,

I am a baptized Catholic seeking an exemption from an immunization requirement. This letter explains how the Catholic Church's teachings may lead individual Catholics, including me, [name], to decline certain vaccines.

The Roman Catholic Church teaches that a person may be required to refuse a medical intervention, including a vaccination, if his or her informed conscience comes to this sure judgment. While the Catholic Church does not prohibit the use of any vaccine, and generally encourages the use of safe and effective vaccines as a way of safeguarding personal and public health, the following authoritative Church teachings demonstrate the principled religious basis on which a Catholic may determine that he or she ought to refuse certain vaccines:[BL 1-4]

- Vaccination is not morally obligatory in principle and so must be voluntary.[1]
- There is a general moral duty to refuse the use of medical products, including certain vaccines, that are produced using human cells lines derived from direct abortions. It is permissible to use such vaccines only under certain case-specific conditions, based on a judgment of conscience.[2]

- A person's informed judgments about the proportionality of medical interventions are to be respected unless they contradict authoritative Catholic moral teachings.3
- A person is morally required to obey his or her sure conscience.4[/BL 1-4]

A Catholic may judge it wrong to receive certain vaccines for a variety of reasons consistent with these teachings, and there is no authoritative Church teaching universally obliging Catholics to receive any vaccine. An individual Catholic may invoke Church teaching to refuse a vaccine developed or produced using abortion-derived cell lines. More generally, a Catholic might refuse a vaccine based on the Church's teachings concerning therapeutic proportionality. Therapeutic proportionality is an assessment of whether the benefits of a medical intervention outweigh the undesirable side-effects and burdens in light of the integral good of the person, including spiritual, psychological, and bodily goods.5 It can also extend to the good of others and the common good, which likewise entail spiritual and moral dimensions and are not reducible to public health. The judgment of therapeutic proportionality must be made by the person who is the potential recipient of the intervention in the concrete circumstances,6 not by public health authorities or by other individuals who might judge differently in their own situations.

At the core of the Church's teaching are the first and last points listed above: vaccination is not a universal obligation and a person must obey the judgment of his or her own informed and certain conscience. In fact, the *Catechism of the Catholic Church* instructs that following one's conscience is following Christ Himself:

> In all he says and does, man is obliged to follow faithfully what he knows to be just and right. It is by the judgment of his conscience that man perceives and recognizes the prescriptions of the divine law: "Conscience is a law of the mind; yet [Christians] would not grant that it is nothing more; . . . [Conscience] is a messenger of him, who, both in nature and in grace, speaks to us behind

a veil, and teaches and rules us by his representatives. Conscience is the aboriginal Vicar of Christ."7

Therefore, if a Catholic comes to an informed and sure judgment in conscience that he or she should not receive a vaccine, then the Catholic Church requires that the person follow this certain judgment of conscience and refuse the vaccine. The *Catechism* is clear: "Man has the right to act in conscience and in freedom so as personally to make moral decisions. 'He must not be forced to act contrary to his conscience. Nor must he be prevented from acting according to his conscience, especially in religious matters.'"8

Sincerely in Christ,

[Name]

NOTES

1 Congregation for the Doctrine of the Faith (CDF), "Note on the Morality of Using Some Anti-COVID-19 Vaccines," December 17, 2020, n. 5: "At the same time, practical reason makes evident that vaccination is not, as a rule, a moral obligation and that, therefore, it must be voluntary."

2 See Pontifical Academy for Life, "Moral Reflections on Vaccines Prepared from Cells Derived from Aborted Human Foetuses," June 9, 2005; Congregation for the Doctrine of the Faith, Instruction *Dignitas personae*, 2008, nn. 34-35; Congregation for the Doctrine of the Faith, "Note on the Morality of Using Some Anti-COVID- 19 Vaccines," nn. 1-3. When there is a sufficiently serious reason to use the product and there is no reasonable alternative available, the Catholic Church teaches that it may be permissible to use the immorally sourced product under protest. In any case, whether the product is used or not, the Catholic Church teaches that all must make their disagreement known and request the development of equal or better products using biological material that does not come from abortions.

3 See United States Conference of Catholic Bishops (USCCB), *Ethical and Religious Directives for Catholic Health Care*

Services, 6th ed. (Washington, DC: USCCB Publishing, 2018), n. 28. Hereafter "*ERDs*."

4 "A human being must always obey the certain judgment of his conscience. If he were deliberately to act against it, he would condemn himself. Yet it can happen that moral conscience remains in ignorance and makes erroneous judgments about acts to be performed or already committed." *Catechism of the Catholic Church* (Vatican City: Libreria Editrice Vaticana, 1993), www.vatican.va, n. 1790. Hereafter "*CCC*."

5 See *ERDs*, nn. 32-33; nn. 56-57; Part Three, Introduction, para. 2; Part Five, Introduction, para. 3.

6 See *ERDs*, nn. 56-57. Both of these directives state that the proportionality of medical interventions is established "in the patient's judgment."

7 *CCC*, n. 1777, citing John Henry Cardinal Newman, "Letter to the Duke of Norfolk," V, in *Certain Difficulties felt by Anglicans in Catholic Teaching II* (London: Longmans Green, 1885), 248.

8 *CCC*, n. 1782, citing Second Vatican Council, *Dignitatis humanae*, December 7, 1965, n. 3.

EVIDENCE ATTACHMENT E

Contractor Guidance

Safer Federal Workforce Task Force

COVID-19 Workplace Safety: Guidance for Federal Contractors and Subcontractors

Issued September 24, 2021

INTRODUCTION

On September 9, President Biden announced his *Path Out of the Pandemic: COVID-19 Action Plan.* One of the main goals of this science-based plan is to get more people vaccinated.

As part of that plan, the President signed Executive Order 14042, *Ensuring Adequate COVID Safety Protocols for Federal Contractors,* ("the order") which directs executive departments and agencies, including independent establishments subject to the Federal Property and Administrative Services Act, 40 U.S.C. § 102(4)(A), to ensure that covered contracts and contract-like instruments include a clause ("the clause") that the contractor and any subcontractors (at any tier) shall incorporate into lower-tier subcontracts. This clause shall specify that the contractor or subcontractor shall, for the duration of the contract, comply with all guidance for contractor or subcontractor workplace locations published by the Safer Federal Workforce Task Force ("Task Force"), provided that the Director of the Office of Management and Budget ("OMB") approves the Task Force Guidance (the or this "Guidance") and determines that the Guidance, if adhered to by covered contractors, will promote economy and efficiency in Federal contracting.

The actions directed by the order will ensure that parties who contract with the Federal Government provide COVID-19 safeguards in workplaces with individuals working on or in connection with a Federal Government contract or contract-like instrument. These workplace safety protocols will apply to all covered contractor employees, including contractor or subcontractor employees in covered contractor workplaces who are not working on a Federal Government contract or contract-like instrument. These safeguards will decrease the spread of SARS-CoV-2, the virus that causes COVID-19, which will decrease worker absence, reduce labor costs, and improve the efficiency of contractors and subcontractors performing work for the Federal Government.

Pursuant to this Guidance, and in addition to any requirements or workplace safety protocols that are applicable because a contractor or subcontractor employee is present at a Federal workplace, Federal contractors and subcontractors with a covered contract will be required to conform to the following workplace safety protocols:

1. COVID-19 vaccination of covered contractor employees, except in limited circumstances where an employee is legally entitled to an accommodation;

2. Compliance by individuals, including covered contractor employees and visitors, with the Guidance related to masking and physical distancing while in covered contractor workplaces; and

3. Designation by covered contractors of a person or persons to coordinate COVID-19 workplace safety efforts at covered contractor workplaces.

The order also sets out a process for OMB and the Safer Federal Workforce Task Force to update the Guidance for covered contractors, which the Task Force will consider doing based on future changes to Centers for Disease Control and Prevention ("CDC") COVID-19 guidance and as warranted by the circumstances of the pandemic and public health conditions. It also sets out a process for the Federal Acquisition Regulatory Council ("FAR Council") to implement such protocols and guidance for covered Federal procurement solicitations and contracts subject to the Federal Acquisition Regulation ("FAR") and for agencies that are responsible for covered contracts and contract-like instruments not subject to the FAR to take prompt action to ensure that those covered contracts and contract-like instruments include the clause, consistent with the order.

Covered contractors shall adhere to the requirements of this Guidance. The Director of OMB has, as authorized by Executive Order 14042, approved this Guidance and has, an exercise of the delegation of authority (see 3 U.S.C. § 301) under the Federal Property and Administrative Services Act determined that this Guidance will promote economy and efficiency in Federal contracting if adhered to by Government contractors and subcontractors. The Director has published such determination in the Federal Register.

DEFINITIONS

Community transmission—means the level of community transmission as set forth in the *CDC COVID-19 Data Tracker County View*.

Contract and contract-like instrument—has the meaning set forth in the Department of Labor's proposed rule, "Increasing the Minimum Wage for Federal Contractors," *86 Fed. Reg. 38,816*, 38,887 (July 22, 2021). If the Department of Labor issues a final rule relating to that proposed rule, this term shall have the meaning set forth in that final rule.

That proposed rule defines a contract or contract-like instrument as an agreement between two or more parties creating obligations that are enforceable or otherwise recognizable at law. This definition includes, but is not limited to, a mutually binding legal relationship obligating one party to furnish services (including construction) and another party to pay for them. The term contract includes all contracts and any subcontracts of any tier thereunder, whether negotiated or advertised, including any procurement actions, lease agreements, cooperative agreements, provider agreements, intergovernmental service agreements, service agreements, licenses, permits, or any other type of agreement, regardless of nomenclature, type, or particular form, and whether entered into verbally or in writing. The term contract shall be interpreted broadly as to include, but not be limited to, any contract within the definition provided in the FAR at 48 CFR chapter 1 or applicable Federal statutes. This definition includes, but is not limited to, any contract that may be covered under any Federal procurement statute. Contracts may be the result of competitive bidding or awarded to a single source under applicable authority to do so. In addition to bilateral instruments, contracts include, but are not limited to, awards and notices of awards; job orders or task letters issued under basic ordering agreements; letter contracts; orders, such as purchase orders, under which the contract becomes effective by written acceptance or performance; exercised contract options; and bilateral contract modifications. The term contract includes contracts covered by the Service Contract Act, contracts covered by the Davis-Bacon Act, concessions contracts not otherwise subject to the Service Contract Act, and contracts in connection with Federal property or land and related to offering services for Federal employees, their dependents, or the general public.

Contractor or subcontractor workplace location—means a location where covered contract employees work, including a covered contractor workplace or Federal workplace.

Covered contract—means any contract or contract-like instrument that includes the clause described in Section 2(a) of the order.

Covered contractor—means a prime contractor or subcontractor at any tier who is party to a covered contract.

Covered contractor employee—means any full-time or part-time employee of a covered contractor working on or in connection with a covered contract or working at a covered contractor workplace. This includes employees of covered contractors who are not themselves working on or in connection with a covered contract.

Covered contractor workplace—means a location controlled by a covered contractor at which any employee of a covered contractor working on or in connection with a covered contract is likely to be present during the period of performance for a covered contract. A covered contractor workplace does not include a covered contractor employee's residence.

Federal workplace—means any place, site, installation, building, room, or facility in which any Federal executive department or agency conducts official business, or is within an executive department or agency's jurisdiction, custody, or control.

Fully vaccinated—People are considered *fully vaccinated* for COVID-19 two weeks after they have received the second dose in a two-dose series, or two weeks after they have received a single-dose vaccine. There is currently no post-vaccination time limit on fully vaccinated status; should such a limit be determined by the Centers for Disease Control and Prevention, that limit will be considered by the Task Force and OMB for possible updating of this Guidance.

For purposes of this Guidance, people are considered fully vaccinated if they have received COVID-19 vaccines currently approved or authorized for emergency use by the U.S. Food and Drug Administration (Pfizer-BioNTech, Moderna, and Johnson & Johnson [J&J]/Janssen COVID-19 vaccines) or COVID-19 vaccines that have been listed for emergency use by the World Health Organization (e.g., AstraZeneca/Oxford). More information is available at Interim Clinical *Considerations for Use of COVID-19 Vaccines | CDC*.

Clinical trial participants from a U.S. site who are documented to have received the full series of an "active" (not placebo) COVID-19 vaccine candidate, for which vaccine efficacy has been independently confirmed (e.g., by a data and safety monitoring board), can be considered fully vaccinated two weeks after they have completed the vaccine series. Currently, the Novavax

COVID-19 vaccine meets these criteria. More information is available at the CDC website *here*.

Mask—means any mask that is consistent with CDC recommendations as set forth in *Types of Masks and Respirators | CDC*. This may include the following: disposable masks, masks that fit properly (snugly around the nose and chin with no large gaps around the sides of the face), masks made with breathable fabric (such as cotton), masks made with tightly woven fabric (i.e., fabrics that do not let light pass through when held up to a light source), masks with two or three layers, masks with inner filter pockets, and filtering facepiece respirators that are approved by the National Institute for Occupational Safety and Health or consistent with international standards. The following do not constitute masks for purposes of this Guidance: masks with exhalation valves, vents, or other openings; face shields only (without mask); or masks with single-layer fabric or thin fabric that does not block light.

GUIDANCE

Covered contractors are responsible for ensuring that covered contractor employees comply with the workplace safety protocols detailed below. Covered contractor employees must also comply with agency COVID-19 workplace safety requirements while in Federal workplaces.

Consistent with applicable law, agencies are strongly encouraged to incorporate a clause requiring compliance with this Guidance into contracts that are not covered or directly addressed by the order because the contract is under the Simplified Acquisition Threshold as defined in section 2.101 of the FAR or is a contract or subcontract for the manufacturing of products.

Agencies are also strongly encouraged to incorporate a clause requiring compliance with this Guidance into existing contracts and contract-like instruments prior to the date upon which the order requires inclusion of the clause.

1. *Vaccination of covered contractor employees, except in limited circumstances where an employee is legally entitled to an accommodation*

Covered contractors must ensure that all covered contractor employees are fully vaccinated for COVID-19, unless the employee is legally entitled to an accommodation. Covered contractor employees must be fully vaccinated no later than December 8, 2021. After that date, all covered contractor employees must be fully vaccinated by the first day of the period of performance on a newly awarded covered contract, and by the first day of the period of performance on an exercised option or extended or renewed contract when the clause has been incorporated into the covered contract.

A covered contractor may be required to provide an accommodation to covered contractor employees who communicate to the covered contractor that they are not vaccinated against COVID-19 because of a disability (which would include medical conditions) or because of a sincerely held religious belief, practice, or observance. A covered contractor should review and consider what, if any, accommodation it must offer. Requests for "medical accommodation" or "medical exceptions" should be treated as requests for a disability accommodation.

Should a Federal agency have an urgent, mission-critical need for a covered contractor to have covered contractor employees begin work on a covered contract or at a covered workplace before becoming fully vaccinated, the agency head may approve an exception for the covered contractor—in the case of such limited exceptions, the covered contractor must ensure these covered contractor employees are fully vaccinated within 60 days of beginning work on a covered contract or at a covered workplace. The covered contractor must further ensure that such employees comply with masking and physical distancing requirements for not fully vaccinated individuals in covered workplaces prior to being fully vaccinated.

The covered contractor must review its covered employees' documentation to prove vaccination status. Covered contractors must require covered contractor employees to show or provide their employer with one of the following documents: a copy of the record of immunization from a health care provider or pharmacy, a copy of the COVID-19 Vaccination Record Card (CDC Form MLS-319813_r, published on September 3, 2020), a copy of medical records documenting the vaccination, a copy of immunization records from a public health or State immunization information system, or a copy of any other official documentation verifying vaccination with information on the vaccine name, date(s) of administration, and the name of health care professional or clinic site administering vaccine. Covered contractors may allow covered contractor employees to show or provide to their employer a digital copy of such records, including, for example, a digital photograph, scanned image, or PDF of such a record.

The covered contractor shall ensure compliance with the requirements in this Guidance related to the showing or provision of proper vaccination documentation.

Covered contractors are strongly encouraged to incorporate similar vaccination requirements into their non-covered contracts and agreements with non-covered contractors whose employees perform work at covered contractor workplaces but who do not work on or in connection with a Federal contract, such as those contracts and agreements related to the provision of food services, onsite security, or groundskeeping services at covered contractor workplaces.

2. *Requirements related to masking and physical distancing while in covered contractor workplaces*

Covered contractors must ensure that all individuals, including covered contractor employees and visitors, comply with published CDC guidance for masking and physical distancing at a covered contractor workplace, as discussed further in this Guidance.

In addition to the guidance set forth below, CDC's guidance for mask wearing and physical distancing in specific settings, including healthcare, transportation, correctional and detention facilities, and schools, must be followed, as applicable.

In areas of high or substantial community transmission, fully vaccinated people must wear a mask in indoor settings, except for limited exceptions discussed in this Guidance. In areas of low or moderate community transmission, fully vaccinated people do not need to wear a mask. Fully vaccinated individuals do not need to physically distance regardless of the level of transmission in the area.

Individuals who are not fully vaccinated must wear a mask indoors and in certain outdoor settings (see below) regardless of the level of community transmission in the area. To the extent practicable, individuals who are not fully vaccinated should maintain a distance of at least six feet from others at all times, including in offices, conference rooms, and all other communal and work spaces.

Covered contractors must require individuals in covered contractor workplaces who are required to wear a mask to:[BL 1-3]

- Wear appropriate masks consistently and correctly (over mouth and nose).
- Wear appropriate masks in any common areas or shared workspaces (including open floorplan office space, cubicle embankments, and conference rooms).
- For individuals who are not fully vaccinated, wear a mask in crowded outdoor settings or during outdoor activities that involve sustained close contact with other people who are not fully vaccinated, consistent with CDC guidance.[/BL 1-3]

A covered contractor may be required to provide an accommodation to covered contractor employees who communicate to the covered contractor that they cannot wear a mask because of a disability (which would include medical conditions) or because of a sincerely held religious belief, practice, or observance. A covered contractor should review and consider what, if any, accommodation it must offer.

Covered contractors may provide for exceptions to mask wearing and/or physical distancing requirements consistent with

CDC guidelines, for example, when an individual is alone in an office with floor to ceiling walls and a closed door, or for a limited time when eating or drinking and maintaining appropriate distancing. Covered contractors may also provide exceptions for covered contractor employees engaging in activities in which a mask may get wet; high intensity activities where covered contractor employees are unable to wear a mask because of difficulty breathing; or activities for which wearing a mask would create a risk to workplace health, safety, or job duty as determined by a workplace risk assessment. Any such exceptions must be approved in writing by a duly authorized representative of the covered contractor to ensure compliance with this Guidance at covered contractor workplaces, as discussed further below.

Masked individuals may be asked to lower their masks briefly for identification purposes in compliance with safety and security requirements.

Covered contractors must check the *CDC COVID-19 Data Tracker County View website* for community transmission information in all areas where they have a covered contractor workplace at least weekly to determine proper workplace safety protocols. When the level of community transmission in the area of a covered contractor workplace increases from low or moderate to substantial or high, contractors and subcontractors should put in place more protective workplace safety protocols consistent with published guidelines. However, when the level of community transmission in the area of a covered contractor workplace is reduced from high or substantial to moderate or low, the level of community transmission must remain at that lower level for at least two consecutive weeks before the covered contractor utilizes those protocols recommended for areas of moderate or low community transmission.

3. Designation by covered contractors of a person or persons to coordinate COVID-19 workplace safety efforts at covered contractor workplaces.

Covered contractors shall designate a person or persons to coordinate implementation of and compliance with this Guidance and the workplace safety protocols detailed herein at covered contractor workplaces. The designated person or persons may be the same individual(s) responsible for implementing any additional COVID-19 workplace safety protocols required by local, State, or Federal law, and their responsibilities to coordinate COVID-19 workplace safety protocols may comprise some or all of their regular duties.

The designated individual (or individuals) must ensure that information on required COVID-19 workplace safety protocols is provided to covered contractor employees and all other individuals likely to be present at covered contractor workplaces, including by communicating the required workplace safety protocols and related policies by email, websites, memoranda, flyers, or other means and posting signage at covered contractor workplaces that sets forth the requirements and workplace safety protocols in this Guidance in a readily understandable manner. This includes communicating the COVID-19 workplace safety protocols and requirements related to masking and physical distancing to visitors and all other individuals present at covered contractor workplaces. The designated individual (or individuals) must also ensure that covered contractor employees comply with the requirements in this guidance related to the showing or provision of proper vaccination documentation.

FREQUENTLY ASKED QUESTIONS

Vaccination and Safety Protocols

Q1: How do covered contractors determine vaccination status of visitors to covered contractor workplaces?

A: Covered contractors should post signage at entrances to covered contractor workplaces providing information on safety protocols for fully vaccinated and not fully vaccinated individuals, including the protocols defined in the masking and physical distancing section above, and instruct individuals to follow the appropriate workplace safety protocols while at the covered contractor workplace. Covered contractors may take other reasonable

EVIDENCE ATTACHMENT E

steps, such as by communicating workplace safety protocols to visitors prior to their arrival at a covered contractor workplace or requiring all visitors to follow masking and physical distancing protocols for not fully vaccinated individuals.

Q2: Do covered contractors need to provide onsite vaccinations to their employees?

A: Covered contractors should ensure their employees are aware of *convenient opportunities to be vaccinated*. Although covered contractors may choose to provide vaccinations at their facilities or workplaces, given the widespread availability of vaccinations, covered contractors are not required to do so.

Q3: What should a contractor employee do if a covered contractor employee has lost or does not have a copy of required vaccination documentation?

A: If covered contractor employees need new vaccination cards or copies of other documentation proof of vaccination, they should contact the vaccination provider site where they received their vaccine. Their provider should be able to provide them with new cards or documentation with up-to-date information about the vaccinations they have received. If the location where the covered contractor employees received their COVID-19 vaccine is no longer operating, the covered contractor employees should contact their State or local health department's *immunization information system (IIS)* for assistance. Covered contractor employees should *contact their State or local health department* if they have additional questions about vaccination cards or vaccination records.

An attestation of vaccination by the covered contractor employee is not an acceptable substitute for documentation of proof of vaccination.

Q4: Who is responsible for determining if a covered contractor employee must be provided an accommodation because of a disability or because of a sincerely held religious belief, practice, or observance?

A: A covered contractor may be required to provide an accommodation to contractor employees who communicate to the covered contractor that they are not vaccinated for COVID-19, or that they cannot wear a mask, because of a disability (which would include medical conditions) or because of a sincerely held religious belief, practice, or observance. A covered contractor should review and consider what, if any, accommodation it must offer. The contractor is responsible for considering, and dispositioning, such requests for accommodations regardless of the covered contractor employee's place of performance. If the agency that is the party to the covered contract is a "joint employer" for purposes of compliance with the Rehabilitation Act and Title VII of the Civil Rights Act, both the agency and the covered contractor should review and consider what, if any, accommodation they must offer.

Q5: Are covered contractor employees who have a prior COVID-19 infection required to be vaccinated?

A: Yes, covered contractor employees who have had a prior COVID-19 infection are required to be vaccinated. More information from CDC can be found *here*.

Q6: Can a covered contractor accept a recent antibody test from a covered contractor employee to prove vaccination status?

A: No. A covered contractor cannot accept a recent antibody test from a covered contractor employee to prove vaccination status.

Workplaces

Q7: Does this Guidance apply to outdoor contractor or subcontractor workplace locations?

A: Yes, this Guidance applies to contractor or subcontractor workplace locations that are outdoors.

Q8: If a covered contractor employee is likely to be present during the period of performance for a covered contract on only one floor or a separate area of a building, site, or facility controlled by a covered contractor, do other areas of the building, site, or facility controlled by a covered contractor constitute a covered contractor workplace?

A: Yes, unless a covered contractor can affirmatively determine that none of its employees on another floor or in separate areas of the building will come into contact with a covered contractor employee during the period of performance of a covered

EVIDENCE ATTACHMENT E

contract. This would include affirmatively determining that there will be no interactions between covered contractor employees and non-covered contractor employees in those locations during the period of performance on a covered contract, including interactions through use of common areas such as lobbies, security clearance areas, elevators, stairwells, meeting rooms, kitchens, dining areas, and parking garages.

Q9: If a covered contractor employee performs their duties in or at only one building, site, or facility on a campus controlled by a covered contractor with multiple buildings, sites, or facilities, are the other buildings, sites, or facility controlled by a covered contractor considered a covered contractor workplace?

A: Yes, unless a covered contractor can affirmatively determine that none of its employees in or at one building, site, or facility will come into contact with a covered contractor employee during the period of performance of a covered contract. This would include affirmatively determining that there will be no interactions between covered contractor employees and non-covered contractor employees in those locations during the period of performance on a covered contract, including interactions through use of common areas such as lobbies, security clearance areas, elevators, stairwells, meeting rooms, kitchens, dining areas, and parking garages.

Q10: Are the workplace safety protocols enumerated above the same irrespective of whether the work is performed at a covered contractor workplace or at a Federal workplace?

A: Yes. The Guidance applies to all covered contractor employees and to all contractor or subcontractor workplace locations. While at a Federal workplace, covered contractor employees must also comply with any additional agency workplace safety requirements for that workplace. Because covered contractor employees working on a covered contract need to be fully vaccinated after December 8, 2021, covered contractor employees who work only at a Federal workplace need to be fully vaccinated by that date as well, unless legally entitled to an accommodation.

Q11: How does this Guidance apply to covered contractor employees who are authorized under the covered contract to perform work remotely from their residence?

A: An individual working on a covered contract from their residence is a covered contractor employee, and must comply with the vaccination requirement for covered contractor employees, even if the employee never works at either a covered contractor workplace or Federal workplace during the performance of the contract. A covered contractor employee's residence is not a covered contractor workplace, so while in the residence the individual need not comply with requirements for covered contractor workplaces, including those related to masking and physical distancing, even while working on a covered contract.

Scope and Applicability

Q12: By when must the requirements of the order be reflected in contracts?

A: Section 6 of the order lays out a phase-in of the requirements for covered contracts as follows:[BL 1-2]

- *Contracts awarded prior to October 15 where performance is ongoing*—the requirements must be incorporated at the point at which an option is exercised or an extension is made.
- *New contracts*—the requirements must be incorporated into contracts awarded on or after
- November 14. Between October 15 and November 14, agencies must include the clause in the solicitation and are encouraged to include the clause in contracts awarded during this time period but are not required to do so unless the solicitation for such contract was issued on or after October 15.[/BL 1-2]

Q13: Must the order's requirements be flowed down to all lower-tier subcontractors and, if so, who is responsible for flowing the clause down?

A: Yes. The requirements in the order apply to subcontractors at all tiers, except for subcontracts solely for the provision of products. The prime contractor must flow the clause down to first-tier subcontractors; higher-tier subcontractors must flow the clause down to the next lower-tier subcontractor, to the point at which subcontract requirements are solely for the provision of products.

Q14: Does the Guidance apply to small businesses?

A: Yes, the requirement to comply with this Guidance applies equally to covered contractors regardless of whether they are a small business. This broad application of COVID-19 guidance will more effectively decrease the spread of COVID-19, which, in turn, will decrease worker absence, reduce labor costs, and improve the efficiency of contractors and subcontractors at workplaces where they are performing work for the Federal Government.

Q15: What steps are being taken to promote consistent application of the order's requirements across agencies?

A: The FAR Council will conduct a rulemaking to amend the FAR to include a clause that requires covered contractors performing under FAR-based contracts to comply with this Guidance for contractor and subcontractor workplace locations. Prior to rulemaking, by October 8, 2021, the FAR Council will develop a clause and recommend that agencies exercise their authority to deviate from the FAR using the procedures set forth in subpart 1.4. Agencies responsible for contracts and contract-like instruments that are not subject to the FAR, such as concession contracts, will be responsible for developing appropriate guidance by October 8, 2021 to incorporate requirements into their covered instruments entered into on or after October 15, 2021.

Q16: If the Safer Federal Workforce Task Force updates this Guidance to add new requirements, do those requirements apply to existing contracts?

A: Yes. Covered contractors are required to, for the duration of the contract, comply with all Task Force Guidance for contractor or subcontractor workplace locations, including any new Guidance where the OMB Director approves the Guidance and determines that adherence to the Guidance will promote economy and efficiency in Federal contracting. The Task Force and OMB plan to ensure any workplace safety protocols reflect what is necessary to decrease the spread of COVID-19.

Q17: What constitutes work performed "in connection with" a covered contract?

A: Employees who perform duties necessary to the performance of the covered contract, but who are not directly engaged in performing the specific work called for by the covered contract, such as human resources, billing, and legal review, perform work in connection with a Federal Government contract.

Q18: Do the workplace safety protocols in the Guidance apply to covered contractor employees who perform work outside the United States?

A: No. The workplace safety protocols in the Guidance do not apply to covered contractor employees who only perform work outside the United States or its outlying areas, as those terms are defined in section 2.101 of the FAR.

COMPLIANCE

Q19: Does this clause apply in States or localities that seek to prohibit compliance with any of the workplace safety protocols set forth in this Guidance?

A: Yes. These requirements are promulgated pursuant to Federal law and supersede any contrary State or local law or ordinance. Additionally, nothing in this Guidance shall excuse noncompliance with any applicable State law or municipal ordinance establishing more protective workplace safety protocols than those established under this Guidance.

Q20: Can a covered contractor comply with workplace safety requirements from the Occupational Safety and Health Administration, including pursuant to any current or forthcoming Emergency Temporary Standard related to COVID-19, instead of the requirements of this Guidance?

A: No. Covered contractors must comply with the requirements set forth in this Guidance regardless of whether they are subject to other workplace safety standards.

EVIDENCE ATTACHMENT E

Q21: What is the prime contractor's responsibility for verifying that subcontractors are adhering to the mandate?

A: The prime contractor is responsible for ensuring that the required clause is incorporated into its first-tier subcontracts in accordance with the implementation schedule set forth in section 6 of the order. When the clause is incorporated into a subcontract, a subcontractor is required to comply with this Guidance and the workplace safety protocols detailed herein. Additionally, first-tier subcontractors are expected to flow the clause down to their lower-tier subcontractors in similar fashion so that accountability for compliance is fully established throughout the Federal contract supply chain for covered subcontractor employees and workplaces at all tiers through application of the clause.

EVIDENCE ATTACHMENT F

Missouri v. Biden

IN THE UNITED STATES DISTRICT COURT
FOR THE EASTERN DISTRICT OF MISSOURI
Case: 4:21-cv-01300
Filed 10/29/21

COMPLAINT

Plaintiffs, the States of Missouri, Nebraska, Alaska, Arkansas, Iowa, Montana, New Hampshire, North Dakota, South Dakota, and Wyoming, bring this action to challenge Defendants' use of federal procurement statutes to create sweeping new power to issue decrees over large swaths of the U.S. economy and take over areas of traditional state power.

Through Executive Order 14042, President Biden has arrogated to the Executive Branch the unilateral power to mandate that all employees of federal contractors be vaccinated. This power grab is sweeping in its scope. Employees of federal contractors constitute one-fifth of the total U.S. workforce. And the mandate goes so far as to demand vaccination even from employees who work entirely within their own home. That is unconstitutional, unlawful, and unwise.

EVIDENCE ATTACHMENT F

PARTIES

Plaintiff State of Missouri is a sovereign State of the United States of America. Missouri sues to vindicate its sovereign, quasi-sovereign, proprietary, and *parens patriae* interests.

Eric S. Schmitt is the 43rd Attorney General of the State of Missouri. Attorney General Schmitt is authorized to bring actions on behalf of Missouri that are "necessary to protect the rights and interests of the state, and enforce any and all rights, interests, or claims any and all persons, firms or corporations in whatever court or jurisdiction such action may be necessary." Mo. Rev. Stat. § 270.060.

Plaintiff State of Nebraska is a sovereign State of the United States of America. Nebraska sues to vindicate its sovereign, quasi-sovereign, proprietary, and *parens patriae* interests.

Douglas J. Peterson is the Attorney General of Nebraska. Attorney General Peterson is authorized to bring legal actions on behalf of the State of Nebraska and its citizens.

Plaintiff State of Alaska is a sovereign State of the United States of America. Alaska sues to vindicate its sovereign, quasi-sovereign, proprietary, and *parens patriae* interests.

Treg R. Taylor is the Attorney General of Alaska. Attorney General Taylor is authorized to bring legal actions on behalf of the State of Alaska and its citizens.

Plaintiff State of Arkansas is a sovereign State of the United States of America. Arkansas sues to vindicate its sovereign, quasi-sovereign, proprietary, and *parens patriae* interests.

Leslie Rutledge is the Attorney General of Arkansas. Attorney General Rutledge is authorized to bring legal actions on behalf of the State of Arkansas and its citizens.

Plaintiff State of Iowa is a sovereign State of the United States of America. Iowa sues to vindicate its sovereign, quasi-sovereign, proprietary, and *parens patriae* interests.

The Attorney General of Iowa is authorized and required to prosecute legal actions on behalf of the State of Iowa and its citizens when requested to so by the Governor.

Plaintiff State of Montana is a sovereign State of the United States of America. Montana sues to vindicate its sovereign, quasi-sovereign, proprietary, and *parens patriae* interests.

The Attorney General of Montana is authorized to bring legal actions on behalf of the State of Montana and its citizens.

Plaintiff State of New Hampshire is a sovereign State of the United States of America.
New Hampshire sues to vindicate its sovereign, quasi-sovereign, proprietary, and *parens patriae* interests.

The Attorney General of New Hampshire is authorized to bring legal actions on behalf of the State of New Hampshire and its citizens.

Plaintiff State of North Dakota is a sovereign State of the United States of America. North Dakota sues to vindicate its sovereign, quasi-sovereign, proprietary, and *parens patriae* interests.

Wayne Stenehjem is the North Dakota Attorney General. Attorney General Stenehjem is authorized to bring legal actions on behalf of the State of North Dakota and its citizens. N.D. Cent. Code 54-12-02.

Plaintiff State of South Dakota is a body politic created by the Constitution and laws of the State; as such, it is not a citizen of any state. This action is brought by the State in its sovereign capacity in order to protect the interests of the State of South Dakota and its citizens as *parens patriae*, by and through Jason R. Ravnsborg, the Attorney General of the State of South Dakota. The Attorney General is acting pursuant to his authority to appear for the State and prosecute any civil matter in which the State is a party or interested when, in his judgment, the welfare of the State demands. S.D. Codified Laws §1-11-1(2).

Plaintiff State of Wyoming is a sovereign State of the United States of America. Wyoming sues to vindicate its sovereign, quasi-sovereign, proprietary, and *parens patriae* interests.

Bridget Hill is the Attorney General of Wyoming. Attorney General Hill is authorized to bring legal actions on behalf of the State of Wyoming and its citizens. Wyo. Stat. Ann. § 9-1-603.

EVIDENCE ATTACHMENT F

Collectively, the States of Missouri, Nebraska, Alaska, Arkansas, Iowa, Montana, New Hampshire, North Dakota, South Dakota, and Wyoming are referred to herein as the "Plaintiff States."

The Plaintiff States have the authority and responsibility to ensure that the United States does not evade its obligations under the Constitution and deprive their citizens of their rights by adopting a rule designed to evade traditional mechanisms of bicameralism and presentment and democratic processes. The Plaintiff States thus bring this suit to obtain a declaration that the contractor vaccine mandate is invalid, enjoin its enforcement, and protect the rights the Defendants have violated.

The Plaintiff States also bring this suit to protect state interests that the contractor vaccine mandate unconstitutionally and unlawfully impairs. The contractor vaccine mandate conflicts with state law, negatively affects the well-being of the residents of the Plaintiff States, and seeks to coopt States into enforcing federal policy—a policy that is unconstitutional.

Defendants are officials of the United States government and United States governmental agencies responsible for implementing the contractor vaccine mandate.

Defendant Joseph R. Biden, Jr., is the President of the United States of America. He is sued in his official capacity.

Defendant United States Office of Personnel Management ("OPM") is an independent federal agency.

Defendant Kiran Ahuja is director of OPM and co-chair of the Safer Federal Workforce Task Force. She is sued in her official capacity.

Defendant General Services Administration ("GSA") is an independent federal agency.

Defendant Robin Carnahan is administrator of GSA and co-chair of the Safer Federal Workforce Task Force. She is sued in her official capacity.

Defendant Office of Management and Budget ("OMB") is an office within the Executive Office of the President of the United States.

Defendant Shalanda Young is Acting Director of the OMB and is a member of the Safer Federal Workforce Task Force. She is sued in her official capacity.

Defendant Safer Federal Workforce Task Force was established on January 20, 2021 by Executive Order 13991.

Defendant Jeffrey Zients is co-chair of the Safer Federal Workforce Task Force and is the Biden Administration's COVID-19 Response Coordinator. He is sued in his official capacity. Defendant Federal Acquisition Regulatory Council ("FAR Council") is responsible for "manag[ing], coordinat[ing], control[ling], and monitor[ing] the maintenance of, issuance of, and changes in the Federal Acquisition Regulation." 41 U.S.C. § 1303(d). The FAR Council issued guidance that is challenged by this suit.

Defendants Lesley A. Field, John M. Tenaglia, Jeffrey A. Koses, and Karla S. Jackson are members of the FAR Council by virtue of their roles in their respective agencies. Defendant Lesley A. Field is the Acting Administrator for Federal Procurement of OMB. Defendant John M. Tenaglia is the Principal Director of Defense Pricing and Contracting of the Department of Defense. Defendant Jeffrey A. Koses is the Senior Procurement Executive & Deputy Chief Acquisition Officer of GSA. Defendant Karla S. Jackson is the Assistant Administrator for Procurement of NASA. They are sued in their official capacities.

JURISDICTION AND VENUE

This Court has jurisdiction pursuant to 5 U.S.C. §§ 702-703 and 28 U.S.C. §§ 1331, 1361, and 2201.

This Court is authorized to award the requested declaratory and injunctive relief under 5 U.S.C. §§ 702 and 706, 28 U.S.C. §§ 1361 and 2201-2202, and its inherent equitable powers.

Venue is proper in this district pursuant to 28 U.S.C. §§ 1391(b)(2) and 1391(e). Defendants are United States agencies or officers sued in their official capacities. Plaintiff State of Missouri is a resident of this judicial district, and a substantial part of the events or omissions giving rise to the Complaint occur within this district.

The Plaintiff States bring this action to redress harms to their sovereign interests, their quasi-sovereign interests, their proprietary interests, and their interests as *parentes patriae*; and to vindicate their interests under 5 U.S.C. § 702 and 41 U.S.C. § 1707.

GENERAL ALLEGATIONS

The Contractor Vaccine Mandate

On January 20, 2021, President Biden signed Executive Order 13991, 86 Fed. Reg. 7045, which established the Safer Federal Workforce Task Force ("Task Force") to provide "ongoing guidance to heads of agencies on the operation of the Federal Government, the safety of its employees, and the continuity of Government functions during the COVID–19 pandemic." 86 Fed. Reg. at 7046. The Task Force is headed by three co-chairs: (1) the Director of OPM; (2) the Administrator of GSA; and (3) the COVID–19 Response Coordinator. The Executive Order also required that GSA "provide funding and administrative support for the" Task Force. *Id.*

On September 9, 2021, President Biden announced his "new plan to require more Americans to be vaccinated" by imposing "new vaccination *requirements*." Joseph Biden, Remarks at the White House (Sept. 9, 2021), https://www.whitehouse.gov/briefing- room/speeches-remarks/2021/09/09/remarks-by-president-biden-on-fighting-the-covid-19- pandemic-3/ (accessed Oct. 28, 2021) (emphasis added).

One of those mandates would "*require* all employers with 100 or more employees, that together employ over 80 million workers, to ensure their workforces are fully vaccinated or show a negative test at least once a week." *Id.* (emphasis added).

The President also announced plans to "*requir[e]* vaccinations" of "those who work in hospitals, home healthcare facilities, or other medical facilities—a total of 17 million healthcare workers." *Id.* (emphasis added).

He further declared that he would "sign an executive order that will now *require* all executive branch federal employees to be vaccinated" and "another executive order that will require federal contractors to do the same." *Id.* (emphasis added).

And finally, the President announced that he would "*require* all of nearly 300,000 educators in the federal paid . . . Head Start program" to get vaccinated. *Id.* (emphasis added).

On September 9, 2021, President Biden signed Executive Order 14042 ("EO 14042"), 86 Fed. Reg. 50,985 (Sept. 14, 2021). EO 14042 required departments and agencies, including independent establishments, to require contractors and subcontractors to "comply with all guidance for contractor or subcontractor workplace locations published by the Safer Federal Workforce Task Force, provided that the Director of the Office of Management and Budget approves the Task Force Guidance and determines that the Guidance ... will promote economy and efficiency in Federal contracting." § 2(a).

EO 14042 delegated the President's Authority under the Federal Property and Administrative Services Act, see 40 U.S.C. §§ 101, 121, to the OMB Director under 3 U.S.C.
§ 301 to "determine whether such Guidance will promote economy and efficiency in Federal contracting . . . ." § 2(c).

EO 14042 said it was effective to new contracts, contract-like instruments, new solicitations for contracts or contract-like instruments, extensions or renewals of contracts or contract-like instruments if the extension or renewal occurred on or after October 15, 2021. § 6.

Acting Director of OMB, Shalanda Young, concluded on September 24, 2021, that compliance with the Task Force's *COVID-19 Workplace Safety: Guidance for Federal Contractors and Subcontractors*, which was also issued on September 24, 2021, would "improve economy and efficiency by reducing absenteeism and decreasing labor costs for contractors and subcontractors working

EVIDENCE ATTACHMENT F

on or in connection with a Federal Government contract." 86 Fed. Reg. 53,691–92 (Sept. 28, 2021).

The Task Force's *COVID-19 Workplace Safety: Guidance for Federal Contractors and Subcontractors* (the "Guidance," attached as Exhibit 1) was never published in the Federal Register. Rather, it is available on the Task Force's website at: https://www.saferfederalworkforce.gov/downloads/Draft%20contractor%20guidance%20doc_ 20 210922.pdf. The Guidance defines and delimits the contractor vaccine mandate.

Neither the OMB nor the Task Force published the Guidance in the Federal Register for public comment, waited 60 days before the Guidance became effective, provided a waiver from
an authorized officer indicating that "urgent and compelling circumstances ma[d]e compliance with" notice and comment and the effective period impracticable, see 41 U.S.C. § 1707(d), or indicated that the Guidance and OMB's conclusion were exempt from notice-and-comment, see 5
U.S.C. § 553(b).

EO 14042 did not provide for any waiver of public comment or effectiveness date for the Guidance.

The Guidance, which includes clarifying FAQs, requires federal contractors and subcontractors to mandate "COVID-19 vaccination of covered contractor employees, except in limited circumstances where an employee is legally entitled to an accommodation." Ex. 1, at 1. The Guidance also requires a clause in covered contracts specifying that the contractor or subcontractor must comply with the contractor vaccine mandate. See Ex. 1, at 3 (defining "covered contract").

The Guidance also imposes mandatory mask policies on contractors, requiring contractors to "ensure that all individuals, including covered contractor employees and visitors, comply with published CDC guidance for masking and physical distancing at a covered contractor workplace." Ex. 1, at 6. __

The FAR Council

EO 14042 provided direction to the FAR Council as well.

Congress established the FAR Council in 1988 "to assist in the direction and coordination of [g]overnment-wide procurement policy and [g]overment-wide procurement regulatory activities in the [f]ederal [g]overnment." Office of Federal Procurement Policy Act Amendments of 1988, Pub. L. No. 100-679, § 4, 102 Stat. 4055, *later codified* at 41 U.S.C. § 1302(a).

The FAR Council consists of the Office of Federal Procurement Policy Administrator, the Secretary of Defense, the Administrator of NASA, and the Administrator of GSA. 41 U.S.C. § 1302(b)(1). These officials are authorized to designate another agency official to serve on the FAR Council. *Id.* § 1302(b)(2).

Subject to limited exceptions,[1] the FAR Council has the authority to issue "a single [g]overnment-wide procurement regulation." *Id.* § 1303(a)(1).

No other agency is authorized to issue government-wide procurement regulations. *Id.* § 1303(a)(2).

Section 1707 further protects Congress's reforms to government procurement practices by requiring that any "procurement policy, regulation, procedure, or form"—whether issued government-wide by the FAR Council or for one agency by that agency—be subject to notice and comment. 41 U.S.C. § 1707(a)-(b). The relevant official may waive that requirement only if "urgent and compelling circumstances make compliance with the requirements impracticable." *Id.* § 1707(d).

EO 14042 instructs the FAR Council to "amend the Federal Acquisition Regulation to provide for inclusion in federal procurement solicitations and contracts subject to this order" a clause

---

1. For example, the Office of Federal Procurement Policy Administrator may issue government-wide regulations if the Department of Defense, NASA, and GSA are unable to agree on or fail to issue regulations, 41 U.S.C. § 1121(d), and may remove a regulation if it is inconsistent with the Federal Acquisition Regulation, *Id.* § 1303(a)(5).

stating that the contractor shall, for the duration of the contract, comply with Task Force Guidance. EO 14042 further instructs agencies to seek to implement this clause in contracts not covered by the Federal Acquisition Regulation ("FAR"). 86 Fed. Reg. 50,985–86.

On September 30, 2021, the FAR Council—purporting to comply with the executive order—issued its "[g]uidance" entitled "Issuance of Agency Deviations to Implement Executive Order 14042" ("FAR Council guidance").[2] Ex. 2, at 1-2. In issuing the FAR Council guidance, the FAR Council did not provide notice or opportunity for public comment.

In its guidance, the FAR Council "encourage[s] [agencies] to make . . . deviations" to the FAR, which should be "effective until the FAR is amended" by the FAR Council. *Id.* at 3.

A deviation is a clause that is inconsistent with the FAR. FAR § 1.401. The FAR prescribes procedures for making individual deviations and class deviations. *Id.* §§ 1.403-04. Deviations are not an appropriate method for implementing a government-wide procurement policy, and "[w]hen an agency knows that it will require a class deviation on a permanent basis, it should propose a FAR revision." *Id.* § 1.404.

The FAR Council guidance contains a draft deviation clause that cites EO 14042 as the single authority for the deviation and contains little substantive content other than requiring compliance with the Task Force Guidance, even if that Guidance is amended during performance of the contract. FAR Council guidance at 3-5.

The FAR Council guidance "reminds" agencies that, under EO 14042, they are "required to include an implementing clause" in new contracts awarded on or after November 14, 2021, new solicitations issued on or after October 15, 2021, and options on existing contracts exercised on or after October 15, 2021. *Id.* at 2.

---

2. See Memorandum from FAR Council to Chief Acquisition Officers et al. re: Issuance of Agency Deviations to Implement Executive Order 14042 (Sept. 30 2021),
https://www.whitehouse.gov/wp-content/uploads/2021/09/FAR-Council-Guidance-on-Agency- Issuance-of-Deviations-to-Implement-EO-14042.pdf.

The Contractor Vaccine Mandate's Scope

The U.S. Department of Labor recognizes that "workers employed by federal contractors" comprise "approximately *one-fifth of the entire U.S. labor force*."[3] This includes similarly large proportions of the labor force in each of the Plaintiff States.

The Guidance's definition section highlights the contractor vaccine mandate's broad scope.

A "contractor or subcontractor workplace location" "means a location where covered contract employees work, including a covered contractor workplace or Federal workplace." Ex. 1, at 3. "Covered contractor employee," in turn, "means any full-time or part time employee of a covered contractor working on or in connection with a covered contract or working at a covered contractor workplace. *This includes employees of covered contractors who are not themselves working on or in connection with a covered contract.*" *Id.* at 4 (emphasis added). "Covered contractor workplace" "means a location controlled by a covered contractor at which any employee of a covered contractor working on or in connection with a covered contract is likely to be present during the period of performance for a covered contract. A covered contractor workplace does not include a covered contractor employee's residence." *Id.* at 4 (emphasis added).

On its face, the contractor vaccine mandate therefore applies to employees of a contractor or subcontractor who is a party to a federal contract, even if the work they do is wholly unrelated to the contract, and even if it is not certain they will ever be working in a location with an employee who is actually working on a federal contract.

The FAQs clarify that "in connection with" includes "[e]mployees who perform duties necessary to the performance of the covered contract, but who are not directly engaged in

---

3. DOL, History of Executive Order 11246, Office of Contract Compliance Programs, https://www.dol.gov/agencies/ofccp/about/executive-order-11246-history (last visited Oct. 28, 2021) (emphasis added).

performing the specific work called for by the covered contract, *such as human resources, billing, and legal review.*" Ex. 1, at 13 (emphasis added). Thus, employees who never work directly on a federal contract; who never directly work with an employee working on a federal government contract; or who never work in the same building or location as an employee who works directly on a federal government contract (*e.g.*, completely back-room people), appear to be subject to the contractor vaccine mandate.

The FAQs also show the sweeping breadth of the "locations" to which the Guidance applies. For example, the Guidance applies "to contractor or subcontractor workplace locations that are outdoors." Ex. 1, at 10. The FAQs also say that even if a contractor's employee works in an entirely separate floor or area or even building or site, they are working in a "covered contractor workplace" "unless a covered contractor can *affirmatively* determine that none of its employees" in the separate area "will come into contact with a covered contractor employee." *Id.* (emphasis added); *see also Id.* at 11. "Contact," the FAQs continue, includes "interactions" in "common areas," such as "elevators," "stairwells," and "parking garages." *Id.* at 10, 11. And if an employee is working completely remotely, but working on a covered federal contract, they still "must comply with the vaccination requirement ... even if the employee never works at either a covered contractor workplace or Federal workplace during the performance of the contract." *Id.* at 11.

Thus, the Guidance ensures that almost any employee of an organization with a federal contract is a "covered contractor employee" subject to the contractor vaccine mandate.

The contractor "must ensure that" all covered employees are "fully vaccinated" by "no later than December 8, 2021" or the "first full day of the period of performance on a newly awarded contract" or a renewed or extended contract. Ex. 1, at 5.

The Guidance FAQs also clarify that the contractor vaccine mandate applies to small businesses. Ex. 1, at 12.

The Guidance FAQs also show that the contractor vaccine mandate preempts any contrary State or local laws or ordinances. Ex. 1, at 13.

The Guidance FAQs also establish that covered contractors must comply with "any new Guidance where the OMB Director approves the Guidance and determines that adherence to the Guidance will promote economy and efficiency in Federal contracting." Ex. 1, at 13. To put it another way, the Task Force may change the Guidance, including the contractor vaccine mandate, at any time, and that change will purportedly be binding.

Exceptions to the Contractor Vaccine Mandate

The Guidance does not exempt from the contractor vaccine mandate employees who have had a prior COVID-19 infection. Ex. 1, at 10.

The Guidance does provide an exemption from the contractor vaccine mandate for those with a disability that prevents them from being vaccinated or who seek an exemption "because of a sincerely held religious belief, practice, or observance." Ex. 1, at 5. The federal contractor is responsible for reviewing and considering "what, if any, accommodation it must offer." *Id.*; *see also Id.* at 7.

The Guidance's FAQs further clarify that federal contractors are "responsible for determining if a covered contractor employee must be provided an accommodation because ... of a sincerely held religious belief, practice, or observance." Ex. 1, 9–10. "The contractor is responsible for considering, and dispositioning, such requests for accommodations regardless of the covered contractor employee's place of performance." *Id.* at 10.

The Guidance—in a section requiring masks in covered contractor workplaces—provides that those who are "not fully vaccinated," which would include those who received religious exemptions, are subject to more onerous masking requirements. Ex. 1, at 6. Specifically, they must wear a mask "regardless of the level of community transmission" and outdoors in crowded settings or where there are "activities that involve sustained close contact with other people who are not fully vaccinated." *Id.* at 6–7. They must also socially distance when practicable. *Id.* at 6. Vaccinated people need not do that.

EVIDENCE ATTACHMENT F

Enforcement of the Contractor Vaccine Mandate

Under the Guidance, the employer (the contractor or subcontractor) is responsible for ensuring that a covered contractor employee is fully vaccinated. See Ex. 1, at 5–6. The contractor or subcontractor "must review its covered employees' documentation to prove vaccination status." *Id.* Specifically, they "must require covered contractor employees to show or provide their employer with one" of several documents. *Id.* at 6.

If an employee loses their vaccine documentation, the Guidance FAQs suggests that they reach out to State authorities. See Ex. 1, at 9.

Federal contractors are responsible for ensuring that subcontractors comply with the contractor vaccine mandate. The FAQs clarify that prime contractors are "responsible for ensuring that the required clause"—which mandates compliance with the Guidance—"is incorporated into its first-tier subcontracts," with subcontractors doing the same if there are lower-tier contractors. Ex. 1, at 13–14.

The Guidance "strongly encourage[s]" contractors to "incorporate similar vaccination requirements into their non-covered contracts and agreements with non-covered contractors whose employees perform work at covered contractor workplaces" but are not otherwise involved with a federal contract. Ex. 1, at 6.

THE FEDERAL CONTRACTOR VACCINE MANDATE HARMS PLAINTIFF STATES

The Guidance, which encompasses the federal contractor vaccine mandate, directly injures the Plaintiff States.

Multiple agencies and political subdivisions of the Plaintiff States are contractors with the federal government and are therefore subject to the contractor vaccine mandate, as delineated in the Guidance. This inflicts direct injury on the Plaintiff States' interests in numerous ways, including but not limited to the following examples:

The State of Missouri has state agencies that are federal contractors and will be directly affected by the contractor vaccine mandate.

The contractor vaccine mandate also purportedly preempts Missouri laws and executive orders regarding the issuance of public health orders and the rights and liberties of its citizens.

The State of Nebraska has various state agencies that are federal contractors and will be directly affected by the contractor vaccine mandate.

The Nebraska Department of Health and Human Services is a contractor for the federal Centers for Disease Control and Prevention ("CDC"). That Nebraska agency currently has a contract with CDC to provide Vital Statistics Cooperative Program data and to perform special projects related to that program. The amount of that contract exceeds the simplified acquisition threshold defined in Section 2.101 of the FAR.

The Nebraska Department of Agriculture is a contractor for the federal Department of Health and Human Services. That Nebraska agency currently has an animal food inspection contract with that federal agency. The amount of that contract exceeds the simplified acquisition threshold defined in Section 2.101 of the FAR.

The Nebraska Department of Education is a contractor for the federal Department of Education. That Nebraska agency currently has a National Assessment of Educational Progress contract with that federal agency. The amount of that contract exceeds the simplified acquisition threshold defined in Section 2.101 of the FAR.

The Executive Office of the State of Nebraska is a contractor for the National Oceanic and Atmospheric Administration ("NOAA")—an agency under the federal Department of Commerce. That Nebraska agency currently has a contract for NOAA Weather Radio maintenance services with that federal agency. The amount of that contract exceeds the simplified acquisition threshold defined in Section 2.101 of the FAR.

EVIDENCE ATTACHMENT F

The State of Alaska has several state agencies—including the Department of Health and Human Services, Department of Public Safety, and Department of Corrections, among others—that are federal government contractors and will be directly affected by the contractor vaccine mandate.

The State of Alaska also has several state instrumentalities—including the University of Alaska System and Alaska Railroad—that will be directly affected by the contractor vaccine mandate.

The University of Alaska System operates world-class research facilities, the interruption of which will cause incalculable damage to the State of Alaska and the national scientific community.

The University of Alaska System also operates the DOD-funded Geophysical Detection of Nuclear Proliferation University Affiliated Research Center, which detects, locates, and assesses the threat potential of nuclear activities worldwide through research, development, testing, and evaluation of scientific and technological capabilities. The disruption of this program would jeopardize national security and public safety.

The contractor vaccine mandate attempts to override Alaskans' fundamental right to privacy as enshrined in Article I, Section 22 of the Alaska Constitution. That fundamental right includes the right to make decisions about medical treatment. The Alaska Supreme Court affirmed that right in *Huffman v. State*, 204 P.3d 339 (Alaska 2009), when it held that an individual's freedom to make medical decisions for themselves is a fundamental right protected under Article I, Section 22.

The contractor vaccine mandate also ostensibly preempts an Alaska statute that broadly protects all Alaskans' rights to object to COVID-19 vaccines "based on religious, medical, *or other* grounds," and that forbids any person from "requir[ing] an individual to provide justification or documentation to support the individual's decision to decline a COVID-19 vaccine." 2021 Alaska Sess. Laws ch. 2, § 17 (emphasis added).

The contractor vaccine mandate also ostensibly preempts Arkansas statutes, including Ark. Code 20-7-143, which prohibits public entities from requiring vaccines, and which is currently in effect; and Ark. Code 11-5-118, which governs private employers (including contractors operating in the state) and requires employees be given a testing option, and which has been enacted and will go into effect in January 2022.

The contractor vaccine mandate also ostensibly preempts a recently enacted Montana statute that generally forbids employers in that State "to refuse employment to a person, to bar a person from employment, or to discriminate against a person in compensation or in a term, condition, or privilege of employment based on the person's vaccination status." Mont. Code Ann. § 49-2-312(1)(b).

The State of South Dakota has several State agencies—including the Department of Transportation, Department of Public Safety, and the Department of Corrections, among others—that are federal government contractors and will be directly affected by the contractor vaccine mandate.

The University of Wyoming, which is a State entity, has a number of federal contracts, including cooperative agreements and subcontracts, with various federal agencies that are either up for a renewal or extension or expected to be awarded to the University in the near future. The contractor mandate will directly affect this State entity.

Because the Guidance requires contractors and subcontractors—which include agencies and political subdivisions of Plaintiff States—to enforce the contractor vaccine mandate among their employees and subcontractors, it directly infringes the State's sovereign authority. Agencies and political subdivisions of the Plaintiff States now have a duty to enforce the federal contractor vaccine mandate.

Because the Guidance requires contractors and subcontractors—which include agencies and political subdivisions of Plaintiff States—to enforce the contractor vaccine mandate among their employees and subcontractors, the Plaintiff States will face increased costs related to the enforcement. *See also* Ex. 1, at 8 (requiring contractors to appoint a person to coordinate implementation and compliance with the Guidance).

Because the Guidance requires contractors and subcontractors—which includes agencies and political subdivisions of the Plaintiff States—to enforce the contractor vaccine mandate, it infringes on rights that the Tenth Amendment guarantees the Plaintiff States by commandeering state officers to enforce federal policy.

The breadth of the Guidance means that numerous employees of the Plaintiff States who are not involved in any federal contract will have to be vaccinated. That will not only increase costs to the Plaintiff States, but will also make it harder to retain and attract employees, as current events involving private companies show that vaccine mandates have led to employees quitting or being fired in large numbers rather than getting vaccinated. Furthermore, if States choose to exercise their sovereign prerogative to not require vaccine mandates, they will face loss of federal funds.

Furthermore, the Guidance's religious exemptions purport to preempt state Religious Freedom Restoration Act (State RFRA) laws and free exercise rights protected by state constitutions. Because the Guidance purports to preempt those laws, see Ex. 1, at 13, it injures the Plaintiff States' ability to comply with their own laws, their sovereign right to enact and enforce their laws, and their interest in protecting the free exercise of religion.

The contractor vaccine mandate, as embodied in the Guidance, harms the Plaintiff States beyond the direct harms that flow from the fact that certain agencies and political subdivisions of the Plaintiff States are contractors subject to the mandate, including but not limited to the following:

Because the Guidance claims to preempt all contrary State law, see Ex. 1, at 13, it injures the Plaintiff States' sovereign, quasi-sovereign, and *parens patriae* interests to set their own laws regarding workplace issues that would otherwise apply to contractors within the States' borders, as well as preempting state religious-liberty protections under state RFRAs and state constitutions as noted above.

Because the Guidance claims to preempt all contrary State law, see Ex. 1, at 13, it injures the Plaintiff States' sovereign, quasi-sovereign, and parens patriae interests to set their own laws regarding public health orders. *See, e.g.,* MO. REV. STAT. § 67.265 (restricting the ability of political subdivisions to issue health orders); Exec. Order No. 21- 10 § 3 (Oct. 28, 2021) (Gov. Parson) (prohibiting state agencies from penalizing individuals or businesses for non-compliance with any federal COVID-19 vaccine mandate if the "non-compliance is the result of an individual's sincerely held religious belief or for medical reasons").

Because the Guidance claims to preempt all contrary State law, see Ex. 1, at 13, it injures the Plaintiff States' sovereign, quasi-sovereign, and *parens patriae* interests to set their own laws regarding workforce vaccination policies under their "police power—a power which the state did not surrender when becoming a member of the Union under the Constitution." *Jacobson v. Massachusetts*, 197 U.S. 11, 24–25 (1905).

The Guidance requires employees to prove vaccination status with documentation, and on information and belief, agencies of the Plaintiff States often possess such documentation. See Ex. 1, at 9. A predictable consequence of the contractor vaccine mandate is thus to increase the number of people seeking documentation from the Plaintiff States regarding vaccination status. See *Dep't of Commerce v. New York*, 139 S. Ct. 2551, 2566 (2019). On information and belief, that will increase costs to the Plaintiff States.

On information and belief, a natural and predictable consequence of the vaccine mandate is that numerous employees may be fired, retire, or quit their jobs, including employees of businesses within the Plaintiff States. This injures the Plaintiff States' quasi-sovereign and *parens patriae* interest in the economic well-being of their citizens. It further injures the Plaintiff States in that it will likely increase the burden on the Plaintiff States' unemployment insurance funds, and it will inflict economic disruption on the States' economies as a whole.

On information and belief, a natural and predictable consequence of the federal contractor vaccine mandate is that employers who are critical to the supply chain, and are also federal contractors, will likely lose significant numbers of employees. It is entirely predictable, therefore, that the contractor vaccine mandate will exacerbate current supply chain issues. As a result, prices will continue to rise and cause direct injuries to the Plaintiff States as purchasers. It will also harm their quasi-sovereign parens patriae interest in the economic well-being of their residents, who will suffer from further supply chain disruptions. *See* Spencer Kimball, *Business Croups Ask White House to Delay Biden COVID Vaccine Mandate Until After the Holidays*, CNBC (Oct.25, 2021), https://www.cnbc.com/2021/10/25/businesses-ask-white-house-to-delay-biden-covid- vaccine-mandate-until-after-holidays.html ("Worried that President Joe Biden's Covid vaccine mandate for private companies could cause a mass exodus of employees, business groups are pleading with the White House to delay the rule until after the holiday season.").

The contractor vaccine mandate as embodied in the guidance discriminates between citizens of the Plaintiff States who are vaccinated and those who are not, and denies the latter employment opportunities available to the former. The States have a quasi-sovereign and *parens patriae* interests in protecting their citizens from discriminatory policies. *See Alfred L. Snapp & Son, Inc. v. Puerto Rico, ex rel., Barez,* 458 U.S. 592, 609 (1982) ("This Court has had too much experience with the political, social, and moral damage of discrimination not to recognize that a State has a substantial interest in assuring its residents that it will act to protect them from these evils.").

As sovereign states, the Plaintiff States have quasi-sovereign interests in protecting the rights of their citizens and vindicating them in court. The States may sue to challenge constitutional violations that "affect the [States'] public at large." *In re Debs*, 158 U.S. 561, 584 (1895).

Declaratory relief announcing that the federal contractor vaccine mandate, as embodied in the Guidance, is unlawful, an injunction enjoining enforcement of that mandate, and an order vacating the Guidance will remedy those harms to the Plaintiff States' interests.

CLAIMS FOR RELIEF

COUNT ONE—VIOLATION OF THE PROCUREMENT ACT (40 U.S.C. §§ 101 and 121)

All preceding Paragraphs of this Complaint are hereby incorporated by reference.

The purpose of the Federal Property and Administrative Services Act (Procurement Act) "is to provide the Federal Government with an economical and efficient system for" enumerated procurement activities. 40 U.S.C. § 101. Those activities include "[p]rocuring and supplying property and nonpersonal services," use and disposal of property, and records management. *Id.*
To fulfill that purpose, the "President may prescribe policies and directives that the President considers necessary to carry out" the Procurement Act. 40 U.S.C. § 121(a). "The policies must be consistent with" the Procurement Act. *Id.*

The contractor vaccine mandate is not consistent with the Procurement Act because it is not a necessary policy or directive "to provide the Federal Government with an economical and efficient system for" procurement, including but not limited to for the following reasons.

Far from increasing economy and efficiency in procurement, the contractor vaccine mandate will have deleterious effects on economy and inefficiency by causing the large-scale resignations of unvaccinated employees of federal contractors. These disruptive consequences will directly oppose both "economy" and "efficiency." A current survey from the Kaiser Family Foundation found that 72 percent of unvaccinated workers say that they will quit rather than submit to a vaccine mandate. See Chris Isidore et al., *72% of unvaccinated workers vow to quit if ordered to get vaccinated*, CNN.com (Oct. 28, 2021), at https://www.cnn.com/2021/10/28/business/covid-vaccine-workers- quit/index.html. Such mass resignations would impose drastic hardship on working families throughout the Plaintiff States and would also cause massive economic disruption for federal contractors and for the economy at large. These concerns far outweigh any perceived benefits to economy and efficiency from the contractor mandate. This is the antithesis of "efficiency and economy."

The reach of the contractor vaccine mandate, as evidenced in the Guidance, is too broad to be consistent with the Procurement Act. Even assuming that vaccinated employees do promote efficiency "by reducing absenteeism and decreasing labor costs," as OMB said, 86 Fed. Reg. 53,692, the Guidance applies to employees who work remotely and employees who have the most fleeting interactions with employees working on federal contracts. Such breadth is unnecessary to prevent the spread of COVID-19, and so completely unconnected with any possible rationale relating to economy and efficiency.

The Guidance's application to subcontractors has no direct connection to federal procurement and thus lies outside the Procurement Act.

Because even vaccinated individuals can spread COVID-19, among other reasons, the contractor vaccine mandate, insofar as it seeks to promote economy and efficiency by limiting the spread of the virus, see EO 14042 § 1, is not appropriately tailored to achieve its goals.

The Guidance undermines economy and efficiency, and exceeds the Government's statutory authorization, in other ways as well.

The contractor vaccine mandate is not statutorily authorized by the Procurement Act.

Nowhere in the Procurement Act is there a clear statement from Congress indicating that the Act permits rules like the contractor vaccine mandate, as embodied in the Guidance. But such a rule is necessary where, as here, the federal action involves issues "of deep 'economic and political significance.'" *King v. Burwell*, 576 U.S. 473, 486 (2015) (quoting *Util. Air Regulatory Grp. v. EPA*, 573 U.S. 302, 324 (2014) (quoting *FDA v. Brown & Williamson Tobacco Corp.*, 529 U.S. 120, 160 (2000))). Likewise, a clear statement is required before a statute is interpreted to push the limits of Congress's authority under the Commerce Clause or disrupt the federal-state balance of authority between the federal government and the States—both of which the Guidance purports to do. No such clear statement appears in this statute.

The contractor vaccine mandate's application to subcontractors has no direct connection to federal procurement, and thus does not fall within the purview of the Procurement Act.

For those reasons, the Guidance is inconsistent with the Procurement Act and is inval*Id*.

COUNT TWO—VIOLATION OF PROCUREMENT POLICY ACT (41 U.S.C. § 1707)

All preceding Paragraphs of this Complaint are hereby incorporated by reference.

Under the Office of Federal Procurement Policy Act (OFPPA), procurement policies must be published for public comment in the Federal Register for 60 days before taking effect if the policy "relates to the expenditure of appropriate funds" and either "has a significant effect beyond the internal operating procedures of the agency issuing the policy" or "has a significant cost or administrative impact on contractors." 41 U.S.C. § 1707(a)(1).

The Guidance, including the contractor vaccine mandate contained therein, is a procurement "policy" and also a procurement "procedure" under 41 U.S.C. § 1707(a).

The Guidance, including the contractor vaccine mandate contained therein, relates to the expenditure of appropriated funds; has a significant effect beyond internal operating procedures; and imposes a significant cost and administrative impact on contractors and offerors.

Defendants failed to publish the Guidance in the Federal Register for public comment, as required by 41 U.S.C. § 1707. Nor did Defendants provide the required 60-day comment period before it became effective. *Id.* This includes OMB's short statement that the Guidance promotes economy and efficiency in the procurement process. Neither the Guidance itself, nor that statement, complied with the procedural requirements of § 1707.

No authorized officer ever waived the requirements of the Procurement Policy Act as applied to the Guidance or to the vaccine mandate contained therein.

Defendants failed to comply with the requirements of the Procurement Policy Act when issuing the Guidance, including the contractor vaccine mandate. The Guidance, including its vaccine mandate, is therefore unlawful.

COUNT THREE—UNLAWFUL USURPATION OF STATES' POLICE POWERS

All preceding Paragraphs of this Complaint are hereby incorporated by reference.

The Tenth Amendment provides that: "The powers not delegated to the United States by the Constitution, nor prohibited by it to the States, are reserved to the States respectively, or to the people."

That power includes the "police power" that is "inherent in the states" and is "reserved from the grant of powers to the federal government by the Constitution." *United States v. Constantine*, 296 U.S. 287, 295–96 (1935). The power to impose vaccine mandates—to the extent that it exists at all—can only be part of the police powers reserved to the States.

The federal government does not possess the general power to impose the contractor vaccine mandate. That power, to the extent it exists at all, remains with the Plaintiff States.

COUNT FOUR—VIOLATION OF ANTI-COMMANDEERING DOCTRINE

All preceding Paragraphs of this Complaint are hereby incorporated by reference.

The Tenth Amendment provides that: "The powers not delegated to the United States by the Constitution, nor prohibited by it to the States, are reserved to the States respectively, or to the people."

That amendment, along with basic structural features of the Constitution, deprives Congress of "the power to issue direct orders to the governments of the States." *Murphy v. NCAA*, 138 S. Ct. 1461, 1476 (2018). The Constitution thus does not tolerate the federal government dragooning State officers "into administering federal law." *Printz v. United States*, 521 U.S. 898, 928 (1997)

The contractor vaccine mandate violates the anti-commandeering doctrine by requiring agencies and political subdivisions of the Plaintiff States to enforce the contractor vaccine mandate against their own employees—including, most egregiously, employees that have nothing to do with federal contracts or those who are working remotely—and against their subcontractors.

COUNT FIVE—PROCEDURAL VIOLATION OF THE APA

(OMB Conclusion)

All preceding Paragraphs of this Complaint are hereby incorporated by reference.

OMB is a federal agency subject to the requirements of the Administrative Procedure Act ("APA").

Under the APA, courts may "hold unlawful and set aside agency action . . . found to be . . . without observance of procedure required by law." 5 U.S.C. § 706(2)(D).

Assuming that OMB's conclusion that the Guidance would "promote economy and efficiency in Federal contracting," which caused that Guidance to apply to all agency contracts with federal contractors, is not subject to the Procurement Policy Act, it is an agency rule within the meaning of the APA. See 5 U.S.C. § 551(4).

That conclusion is a major agency action that could not be lawfully conducted without compliance with APA procedures, such as notice-and-comment rulemaking.

OMB did not seek input from stakeholders or the public, and did not provide any public notice and comment period before concluding that the Task Force's Guidance would promote economy and efficiency in federal contracting.

The adoption and promulgation of the Guidance, including the federal contractor vaccine mandate, is a major agency action that could not lawfully be conducted without compliance with APA procedures such as notice-and-comment rulemaking.

OMB's conclusion that the Guidance would promote economy and efficiency, thus promulgating the Guidance as a binding rule on agencies and federal contractors, did not comply with APA procedural requirements and should be held unlawful and set aside.

COUNT SIX—SUBSTANTIVE VIOLATION OF THE APA

(OMB Conclusion)

All preceding Paragraphs of this Complaint are hereby incorporated by reference.

OMB is a federal agency subject to the requirements of the APA.

OMB's adoption and promulgation of the Guidance on the basis that it would promote economy and efficiency in federal contracting was a major agency action that could not lawfully be conducted without compliance with the APA.

Under the APA, a court must "hold unlawful and set aside agency action" that is arbitrary or capricious or otherwise not in accordance with law or contrary to the Constitution. 5 U.S.C. § 706(2)(A).

The APA also prohibits agency action that is "in excess of statutory jurisdiction, authority, limitations, or short of statutory right." 5 U.S.C. § 706(2)(C).

Under the APA, federal administrative agencies are required to engage in "reasoned decision-making." *Allentown Mack Sales & Serv., Inc. v. NLRB*, 522 U.S. 359, 379 (1998) (cleaned up). In other words, "agency action is lawful only if it rests on a consideration of the relevant factors" and "important aspects of the problem."

Michigan v. EPA, 576 U.S. 743, 750- 52 (2015) (cleaned up). Failing to consider important costs of a new policy or the efficacy of a policy, for example, renders the policy arbitrary and capricious. In adopting the Guidance and determining that it would promote economy and judicial efficiency in federal contracting, OMB did not engage in reasoned decisionmaking.

First, on information and belief, OMB failed conduct its own independent analysis but relied heavily on the Guidance. The Guidance does not display reasoned decisionmaking, but instead ignored important aspects of the problem, including but not limited to economic impacts, cost to States, cost to citizens, labor-force and supply-chain disruptions, the current risks of COVID-19, and basic distinctions among workers such as those with natural immunity to COVID- 19 and those who work remotely or with limited in-person contacts, among other important aspects of the problem.

Second, there is no evidence to conclude that OMB engaged in "decisionmaking" at all—whether reasoned or not. OMB's conclusion that Guidance would "promote economy and efficiency in Federal contracting" contained no explanation at all, so it did not "rest[ ] on a consideration of the relevant factors." Michigan v. EPA, 576 U.S. 743, 750 (2015). For instance, OMB's reasoning ignores costs to the States, State agencies, citizens, and the economy, which is a "centrally relevant factor when deciding whether to regulate," *Id.* at 752-53, especially when directed to determine whether the regulations would "promote economy and efficiency."

There is also additional evidence that OMB failed to engage in reasoned decisionmaking. Among other reasons:

OMB also did not consider the effect of large-scale resignations of unvaccinated employees of federal contractors, especially in an economy already experiencing high levels of inflation, labor shortages, and a supply-chain crisis.

OMB did not consider the effect this would have on States, which incur costs associated with enforcing the vaccine mandate within their agencies and political subdivisions that are federal contractors.

OMB did not provide an exemption to persons with natural immunity to COVID-19, even though natural immunity exists and is at least as effective as vaccination in preventing re-infection, transmission, and severe health outcomes.

OMB did not provide an exemption for contractors who work in their own homes or who are otherwise isolated from others while working.

OMB failed to consider whether the Guidance's religious exemption was consistent with State RFRAs or the Federal RFRA. Instead, OMB unlawfully delegated authority to private entities, i.e., federal contractors, to dictate the scope of their own employees' religious exemptions, instead of protecting employees' religious freedom as required by federal law.

On information and belief, the Guidance and OMB's approval of it failed to consider the fact that contractor vaccine mandate will have a disparate impact on minority and economically disadvantaged communities that have relatively low rates of vaccination, and will inflict disproportionately greater unemployment, job losses, and economic injury on those disadvantaged communities.

OMB failed to consider the fact that its actions were contrary to law, as they were not authorized by the Procurement Act, the Procurement Policy Act, federal RFRA, or any other federal statute, and were also unconstitutional, as the Guidance violates the Tenth Amendment and was premised on an unconstitutional Executive Order.

Ultimately, OMB's decision that the Guidance would improve efficiency by reducing absenteeism and decreasing labor costs is facially pretextual. The OMB rule, in reality, is a blatant attempt to federalize public health. See Ex. 2, at 3 (encouraging agencies "to apply [the Guidance] broadly" "[t]o maximize the goal of getting more people vaccinated and decrease the spread of COVID-19").

Thus, OMB's promulgation of the Guidance, including the contractor vaccine mandate and masking rules, via its conclusion that it will promote economy and efficiency, is arbitrary, capricious, and unlawful under the APA and should be set aside.

COUNT SEVEN—SUBSTANTIVE VIOLATION OF THE APA AGENCY ACTION NOT IN ACCORDANCE WITH LAW AND IN EXCESS OF AUTHORITY

(OMB Conclusion)

All preceding Paragraphs of this Complaint are hereby incorporated by reference.

Under the APA, a court must "hold unlawful and set aside agency action" that is "not in accordance with law" or "in excess of statutory . . . authority, or limitations, or short of statutory right." See 5 U.S.C. § 706(2)(A), (C).

The OMB rule adopting the Task Force guidance is contrary to law for at least four reasons.

First, the OMB rule violates 41 U.S.C. § 1303(a) because it is a government-wide procurement regulation, which only the FAR Council may issue.

EO 14042 apparently seeks to circumvent § 1303 by delegating the President's Procurement Act power to the OMB Director.

That attempt is unlawful because the President has no authority to issue regulations under § 1303—only the FAR Council may issue government-wide procurement regulations. See *Centralizing Border Control Policy Under the Supervision of the Attorney General*, 26 Op. OLC 22, 23 (2002) ("Congress may prescribe that a particular executive function may be performed only by a designated official within the Executive Branch, and not by the President.")

Second, and relatedly, the OMB rule is contrary to law because the Procurement Act does not otherwise grant the President the power to issue orders with the force or effect of law. Congress authorized the President to "prescribe policies and directives that the President considers necessary to carry out" the Procurement Act. 40 U.S.C. § 121(a). "[P]olicies and directives" describe the President's power to direct the exercise of procurement authority throughout the government. It does not authorize the President to issue regulations himself.

Congress knows how to confer the power to "prescribe regulations," as it expressly authorized the GSA Administrator to do so

in the same section. *Id.* § 121(c); *see also Sosa v. Alvarez-Machain*, 542 U.S. 692, 711 n.9 (2004) ("[W]hen the legislature uses certain language in one part of the statute and different language in another, the court assumes different meanings were intended."). And Congress has given the President the power to "prescribe regulations" in other contexts, typically in the realm of foreign affairs and national defense. See, e.g., 18 U.S.C. § 3496 ("The President is authorized to prescribe regulations governing the manner of executing and returning commissions by consular officers. . . ."); 32 U.S.C. § 110 ("The President shall prescribe
regulations, and issue orders, necessary to organize, discipline, and govern the National Guard.").

Third, even if the Procurement Act authorized the President to issue orders with the force or effect of law, it would not authorize approval of the Task Force guidance. The President appears to assume that the Procurement Act authorizes him to issue any order that he believes, as the Procurement Act's statement of purpose states, promotes "an economical and efficient" procurement system. 40 U.S.C. § 101; see 86 Fed. Reg. at 50,985 ("This order promotes economy and efficiency in [f]ederal procurement."). But that mistakes a prefatory purpose statement for a grant of authority. *D.C. v. Heller*, 554 U.S. 570, 578 (2008) ("[A]part from [a] clarifying function, a prefatory clause does not limit or expand the scope of the operative clause.").

And even if the Procurement Act did authorize the President to issue binding procurement orders solely because they may promote economy and efficiency, the OMB rule does not adequately do so. Providing the federal government with an "economic and efficient system for" procurement is not a broad enough delegation to impose nationwide social policy that Congress has not separately authorized. Further, EO 14042 is divorced from the practical needs of procurement. It will exclude otherwise competitive bidders, cause contractors to suffer labor shortages, and is substantially overbroad in, for example, refusing to account for natural immunity and the low transmission risk for COVID-19 outdoors.

Fourth, the OMB rule is inconsistent with the requirements of the Competition in Contracting Act, which requires federal agencies to provide for "full and open competition through the use of competitive procedures." 41 U.S.C. § 3301; see 40 U.S.C. § 121(a) (requiring "policies" issued by the President pursuant to the Procurement Act to be "consistent with this subtitle"); *Id.* at § 111 (defining "this subtitle" in 40 U.S.C. § 121(a) as to also refer to division C (except

§§ 3302, 3501(b), 3509, 3906, 4710, and 4711) of subtitle I of title 41).

Because the OMB rule violates § 1303(a), seeks to exercise a delegated power the President does not possess, relies on a misreading of FPASA, and violates § 3301, it is contrary to law.

COUNT EIGHT—APA VIOLATIONS

AGENCY ACTION THAT IS NOT IN ACCORDANCE WITH LAW AND IS IN EXCESS OF AUTHORITY

(FAR Guidance)

All preceding Paragraphs of this Complaint are hereby incorporated by reference.

The Guidance issued by the FAR Council, while stylized as "guidance," is in reality binding on regulated parties and so reviewable. *See Iowa League of Cities v. EPA*, 711 F.3d 844, 862–63 (8th Cir. 2013).

The Guidance does not explain what authority enables the FAR Council to create a government-wide procurement regulation mandating vaccines for contractors. For the reasons set forth above, the Procurement Act does not provide that authority.

The Guidance issued by the FAR Council is unlawful and in excess of statutory authority for all the reasons stated above with respect to the actions of OMB.

EVIDENCE ATTACHMENT F

COUNT NINE—APA AND STATUTORY VIOLATIONS

ARBITRARY AND CAPRICIOUS AGENCY ACTION AND VIOLATION OF NOTICE- AND-COMMENT REQUIREMENTS

(FAR Guidance)

All preceding Paragraphs of this Complaint are hereby incorporated by reference.

Under the APA, a court must "hold unlawful and set aside agency action" that is arbitrary or capricious or otherwise not in accordance with law or contrary to the Constitution. 5 U.S.C. § 706(2)(A).

The APA also prohibits agency action that is "in excess of statutory jurisdiction, authority, limitations, or short of statutory right." 5 U.S.C. § 706(2)(C).

The APA also prohibits agency action that was conducted "without observance of procedure required by law," 5 U.S.C. § 706(2)(D), and it requires procedures such as notice-and- comment rulemaking, see 5 U.S.C. § 553.

41 U.S.C. § 1707 likewise requires the FAR Council to engage in notice-and- comment rulemaking in this context.

The FAR guidance is arbitrary and capricious for the same reasons that OMB's adoption of the Task Force guidance was, as described more fully in the counts above.

The FAR guidance violates the APA because it was issued without engaging in procedures required by law, including notice-and-comment rulemaking procedures, as described more fully in the allegations above.

COUNT TEN—SEPARATION OF POWERS

All preceding Paragraphs of this Complaint are hereby incorporated by reference.

RELIGIOUS EXEMPTIONS FROM FEDERAL VACCINE MANDATES

Our Constitution creates a federal government of limited and enumerated powers, and this limitation applies to the Executive Branch.

Any action of the Executive Branch must come from one of two sources of authority: (1) a valid delegation of authority by statute enacted by Congress, or (2) a direct exercise of one of the President's enumerated powers in Article II. "The President's power, if any, to issue [an] order must stem either from an act of Congress or from the Constitution itself." *Youngstown Sheet & Tube Co. v. Sawyer*, 343 U.S. 579, 585 (1952).

Where "[t]here is no statute that expressly authorizes the President to take" an action and no "act of Congress ... from which such a power can fairly be implied," the action is not authorized by an act of Congress. *Id.*

In the absence of such an express or implied authorization by act of Congress, "if the President had authority to issue the order he did, it must be found in some provisions of the Constitution." *Id.* at 587.

Article II confers no authority on the President to exercise any legislative function without a delegation of authority by statute enacted by Congress.

EO 14042 purports to bind federal agencies to require in all contracts a clause incorporating the Guidance, including the contractor vaccine mandate and mask requirements, based on OMB's conclusion that the Guidance would "promote economy and efficiency." See EO 14042 § 2(a). That includes parts of the Guidance applying to employees with little to no nexus to federal contracting programs.

By purporting to bind agencies and contractors to the Guidance—including the contractor vaccine mandate and masking requirements—after a finding of economy and efficiency by OMB, EO 14042 unconstitutionally and unlawfully seeks to exercise a quintessentially legislative power that the Constitution vests exclusively in Congress under Article I, Section 1.

To put it another way, the delegation that EO 14042 purported to give to OMB is the type of delegation that is inherently legislative, and so that delegation needed to go through bicameralism and presentment.

Congress did not delegate the authority to dictate vaccine and mask mandates on federal contractors—which would include agencies and political subdivisions of States—to the President or OMB. Indeed, consistent with the non-delegation doctrine, Congress likely could not have validly delegated such sweeping and indeterminate authority, with enormous potential impact on the U.S. economy, to a single federal agency—and certainly could not have done so without an extremely clear statement of congressional intent. No such statement—and no such statute—exists here.

Accordingly, EO 14042 violates the Constitution's separation of powers.

COUNT ELEVEN—VIOLATION OF TENTH AMENDMENT AND FEDERALISM

All preceding Paragraphs of this Complaint are hereby incorporated by reference.

The structure of the U.S. Constitution and the text of the Tenth Amendment protects federalism.

The powers not delegated by the Constitution to the United States or prohibited by it to the States are reserved to the States.

Defendants, through their vaccine mandate, have exercised power far beyond what was delegated to the federal government by constitutional mandate or congressional action.

Neither Article II of the U.S. Constitution nor any act of Congress authorizes Defendants to implement their vaccine mandate.

The power to impose vaccine mandates, to the extent that any such power exists, is a power reserved to the States.

By interfering with the traditional balance of power between the States and the federal government, and by acting pursuant to ultra vires federal action, Defendants violated the Tenth Amendment and structural principles of federalism.

Defendants' mandate was thus adopted pursuant to an unconstitutional exercise of authority and must be invalidated.

COUNT TWELVE—UNCONSTITUTIONAL EXERCISE OF THE SPENDING POWER

All preceding Paragraphs of this Complaint are hereby incorporated by reference.

The contractor vaccine mandate is an unconstitutional condition on the Plaintiff States' receipt (by and through their agencies and political subdivisions who are federal contractors) of federal funds.

"[I]f Congress intends to impose a condition on the grant of federal moneys, it must do so unambiguously," so "States [can] exercise their choice knowingly," *Pennhurst State Sch. & Hosp. v. Halderman*, 451 U.S. 1, 17 (1981).

Federal contracts are an exercise of the Spending Clause, yet the challenged actions ask the Plaintiff States to agree to an ambiguous contract term—specifically, agreeing to comply with Guidance that can be changed at any time.

Nor does the Procurement Act provide the requisite notice to States who are federal contractors or have agencies and political subdivisions that are federal contractors, like the Plaintiff States, that the contractor vaccine mandate would be a condition of their contract.

"[C]onditions on federal funds must be related to the federal interest in particular national projects or programs." *Van Wyhe v. Reisch*, 581 F.3d 639, 650 (8th Cir. 2009).

Because the contractor vaccine mandate is not necessary, nor necessarily effective, at preventing the spread of COVID-19, and, on information and belief, will lead to employees either being fired or resigning, it is not rationally related to any federal interest in a particular project or program that is the subject of a federal contract.

Because the contractor vaccine mandate, as embodied in the Guidance, covers employees who have no connection to the federal contract beyond just being coworkers with an employee who works on such a contract and being likely to come into contact with them, the mandate is not rationally related to any federal interest in a particular project or program that is the subject of a federal contract.

"[C]onditions must not be prohibited by other constitutional provisions." Van Wyhe, 581 F.3d at 650.

As described above, the contractor vaccine mandate is prohibited by the Tenth Amendment and Free Exercise Clause.

PRAYER FOR RELIEF

Wherefore, the Plaintiff States ask this Court to issue an order and judgment:

Declaring unconstitutional, pursuant to 28 U.S.C. § 2201, the Guidance, including the contractor vaccine mandate;

Declaring unconstitutional, pursuant to 28 U.S.C. § 2201, EO 14042 as violating the separation of powers;

Declaring unconstitutional and unlawful, pursuant to 28 U.S.C. § 2201, the FAR Council guidance;

Declaring, pursuant to 28 U.S.C. § 2201, that OMB's conclusion that the Guidance promotes economy and efficiency is unlawful under the Federal Procurement Act and the Procurement Policy Act;

Declaring, pursuant to 28 U.S.C. § 2201, that OMB's conclusion that the Guidance promotes economy and efficiency is unlawful and arbitrary and capricious under the APA;

Declaring, pursuant to 28 U.S.C. § 2201, that the Task Force Guidance, including the contractor vaccine mandate, is unlawful under the Federal Procurement Act and the Procurement Policy Act;

Declaring, pursuant to 28 U.S.C. § 2201, that the Task Force Guidance, including the contractor vaccine mandate, is unlawful and arbitrary and capricious under the APA;

Declaring, pursuant to 28 U.S.C. § 2201, that the Task Force Guidance, including the contractor vaccine mandate, is not a constitutional exercise of Congress's spending power;

Declaring, pursuant to 28 U.S.C. § 2201, that the FAR Council guidance, including the contractor vaccine mandate, is unlawful under the APA;

Declaring, pursuant to 28 U.S.C. § 2201, that the FAR Council guidance, including the contractor vaccine mandate, is arbitrary and capricious under the APA;

Enjoining Defendants from imposing the Guidance, including the vaccine mandate and masking requirements, on federal contractors;

Enjoining Defendants from imposing the FAR Council guidance, including the vaccine mandate and masking requirements, on federal contractors;

Enjoining Defendants from issuing any COVID-19 requirements on federal contractors without first following the required notice-and-comment procedures of the Procurement Policy Act and APA;

Set aside OMB's conclusion that the Task Force Guidance promotes economy and efficiency;

Set aside the FAR Council's guidance; and

Grant any and all other relief the Court deems just and proper.

Dated: October 29, 2021

EVIDENCE ATTACHMENT G

Navy Ruling

UNITED STATES DISTRICT COURT
MIDDLE DISTRICT OF FLORIDA
TAMPA DIVISION

NAVY SEAL 1, et al.,
Plaintiffs,
CASE NO. 8:21-cv-2429-SDM-TGW
LLOYD AUSTIN, et al.,
Defendants.

ORDER

The defendants move (Doc. 118) on an emergency basis (1) for a stay pending appeal from a February 18, 2022 preliminary injunction (Doc. 111) and (2) for an "immediate administrative stay" pending resolution of the motion (Doc. 118) to stay. The preliminary injunction order enjoins the defendants:

(1) from enforcing against Navy Commander and Lieutenant Colonel 2 any order or regulation requiring COVID-19 vaccination and

(2) from any adverse or retaliatory action against Navy Commander or Lieutenant Colonel 2 as a result of, arising from, or in conjunction with Navy Commander's or Lieutenant Colonel 2's

requesting a religious exemption, appealing the denial of a request for a religious exemption, requesting reconsideration of the denial of a religious exemption, or pursuing this action or any other action for relief under RFRA or the First Amendment. (Doc. 111 at 47–48)

The defendants contend that, among other things, the preliminary injunction "allows two officers who have refused a lawful order to continue to serve in assignments over the Navy's objection." (Doc. 118 at 15) The defendants report that "the Navy has lost confidence in [Navy Commander's] ability to lead" because Navy Commander "disobeyed an order that he is also expected to enforce" and because Navy Commander "further compromised his trustworthiness" by allegedly "misleading his commander regarding taking leave out of the area," by allegedly making misleading statements about communications with his Executive Officer," and by allegedly "expos[ing] dozens of his crew to COVID-19 when he decided not to test himself after experiencing symptoms." (Doc. 118 at 15–16)

In other words, the defendants contend that the sudden eagerness to remove Navy Commander from command of a destroyer results from "other neutral fac- tors," *U.S. Navy Seals 1-26 v. Biden*, No. 22-10077, 2022 WL 594375 at *12 (5th Cir. Feb. 28, 2022), and not from a retaliatory animus toward Navy Commander's legally protected pursuit of the relief that Congress through RFRA secures in federal court for every service member. Presented at the preliminary injunction hearing with declarations endeavoring to establish Navy Commander's untrustworthiness (and consequently his unsuitability for command), the preliminary injunction order (Doc. 111) states:

> Because I heard the testimony of Navy Commander and carefully observed his demeanor and listened attentively to the content of his testimony, I fully credit his testimony, even the parts inconsistent with the un-cross-examined, last-minute affidavits. A determination of the credibility of the statements in the [defendants'] affidavits must await live testimony and further exploration

(these two witnesses are at the disposal of, and under the command of, the defendants, who neither offered their live testimony nor notified the plaintiffs of the fact of, or the content of, their affidavits). Cross-examination is necessary in this circumstance to permit assessment of, among other things, the extent to which "command influence" might have affected the presence or content of the affidavits.

(Doc. 111 at 12 n.3) Accordingly, the defendants' proffered basis to stay the injunction to permit the re-assignment of Navy Commander and Lieutenant Colonel 2 (despite the likely unlawful denial of their religious exemptions) warrants a prompt evidentiary hearing.[1]

A Necessary Preface About RFRA

In Article I, Section 8, the Constitution empowers (but does not compel) the Congress to "raise and support" the armed forces of the United States and "to make rules for the government and regulation of the . . . forces." These constitutional clauses were informed preeminently by the unfortunate English experience, fresh in the minds of the Constitution's authors, with James II and his royal army, which was raised without the consent of Parliament, which led to the Glorious Revolution of 1688, and which ended with the Bill of Rights of 1689, which stated that "raising or keeping a standing army within the kingdom in time of peace, unless it be with the consent of Parliament, is against the law."

Fortunately, Congress raised and has maintained the armed forces (at some times more generously than at others) throughout the ensuing years, and these forces have preserved and defended the Constitution of the United States by defeating aggression and tyranny whenever and wherever necessary; under whatever

---

1. The defendants contend that Lieutenant Colonel 2, among other things, allegedly cannot reliably enforce the vaccination order against subordinates, convene administrative separation proceedings for service members refusing COVID-19 vaccination, or deploy worldwide in foreign countries requiring that foreign service members accept COVID-19 vaccination. (Doc. 118 at 17)

circumstance, no matter how brutal and merciless; and at whatever cost proved necessary (for one historic example, read the riveting and unforgettable *With the Old Breed* by E. B. Sledge).

A signal feature of the Constitution that the armed forces have vigilantly preserved and defended is the Free Exercise Clause of the First Amendment. One of the "rules for the government and regulation of the . . . forces" that the Congress has enacted and that the President (who is, of course, also the Commander-in-Chief of the armed forces) has signed into law is the Religious Freedom Restoration Act of 1993, Public Law 103-141, which creates for the free exercise of religion a renewed protection against impingement by the government, including the armed forces. RFRA was a bipartisan enactment (although in 1993 the President, the Speaker of the House, and the Majority Leader in the Senate were Democrats). Specifically, two months after then-Representative Chuck Schumer (and more than one hundred other representatives, both Republicans and Democrats) introduced RFRA, H.R. 1308, 103d Cong. (1993), the House of Representatives passed the bill by a two-thirds voice vote. 139 Cong. Rec. 9,687 (1993). The Senate amended the bill and passed the amended version by a vote of 97 yeas to 3 nays. 139 Cong. Rec. 26,416. After unanimously consenting to the Senate's amendment, 139 Cong. Rec. 27,241, the House presented RFRA to President Clinton on November 5, 1993. 139 Cong. Rec. 32,215. President Clinton promptly signed RFRA.

The statutorily stated purpose of RFRA is "to restore the compelling interest test . . . in all cases where free exercise of religion is substantially burdened and to provide a claim or defense to persons whose religious exercise is substantially burdened by government." To enable those, including service members, whose free exercise rights are improperly restricted to pursue RFRA's statutory remedy, RFRA amends 42 U.S.C. § 1988, the Civil Rights Attorney's Fees Awards Act of 1976, Pub- lic Law 94–559, to allow in a RFRA action an award to the prevailing party, other than the United States, of a reasonable attorney's fee and costs, including expert witness fees.

RFRA includes specific and unequivocal commands to the government, defined to include every "branch, department, agency, instrumentality, and official (or other person acting under color of law) of the United States." Obviously, RFRA includes everyone from the President to a park ranger, from the Chief Justice of the United States to a probation officer, from the Speaker of the House to a member's district office staffer, from the Chairman of the Joint Chiefs of Staff to a military recruiter—even if they don't like it and even if they don't agree with it. The Free Exercise Clause and RFRA are the law of the land.

Among RFRA's express and explicit findings are that the government "should not substantially burden religious exercise without a compelling justification" and that the "compelling interest test" that RFRA restores is a "workable test" that demands "striking a sensible balance between religious liberty and competing prior governmental interests." With the notions of a "workable test" and a "sensible balance" featured conspicuously, the statute proscribes any substantial burden on Free Exercise unless the government "demonstrates" (a statutorily defined term) that the substantial burden (1) "is in furtherance of a compelling governmental interest" and (2) "is the least restrictive means of furthering that compelling governmental interest." Explaining that the government must meet a "burden of proof," RFRA defines "demonstrates" as "meets the burdens of going forward with the evidence and of persuasion." That burden is the same for preliminary or permanent injunctive relief.

The unanimous decision in *Gonzalez v. O Centro Espirita Beneficente Uniao Do Vegetal*, 126 S. Ct. 1211 (2006), authored by the Chief Justice, exemplifies the proper method for applying RFRA. In O Centro, a Christian "religious sect" used a "sacramental tea," *hoasca*, containing dimethyltryptamine, a Schedule 1 controlled substance under the Controlled Substances Act, 21 U.S.C. §§ 801–971, which imposes on the hallucinogen in *hoasca* "an outright ban on all importation and use, except pursuant to strictly regulated research projects." The religious sect sued in the district court under RFRA for preliminary and permanent injunctive relief against both the government's seizure of shipments of hoasca and the government's threatened prosecution for continued use of hoasca. In sum, a statute containing a prohibition against the acquisition and use of a dangerous controlled substance and providing for the necessary enforcement mechanism, including prosecution—a statute fundamental to the well-being and security of the United States—conflicted directly with the sacramental observations, using hoasca, of the sectarian plaintiffs, who relied on RFRA to resolve the conflict.

After finding the evidence introduced at the preliminary injunction hearing to stand "in equipoise," the district court determined that the government failed to satisfy RFRA's statutory burden of "demonstrating" that seizure and prosecution were the "least restrictive means" to preserve the compelling governmental interests expressed in the Controlled Substances Act and issued a preliminary injunction against the government. The Tenth Circuit affirmed, and the Supreme Court granted certiorari.

After confirming that the lower courts properly assigned the burden of proof to the government in accord with RFRA, the Chief Justice explained a fundamental flaw in the government's approach:

> RFRA, and the strict scrutiny test it adopted, contemplate an inquiry more focused than the Government's categorical approach. RFRA requires the Government to demonstrate that the compelling interest test is satisfied through application of the challenged law "to the person"—the particular claimant whose sincere exercise of religion is being substantially burdened.

126 S. Ct. at 1220. Similarly, responding to the government's argument that granting an exception to the Controlled Substances Act was not within the proper domain of the judiciary, the Chief Justice responded authoritatively:

> RFRA, however, plainly contemplates that courts would recognize exceptions—that is how the law works. See 42 U.S.C. § 2000bb-1(c) ("A person whose religious exercise has been burdened in violation of this section may assert

EVIDENCE ATTACHMENT G

that violation as a claim or defense in a judicial proceeding and obtain appropriate relief against a government.") RFRA makes clear that it is the obligation of the courts to consider whether exceptions are required under the test set forth by Congress.

126 S. Ct. at 1222. (Supreme Court's emphasis). The message from *O Centro* and later decisions is unmistakable.

Despite the unmistakable message of the Free Exercise Clause, RFRA, and *O Centro*, the defendants argue as if none of the three exists (or, at least, as if none of the three affects the command discretion of the armed forces). The defendants begin their present motion by declaring, "The Supreme Court has made clear: 'Judges are not given the task of running the Army,'" a quote from *Orloff v. Willoughby*, 345 U.S. 83, 93 (1953), a dispute resolved forty years before enactment of RFRA. Although certainly not "given the task of running the Army," the courts in the narrow instance of RFRA are given the task of ensuring that those who are given the task of running the Army (and the armed forces in general and every other component of the federal government) conform their actions to the governing law, to RFRA, to which the admirals and the generals and commandants are unquestionably subordinate—just like the President, the Speaker of the House, the Chief Justice, and every other person in the federal government. This order and this action will proceed accordingly.

Discussion

The defendants move (Doc. 118) for a stay pending appeal and for an "immediate administrative stay." The defendants announce menacingly in the opening sentences of the motion, filed at 6:27 p.m. EST on February 28, 2022, that "by the end of the day March 2, 2022 . . . if relief has not been granted, Defendants will seek relief from the U.S. Court of Appeals for the Eleventh Circuit." The opening sentences of the motion, along with much of the remainder of the motion, attempt to evoke the frightening prospect of a dire national emergency resulting from allegedly reckless and unlawful overreaching by the district judge, an exigency sufficient to warrant depriving the plaintiffs of a fair opportunity to respond to the motion, depriving the district court of a fair opportunity to consider and resolve the motion, and finally and effectively depriving the two immediately affected service-member plaintiffs of a right explicitly secured by RFRA.

A review of the defendants' motion reveals that the defendants persistently and resolutely cling to the belief that their accustomed and unfettered command discretion need not yield—on the narrow and specific question of the free exercise of religion—to the statutory command of RFRA or to an order under RFRA from a district court (actually, at this moment, orders from several district courts and a circuit court of appeals), the forum selected by Congress and enacted in RFRA to resolve a dispute under RFRA (in other words, Congress and the President, not the district court, chose the district court as the proper forum for service members to assert the RFRA claim asserted in this action).

In the motion, filed in response to the preliminary injunction granted to one Navy officer and one Marine officer, the defendants first feature a series of alarums, including the specter of "a direct and imminent threat to the national security" and "an indefinitely sideline[d]" Navy warship," which putatively create a circumstance of "utmost urgency," the severity of which compels the defendants to demand an immediate ruling from the district court, failing which the defendants promise an emergency motion in the court of appeals. In contrast, this order prescribes an accelerated but reasonable time for the plaintiffs to respond and schedules a hearing at which the parties can offer evidence, including live testimony, and both legal and factual argument on the merits of the defendants' motion. Also, because the defendants, if dissatisfied with the stated schedule, promise to move in the court of appeals, this order responds in general terms (all that time permits) to the defendants' characterization of the preliminary relief granted to Navy Commander and Lieutenant Colonel 2.

The first heading of the defendants' motion suggests that the preliminary in- junction "exceeds the court's authority"; mentions

EVIDENCE ATTACHMENT G

that the executive branch and the legislative branch, not the court, properly direct "the composition, training, equipping, and control" of the armed forces; insists that "who is placed in command" is "beyond the judiciary's competence"; and recalls that "challenges to military assignment decisions" are "routinely" found non-justiciable. Although those claims are largely correct, none takes cognizance of RFRA; none mentions the narrow and specific instruction in RFRA to the district court to provide an "appropriate remedy" for violation of RFRA by any component of the federal government, including the military. The defendants argue as if RFRA does not exist or has no application to the military or is a matter subject to the command discretion of the military. Stated plainly: Yes, the Congress and the President, not the courts, govern the military. But the Congress and the President in governing the military and by enacting RFRA have established—for the narrow category of free exercise of religion—an action and a remedy in the district court, have specified and placed the burden of proof on the military, and have allowed for an "appropriate remedy" to ensure a service member's right to free exercise. That is not a fairly contestable proposition, and the military must acquiesce to the command of the Congress and the President in that respect.

Further the preliminary injunction includes no instructions to the military about composing, training, equipping, or otherwise controlling the military or about assigning, promoting, or demoting anyone. On the contrary and in accord with RFRA, the preliminary injunction—as an "appropriate remedy" pending a final order—merely preserves the status quo, that is, preserves for Navy Commander and Lieutenant Colonel 2 the assignments granted by the military, not by the court. The preliminary injunction preserves the state of affairs established by the military before Navy Commander and Lieutenant Colonel 2 sought under RFRA a religious exemption from vaccination. As an interim "appropriate remedy," the preliminary injunction prevents an adverse action by the military against Navy Commander and Lieutenant Colonel 2 based on their resort to the court in an effort to acquit their statutory rights under RFRA.

If the military has a non-retaliatory reason for some adverse action against Navy Commander and Lieutenant Colonel 2, the military can move for a modification of the injunction, which is always an option for a party subject to a preliminary, or even a permanent, injunction. In this instance, Navy Commander and Lieutenant Colonel 2 testified most credibly in person at the hearing. Before the hearing, the Navy submitted affidavits that claim the Navy has "lost confidence" in Navy Commander. This peculiarly subjective determination of "lost confidence," arriving suddenly after seventeen stellar years of service by Navy Commander and after, to say the least, tense exchanges with his superior officer about vaccination and about his RFRA claim does not warrant immediate deference but, rather, demands a closer examination, which is readily and reasonably promptly available. Surely the free exercise rights restored by RFRA are not subject to evisceration or circumnavigation by a notion as subjective and illusory —and, according to the defendants, unreviewable by the judiciary—as a sudden "loss of confidence" by a superior officer who sends a declaration to the court. The same reasoning applies to Lieutenant Colonel 2 and any non-retaliatory basis the military might have with respect to her assignments.

The defendants conclude the first heading with the startling accusation that the preliminary injunction "is broad enough to prevent the military from imposing discipline or convening a court martial with respect to either plaintiff, even for potential violations of the Uniform Code of Military Justice." This novel formulation is wholly unwarranted, except that admittedly the preliminary injunction likely prohibits, because RFRA prohibits, the military's disciplining or court martialing either plaintiff in retaliation for their requesting a religious exemption under RFRA.

This odd inclusion in the defendants' argument of the prospect of a court martial for the plaintiffs perhaps originates in the defendants' frequently repeated idea that the plaintiffs are subject to discipline and separation because they have "disobeyed a lawful order" to accept vaccination. Admittedly, the order to accept vaccination is lawful. But, owing to RFRA, the order to accept

EVIDENCE ATTACHMENT G

vaccination is a lawful order with respect to which the plaintiffs, based on the present record, are likely entitled to an exemption. In other words, what we have here is a failure to communicate. The military sees the plaintiffs' request for a lawful exemption from a law- ful order as a refusal to obey a lawful order and as a basis for discipline. But, although the matter remains momentarily unresolved, the plaintiffs might enjoy—likely enjoy—a lawful exemption from compliance with a lawful order. Thus far, the defendants seem to comprehend, or at least to acknowledge, only half—the "lawful order" half—of the governing legal reality and seem studiously and purposefully to ignore the other half, the religious exemption half, ensured by RFRA.

The second portion of the defendants' motion advances the "judicial overstep- ping" claim. In particular, the second portion claims that two footnotes in the pre- liminary injunction (Doc. 111 at 37, n.10 and at 43, n. 11) somehow "discount[] the effect of refusers on good order and discipline in the military" and "by second-guessing the scientific and military evidence that vaccination is the most effective means to protect the health and safety of the force." (The term "refusers" is a tellingly offen- sive term that the defendants must employ no further in this court. A RFRA claimant is not a "refuser," not an outcast subject to shunning.)

First, the footnote on page 37 of the preliminary injunction order notes—with a lengthy quote from, and citation to, a January 28, 2022 CDC publication—that the matter of natural immunity and vaccination in several combinations "remain under careful study and constant evolution," which is not surprising, is not news, and is not an adjudication or a "second guessing" of any kind. The footnote on page 43 of the order notes then-current Department of Defense data that shows a remarkable surge in COVID-19 (Omicron) cases in the military immediately after the vaccination deadline and despite about a 97% vaccination rate among service members. The footnote draws no conclusion from the Department of Defense's data, adjudicates nothing, and second-guesses nothing.

Second, no dispute exists in the action (not even the plaintiffs suggest otherwise) that the military must combat COVID-19 (and other diseases) and that vaccination helps maximize the health and safety of the force. Of course it does. And in excess of 99% of the armed forces is fully vaccinated today. Neither this action nor the plaintiffs' claims nor the preliminary injunction raises any question about that. The defendants might prefer to argue that question, but the plaintiffs and the court address only the question presented in this RFRA claim. The plaintiffs concede that the military has a compelling governmental interest in the "health and safety of the force" and consequently in vaccinating the force. The question presented in this action and presented by the explicit language of RFRA is whether vaccinating Navy Commander or Lieutenant Colonel 2 over their religious objection, that is, athwart the right of each to the free exercise of religion, is "the least restrictive means of furthering that compelling governmental interest." RFRA establishes that explicit test and places the burden of proof on the government.

Proving the obvious, that vaccination is best for "the force" and necessary for "the force," fails to satisfy the "to the person" test required by RFRA. The military designs to avoid the "to the person" test, but the statute is unflinching.

Earlier orders discuss—without any limitations and for suggestive, not directional, purposes—what sort of evidence might gravitate favorably for the defendants. For example, reason suggests that the defendants might show why the Navy cannot—in the facts of his actual performance—accommodate Navy Commander's service on his surface missile destroyer now, when 99% of the force is vaccinated and the relatively weak and transient Omicron variant is dominant, even though Navy Commander served in the same command on the same destroyer, including on a 300-day mission with his 320-member crew, entirely without vaccination during the many months of the height of the pandemic and without any unmanageable consequence. Navy Commander's unrebutted testimony about the feasibility of that accommodation was compelling (history is difficult to rebut). Perhaps the defendants have a good

EVIDENCE ATTACHMENT G

response—directed "to the person" of Navy Commander—but, because they fail to acknowledge the correct issue (or, at least, the correct focus of the issue), the defendants' presentation was largely unresponsive to the issue governing the preliminary injunction.

Also, as stated in a November 22, 2021 order (Doc. 40), the defendants might consider offering evidence probative of:

> not whether COVID adversely affects the force (or course it does) but whether the readiness and fitness of the force is more adversely affected (1) by granting exemptions and accommodations to a stated number of sincere objectors or (2) by punishing, separating, and discharging that same stated number of skilled and experienced personnel, notwithstanding the time, energy, and money expended to train those service members and necessarily spent again to locate, recruit, and train a successor, including the cost of the successors' acquiring similar experience and the deficit in fitness and readiness experienced in the interim.

To illustrate the deeply entrenched failure of the defendants to respond effectively to the requirements of RFRA, Part A of Section III (Doc. 118 at 10–14) of the defendants' motion offers a graphic exemplar. The defendants claim that the preliminary injunction "causes irreparable harm because these unvaccinated individuals place themselves and their units at higher risk of illness, hospitalization and death, and this creates a greater risk of mission failure." To support this dramatic and broad claim, the defendants cite declarations submitted by Lescher, Yun, and Rans. A definitive review of the probative value of these declarations and others requires a hearing and an opportunity for cross-examination. And a detailed discussion of these declarations is beyond the scope of, and the time available for, this order. But the affidavits fail, consistent with the balance of the defendants' presentation, to focus on the assignment, duty, and performance of Navy Commander and Lieutenant Colonel 2. Further, for the most part, the declarations contain generalizations and conclusions about "the force" as a whole or aggregated portions of the whole force. The declarations

215

fail, at a minimum, to disaggregate by age, by medical characteristics (for example, BMI, diabetes, high blood pressure, etc.), by assignment, and the like. The declarations evidence mostly historical data from the 2020 and 2021 pre-Omicron, pre-vaccine phase of the pandemic. In sum, the declarations, both bulky and full of numbers, say little or nothing about, for example, the marginal risk, if any, that Navy Commander, who is triumphantly fit and slim and strong, who is robustly healthy, who is young, who has already caught and recovered from COVID-19 with only trivial symptoms, who has commanded the same destroyer "underway" on a 300-day mission with a 320-sailor crew, and who has designed and implemented successfully an anti-COVID protocol customized to the needs of his vessel cannot serve—consistent with his sincerely held religious beliefs—without vaccination as a reasonable accommodation that both preserves the compelling governmental interest and reasonably accommodates the free exercise of religion. That is the question, as to Navy Commander, the defendants scrupulously avoid. But that is the question that RFRA burdens the defendants to answer. They have not.

As well stated in *U.S. Navy Seals 1–26 v. Biden*, No. 22-10077, 2022 WL 594375 at *9–10 (5th Cir. Feb. 28, 2022), in denying a stay in a strikingly similar circumstance:

> The Navy has been extraordinarily successful in vaccinating service members, as at least 99.4% of whom are vaccinated. But that general interest is nevertheless insufficient under RFRA. The Navy must instead "scrutinize[ ] the asserted harm of granting specific exemptions to particular religious claimants." O Centro, 546 U.S. at 431, 126 S. Ct. at 1220. "The question, then, is not whether [the Navy has] a compelling interest in enforcing its [vaccination] policies generally, but whether it has such an interest in denying an exception to [each Plaintiff]." Fulton, 141 S. Ct. at 1881. And RFRA "demands much more[]" than deferring to "officials' mere say-so that they could not accommodate [a plaintiff's religious accommodation] request." Holt, 574 U.S. at 369, 135 S. Ct. at 866 (RLUIPA context). That is because "only the gravest

EVIDENCE ATTACHMENT G

abuses, endangering para-mount interests, give occasion for permissible limitation[ ]" on the free exercise of religion. Sherbert v. Verner, 374 U.S. 398, 406, 83 S. Ct. 1790, 1795, 10 L.Ed.2d 965 (1963).

(Because the defendants in this action assert in the Fifth Circuit action many arguments and theories rejected by the Fifth Circuit, the quoted opinion is immensely instructive and endorsed entirely.)

Time will not permit further comment about the defendants' motion for a stay. However, a comment on the progress of the action is required. The complaint (Doc. 1) and a motion (Doc. 2) for injunctive relief were filed on October 15, 2021. The defendants responded (Doc. 23) to the motion on November 3, 2021. The first hearing on the motion occurred on November 15, 2021. A November 22, 2021 order (Doc. 40) denied the motion for a temporary restraining order and denied the motion for a preliminary injunction as to the civilian plaintiffs, some defendants, and some counts but deferred ruling on the preliminary injunction as to the First Amendment and RFRA counts pending. Also, the order directed certain reporting by the defend- ants and permitted another hearing, which occurred on February 10, 2022, after additional briefing and supplemental material. Navy Commander and Lieutenant Colonel 2 were the only witnesses testifying at the hearing.

The amended complaint (Doc. 75) had arrived on February 7, 2022. Later, an order (Doc. 89) severed misjoined parties and opened separate actions (assigned to the same district and magistrate judge) in an effort to manage this abundance of parties and claims more effectively. The order (Doc. 111) granting preliminary relief was entered on February 18, 2022.

In sum, this difficult and unprecedent action, along with similar actions pending in this court and elsewhere, presents not only a somewhat novel legal problem (the application of RFRA to the armed forces) but a daunting management problem (hundreds or more of disappointed RFRA applicants asserting claims in different districts in different circuits, some including class allegations, as in this action, and some not, and some with plaintiffs serving on one branch or two branches of the armed forces and this action, with plaintiffs in each branch of the service). To further illustrate the management problem, at 1:56 p.m. today, during the hurried composition of this order, the plaintiffs filed another motion (Doc. 121) for preliminary relief on behalf of another plaintiff who is ordered to receive vaccination and offered only two days to either accept vaccination or face discipline. The military, despite several adverse orders, continues on the path determined months ago. A more organized and encompassing approach must attach soon.

In finalizing a plan, the district judge must consider the full array of options available for conditional and final class certification, along with an array of other formidable issues. Mindful of these and other considerations and mindful both of the public interest and the interest of the litigants (not necessarily divergent in many or most respects), this action has proceeded expeditiously but carefully (with simultaneous mediation underway before the magistrate judge). Unless ordered otherwise, the district judge will continue to proceed apace to resolve the organizational, legal, and remedial complexities (assuming some successful claims) in accord with governing law.

Conclusion

The motion for an "immediate administrative stay" is **DENIED**. Not later than **MARCH 8, 2022**, (1) the plaintiffs must respond to the motion (Doc. 118) to stay and (2) the parties must submit a witness and exhibit list. An evidentiary hear- ing on the motion to stay is scheduled for **MARCH 10, 2022**, at 10:00 A.M. in Courtroom 15A, United States Courthouse, 801 N. Florida Avenue, Tampa, Florida, 33602.

ORDERED in Tampa, Florida, on March 2, 2022.
STEVEN D. MERRYDAY
UNITED STATES DISTRICT JUDGE

www.ingramcontent.com/pod-product-compliance
Lightning Source LLC
Chambersburg PA
CBHW070252230426
43664CB00014B/2499